Asle Knudsen

In His Own Words

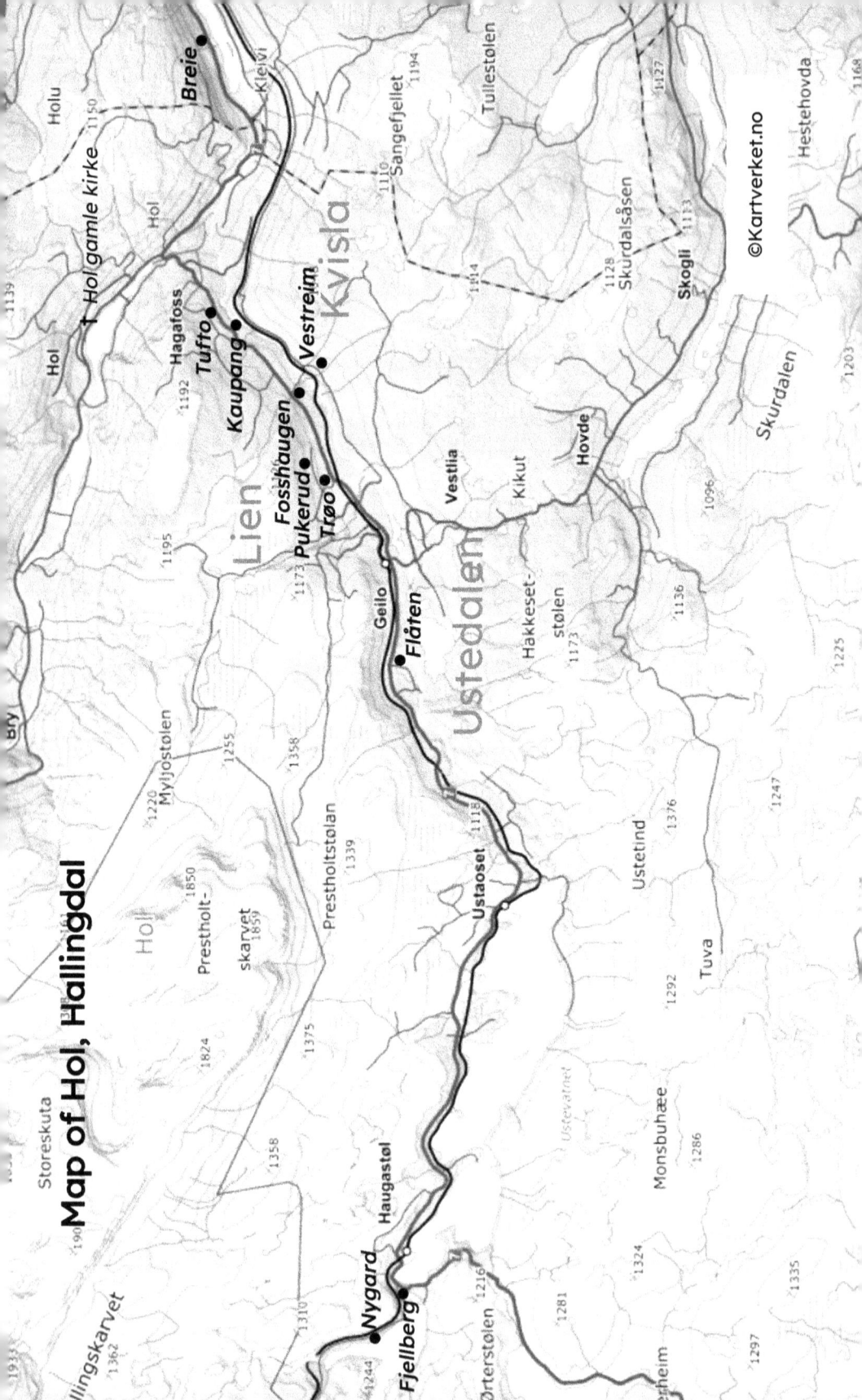

Asle Knudsen

In His Own Words

Memories of a Circuit-Riding Pioneer Preacher

James M. Larson

2025

Immigrant Ancestor Books
Mission Viejo, California

Asle Knudsen, In His Own Words
Text copyright © 2025 by James M. Larson

All rights reserved.

No part of this book may be used or reproduced in any manner whatsoever without written permission except for brief quotations embodied in critical articles or reviews.

All photographs are the property of their respective owners and are used by permission.

Front cover photograph courtesy of the author. Portrait by Halmrast Studio, Minneapolis.

Back cover photograph of the interior of the Washington Prairie Church by Dorothy Petersen Swaney, courtesy of Stan Petersen.

Back cover quote is from J. Sanaker, "Amerikabrev," *Kristelig Tidende*, 23 July 1909, page 239, column 1.

Map of Hol copyright © Kartverket.no. Overlay of farm names by the author.

Library of Congress Control Number: 2024926371

ISBN: 979-8-9992745-0-2 (paperback)
ISBN: 979-8-9992745-1-9 (hardcover)

PUBLISHED BY
Immigrant Ancestor Books
Mission Viejo, California

books@ourimmigrantancestors.com

https://knudsen.familyarchive.online

Table of Contents

List of Illustrations vii
Acknowledgments ix
Glossary xi

Introduction

Growing Up In Norway 3
Norway to America 7
Haugeanism to Methodism 13
Early Pastorates 19
Presiding Elder 27
Later Pastorates 35
Retirement 41

Asle's Diary

Early Years 57
Grand Meadow and Plainview 65
Plainview and Belvidere 71
Washington Prairie and Big Canoe 75
Newburg and South Fork 81
Plainview, Belvidere, Red Wing, and Grand Meadow 85
Saint Paul District 87
Red River Valley District 91
Eidsvold, Deer Park, Minneapolis, Diamond Bluff, Chicago, and Lake Mills 93

Letters to the Editor

Des Moines and Lake Mills, Iowa 105
From the St. Lawrence River, New York 120
A Camp Meeting in Old Times 129
A 50th Anniversary 146
Crumbs from the Journey to the West...171
Lake Mills, Iowa 191

Other Writings

Vinter!... 201
A Brief Visit to Hol, Hallingdal, in 1902 203

Appendix

Lineage of Asle Knudsen 209

Illustration Credits 241
Resources 245
Index 253
Next Steps.. 267

List of Illustrations

Nygard farm, circa 1920 4
The steamship *Belgian*, formerly *Hammonia* 8
Map of Knudsen, Fosse, and Foss farms 10
Asle's Pastoral Appointments 12
Washington Prairie Norwegian Methodist Church 22
First Norwegian-Danish Methodist Church 33
Bethlehem Methodist Church, North Minneapolis 38
Asle Knudsen on his 94th birthday 46
1925 Norse-American Centennial program 49
Asle's relatives in Winneshiek County 56
Map of nearby farms in the Big Canoe area 60
Railroad map of southeast Minnesota, circa 1885 63
Family members Asle joined in marriage in 1874 70
Asle Knudsen, circa 1875 80
Oakwood Methodist Church, 1881 84
A page from Asle's handwritten history of Bethlehem Church
.... 96
1819 Engraving of a Methodist camp meeting 130
Trinity Methodist Church, Deer Park, 1910 134
Veterans C. F. Eltzholtz and A. Knudsen 142
Four generations 174
Asle's relatives in California 180
Lake Mills Norwegian Methodist Church 192
Knudsen family, circa 1904 208

Acknowledgments

I have always known that my great-great-grandfather, Asle Knudsen, was a Methodist minister. Growing up, I assumed he was just like the pastor at the Lutheran church we attended; he trained at the seminary, was called to serve a congregation, and served that same congregation until retirement. It wasn't until I began to research Asle's life story that I realized that he was, in fact, a circuit-riding pioneer preacher on what was then the American frontier.

I first became aware of the existence of Asle's diary when Sue Daigle posted excerpts from it on *Facebook* many years ago. Sue was kind enough to send me a copy of the diary, which I transcribed, annotated, and posted on my website, *Our Immigrant Ancestors.*

Later, I discovered that Asle had been a regular contributor of letters to the editors of the Norwegian-Danish Conference newspaper. It was then that I realized that I had the makings of a book. My annotations from the website formed the basis of the introduction, which, along with the diary, the letters to the editor, and a three-generation paternal lineage, became the book you hold today.

Much research was required to produce this book. I want to thank the Minnesota Conference United Methodist Church archivists in Minneapolis for their help. Heidi Heller provided me with copies of Asle's Presiding Elder reports from the Conference minutes and was most helpful in explaining Methodist terminology. Her predecessor, Kathy

Johnson, gave me access to the Belvedere Church papers, which included the Record Book.

I would also like to thank Kristina Warner, archivist at the Norwegian-American Historical Association, for giving me access to their Congregational Papers collection and making high-quality scans of the documents I needed; Christine Klauer, Senior Researcher at the Vesterheim Genealogy Center and Naeseth Library, for sending me copies of pages from the Ål bygdebok; Spencer Schwartz at the Gale Family Library in the Minnesota Historical Society who went above and beyond to make scans of pages from *Evangelisk Tidende*.

Jennifer Kovarik, Collection Manager at the Vesterheim Norwegian-American Museum, sent me scans of photographs of Asle and the Lake Mills church from their collection; Stacey Gossling and the Winneshiek County Historical Society staff kindly gave me access to the Washington Prairie Methodist Church Record Book; Kevin Lee provided access to digital images of the contents of the Washington Prairie folders held at Decorah First United Methodist Church.

I would also like to thank family members who contributed documents and photographs. Stan Petersen allowed me to scan his collection of photos taken by Dorothy Petersen Swaney. Bob Swaney, Dorothy's son, sent me copies of her manuscript, "Nygaard-Knudsen and Related Families from Norway."

Special thanks to my sister, Karen Noecker, and my niece, Dr. Jennifer Schmitt Carnell, who edited and proofread this work. Their suggestions and advice proved to be invaluable.

JML

Glossary

Methodist Terminology

The definitions below are based on the 1876 edition of *The Doctrines and Discipline of the Methodist Episcopal Church* and may differ from modern usage.

Camp Meeting — a popular religious event on the frontier in the nineteenth century. These week-long events, held in an open field, attracted people from 30-40 miles around who set up tents and lived there for the duration. The meetings were like an open-air church service with nearly continuous preaching and hymn singing.

Charge — a preacher's appointment for the year. A charge could be a single church (a station) or a group of churches (a circuit). Preachers received their appointment at the Annual Conference meeting and were under obligation to serve where appointed.

Church Extension Society — a board composed of equal numbers of clergy and laymen whose mission is to provide financial aid to local congregations for acquiring land, erecting church buildings, and paying debts.

Circuit — a group of congregations and preaching points served by the same pastor. Circuits were fluid and could change from year to year. See *Charge.*

Conference — a regional organizational unit of the Methodist Church. Each conference held annual meetings, which were presided over by a bishop. At these meetings, the bishop would give each preacher his appointment for the upcoming year.

Deacon — an ordained minister authorized to administer baptism, solemnize marriage, and assist the Elders in administering communion. Deacons were elected by the Annual Conference and ordained by a bishop.

District — a sub-division of a Conference. Districts were overseen by a Presiding Elder, today known as the District Superintendent. District meetings were held quarterly.

District Superintendent — see *Presiding Elder.*

Elder — an ordained minister authorized to administer communion in addition to the other sacraments. Elders were elected by the Annual Conference and solemnized by a bishop's laying on of hands.

Epworth League — a Methodist young adult association for people aged 18 to 35. Its modern equivalent is the United Methodist Youth Fellowship.

Exhorter — a layperson licensed to hold prayer meetings.

Freedmen's Aid Society — an organization that funded schools and teachers in the post-Civil War South to help educate formerly enslaved people and their children.

Itinerancy — a system by which traveling preachers are appointed to a charge. In the early days, preachers were not to serve a charge for more than three years.

Lay Preacher — a licensed preacher who could conduct worship services and preach but could not administer the sacraments.

Local Preacher — a licensed part-time preacher assigned to a station under the supervision of a district superintendent. Local preachers do not receive a salary and are required to attend district meetings. A local preacher could be ordained and was eligible to become a deacon after four years of service and an elder after an additional four years.

Methodist Episcopal Church (MEC) — the mainline Methodist denomination founded in 1784. In 1939, the MEC merged with two other Methodist denominations to form the Methodist Church. In 1968, the Methodist Church merged with the United Brethren Church to form the present-day United Methodist Church.

Missionary Rules — under missionary rules, the Annual Conference had the authority to elect an elder before he had completed his required time as a deacon if it was deemed necessary.

Parsonage — a dwelling place for the traveling preachers, usually a house on a parcel of land owned by the Church.

Preaching Point — a place where regular services were held but which had not yet been organized into a congregation.

Presiding Elder — the duties of the Presiding Elder were to supervise all of the elders, deacons, and local preachers in his district and to preside at the quarterly district meetings. Presiding Elders, chosen by the bishops, could not serve the same district for more than six years.

Station — see *Charge*.

Superannuated — a minister who was unable, due to old age or health issues, to perform the duties of a traveling preacher. Superannuated preachers were given appointments that required minimal travel. The early Conference minutes referred to superannuated preachers as "worn-out" preachers.

Tract Society — The purpose of the Tract Society is to spread religious knowledge by publishing evangelical tracts, inexpensive books, and other publications.

Traveling Preacher — a licensed full-time preacher appointed to a circuit under the supervision of a district superintendent. A traveling preacher receives a salary and a place to live and is required to attend the Annual Conference meetings. A traveling preacher was eligible to become a deacon after two years of service and an elder after an additional two years.

United Methodist Church (UMC) — the present-day denomination formed in 1968 by merging the Methodist Episcopal Church with the United Brethren Church.

Some Norwegian Words and Phrases

Bygdebok — farm history book. Every kommune in Norway has a local genealogist who has published histories of the farms and families in the kommune.

Bygdelag — a social organization for people from a specific region of Norway.

Digitalarkivet — the website of the National Archives of Norway.

Gamle kirke — old church.

Goro — a kind of wafer baked on a patterned, rectangular iron.

Grend — a rural neighborhood, a group of farms.

Halling — a person from Hallingdal.

Hallingen — the monthly publication of the Hallinglag of America, a social organization for immigrants from Hallingdal and their descendants.

Husmann — a person who rented a cottage on a farm and paid rent to the farm owner, usually by providing a specified number of hours of labor each month to the farmer.

Husmann med jord — a husmann with land. In addition to a cottage, this person also rented a couple of acres of land, which he could work for himself.

Juletræfest — Christmas Tree Party, an after-Christmas party when the tree is re-lighted, and candies, etc., are taken from the tree and eaten.

Kommune — a local administrative area similar to a township in the United States.

Klokker — the sexton or pastor's assistant, whose duties may include ringing the church bell (*klokke*), leading the singing in the church, and maintaining the klokkerbok.

Klokkerbok — a duplicate church record book maintained by the klokker, the pastor's assistant. Not every parish has a set of klokkerboker. See *Ministerialbok*.

Lag — a group of people. See *Bygdelag*.

Ministerialbok — a church book maintained by the Pastor, containing a record of baptisms, marriages, funerals, etc. The ministerialboker and klokkerboker were stored in separate places to prevent a total loss of records in case of a disaster. See *Klokkerbok*.

Prim — a soft, spreadable cheese made from whey.

Rømmegrøt — porridge made from either sweet or sour cream, a Norwegian delicacy.

Rosemaling — a style of decorative, floral painting.

Seter — a mountain summer farm.

Slekt og data — literally kin and data, this is the name of the website of the Genealogy Society of Norway.

Stavkirke — stave church.

Stevne — a large gathering or convention. In America, the Hallinglag used this term for their annual reunion.

Introduction

> "In the land of the midnight sun lies the beautiful valley of Hallingdal. Here, on an old mountain farm in Aals parish, Asle Knudsen was born.... The grand and majestic nature in which he spent his childhood left a lasting impression on his character. He carried with him ever after the ruggedness of the mountain and the gentleness of the valley."
>
> — C. W. Schevenius

Growing Up In Norway

Asle Knudsen was born on 19 January 1844 in what was then known as the Hol Annex to Ål *kommune* (a rural community). Hol later separated from Ål and became a kommune in its own right.[1]

Asle's father, Knud Aslesen, his aunt Kristi, and his uncles Hermund and Elling were born on the Nygard farm in Hol and grew up there. *Nygard i fjellet* (Nygard on the mountain) is the highest farm in Hol and, indeed, the highest in Norway, at 1,000 meters (3,280 feet) above sea level.[2]

The land is very rocky and not suitable for farming. However, the family was able to grow a small number of potatoes. They raised domesticated reindeer and cattle, supplementing their diet by hunting and fishing in Nygardvatnet, a nearby lake.[3]

---

[1] The quote on the facing page is from C. W. Schevenius, "Asle Knudsen," *Evangelisk Tidende*, 26 October 1939, page 2. Citations for birth, marriage, and death events are found in the "Lineage of Asle Knudsen" in the Appendix.

[2] Sigurd S. Reinton, "Hol Herad" in Lars Berg, *Norske Gardsbruk*, volume 7, *Buskerud Fylke I* (Oslo: Norske Gardsbruk, 1948), page 483.

[3] Lars Reinton and Sigurd S. Reinton, *Folk og Fortid i Hol*, volume 7, *Ætt og Eige: Ustedalen og Skurdalen* (Oslo: Hol Sparebank, 1979), pages 403, 407-408.

Hol Bygdearkiv

Nygard farm, circa 1920

As reported in the 1845 census, Nygard had six cattle, six pigs, and 40 reindeer.[4]

Further down the valley, in the vicinity of the modern town of Geilo, lies the Flåten farm where Asle's mother, Birgit Knudsdatter, was born and raised. This area is the site of an Iron Age settlement, and a Viking-era burial mound lies not far from Flåten. In addition to artifacts found in the burial mound, several items were discovered on the Flåten farm, including an unusually beautiful and well-preserved iron axe typical of the Viking age.[5]

In 1845, Flåten reported three acres of cultivated land in barley and potatoes, 18 acres of natural pasture, 14 acres of outlying and mountain meadows, access to a lake, and some woodland but little timber.[6]

---

[4] 1845 Census of Norway, Buskerud Amt, Aals Præstegjeld, Hoels Sogn, folio 92, entry 540/541; digital image, National Archives of Norway, *Digitalarkivet* (media.digitalarkivet.no).

[5] Reinton and Reinton, *Folk og Fortid i Hol*, volume 7, page 121.

[6] Ibid., page 124.

Knud and Birgit married in 1841 and lived on Flåten, where Asle and his older sister, Eli, were born. They later moved to Annfinnset and finally to Kaupang, where Asle's sister Astrid was born.[7]

Asle's mother died in 1850 when Asle was six years old, and later he went to live with his uncle Hermund. Hermund had been fortunate enough to marry a widow who owned a prosperous farm in Ål kommune called Nordre Breie. Breie had 8.6 acres under cultivation in barley and potatoes, 13 acres of natural meadow, 31 acres of outlying meadow, and three *seter* (summer farms). Breie also included some forested land and a sawmill.[8]

In his diary, Asle states he was a herdsboy on Uncle Hermund's farm for four years. Typically, children were expected to begin helping with the farm work at 12 years of age. Every spring, the cattle would be moved to a seter higher up in the mountains. The primary activity on the seter was dairy farming. It was the children's job to take care of the cattle, milk the cows, and make cheese and butter. Usually, a woman from the farm would go along to supervise. The older girls would churn the butter and make the cheese, while the boys and younger girls would care for the animals. Once a week, a man from the farm would bring provisions to the seter and take the cheese and butter produced back to the main farm. The children spent the entire summer at the seter until it was time to move the cattle down to the main farm in the fall.[9]

---

[7] These three farms, Flåten, Annfinnset, and Kaupang, are in Hol kommune.

[8] Warberg, Thor, *Aal Bygdesoga,* volume 9, *Breie (Grn. 125-130), Andre bygdefolk* (Ål, Norway: Ål Kommune/Sparebank, 2008), page 123.

[9] Ann Urness Gesme, *Between Rocks and Hard Places* (Hastings, Minnesota: Caragana Press, 1993), pages 34-36.

Years later, Asle recalled "the good old days" when the young people began to move up to the seter in the springtime:

> *It was hard work preparing and mounting the heavy load on the little pack horse. Those small horses were strong, though.*
>
> *It was great fun up there on the mountain! There, we got to eat 'milk foods' such as real buttermilk, curds and whey, cheese and prim, and rømmegrøt made with either sweet or sour cream and floating in butter.*[10]

At 16, Asle was confirmed in the Ål *stavkirke* (stave church).[11] Shortly after that, he moved with Uncle Hermund to Lier kommune, which borders the city of Drammen, a port city 27 miles southwest of Oslo. Asle attended an agricultural school in Lier for two years to learn modern farming techniques.[12] While Asle was attending school, Uncle Hermund purchased the Thorrud farm in neighboring Skoger kommune. After graduating, Asle was the manager of Uncle Hermund's farm for two years.

---

[10] [Edna Rude], "From Pastor Asle Knutson to the Hallinglag," handwritten manuscript, page 2; photocopy provided by Sue Daigle. This document is a translation of "Fraa pastor Asle Knutson til Hallinglaget," *Hallingen*, 15 September 1920.

[11] Ål Parish (Buskerud County, Norway), Ministerialbok nr. 6 (1849-1864), page 115, line 23; Family History Library (FHL) microfilm 0,278,233.

[12] Lars Reinton and Sigurd S. Reinton, *Folk og Fortid i Hol*, volume 2, *Frå 1815 til Vår Tid* (Oslo: Grøndahl & Søn, 1943), page 68.

Norway to America

Asle emigrated from Norway to America in 1865. His uncle, Elling Foss, who had emigrated in 1850, had offered him a place to stay if he came to the United States.[1] The first leg of the journey was by steamer from Drammen to Hull on the east coast of England, then by train across England to Liverpool. Along the way, Asle picked up two traveling companions: Andrew Johnsen, listed as Anders Jansen in the ship's passenger list, and Peter Linam, listed as Peder Pedersen.[2]

After waiting three days in Liverpool, Asle and his friends boarded the steamship *Belgian*, bound for Quebec, Canada. Family legend holds that this was the first steamship to cross the Atlantic between England and America,[3] but this

---

[1] Dorothy Petersen Swaney, "Nygaard-Knudsen and Related Families from Norway," typescript, final draft (1985), page 1; copy privately held by Bob Swaney, son of Dorothy Swaney. As part of her research, Dorothy traveled to Norway in the 1970s where she interviewed descendants of these families.

[2] Passenger List, SS *Belgian*, page 6, entry 888 (Peder Pedersen) and entry 889 (Anders Jansen); "Passenger Lists: Quebec 1865–1921," digital image, *Library and Archives Canada* (collectionscanada.gc.ca).

[3] This assertion is found in a letter from Adella (Knudsen) Swenson to her great-niece, Doris (Helgeson) Larson, dated 7 July 1957, and also in Schevenius' memorial to Asle in the October 26, 1939 issue of *Evangelisk Tidende*.

Courtesy of Norway-Heritage

The steamship *Belgian*, formerly *Hammonia*

is untrue. That distinction belongs to the *Great Britain,* which carried passengers from Liverpool to New York in 1845. Although other steam-powered ships had made the cross-Atlantic journey earlier, *Great Britain* was the first iron-hulled, propeller-driven passenger ship to do so.[4]

The *Belgian*, erroneously referred to as the *Hamilton* in Asle's diary, was built in 1855 for the Hamburg-America Line. She was *their* first steamship, the flagship of their fleet, and was christened *Hammonia* (the Latin name for Hamburg). She had one funnel and three masts and could carry 510 passengers. In 1864, she was sold to the Allen Line, re-christened *Belgian*, and put into service on the Liverpool–Quebec route.[5]

---

[4] "SS Great Britain," *Wikipedia, The Free Encyclopedia* (en.wikipedia.org : accessed May 11, 2021).

[5] Geo. Henry Preble, *A Chronological History of the Origin and Development of Steam Navigation* (Philadelphia: L. R. Hamersly & Co., 1883), pages 340–341. Also:

INTRODUCTION

After a voyage of 11 days and enduring a storm that lasted one night, the *Belgian* arrived in Quebec City on 2 June. From there, Asle and his companions "continued over land," indicating they traveled by train. Their most likely route would have been on the Grand Trunk Railway from Quebec to Detroit, Michigan. There, they would have transferred to the appropriately named Detroit, Grand Haven, and Milwaukee Railway, which took them to Grand Haven, Michigan, on the eastern shore of Lake Michigan and then via ferry to Milwaukee, Wisconsin.[6] Here, Asle parted ways with his two traveling companions.

After spending the night in Milwaukee, Asle got on the wrong train and found himself in La Crosse, Wisconsin, instead of his intended destination, Prairie du Chien, Wisconsin. From there, he took a boat down the Mississippi River to Lansing, Iowa, where he found a ride with Lewis T. Fosse to his uncle Elling's farm in the Big Canoe area of Winneshiek County, Iowa.

Asle immediately went to work as a laborer on farms in the area and attended English school during the winter.

On 27 November 1866, Asle married Susan T. Fosse, daughter of Torkel Torkelsen Fosse and Christi Anfindsdatter Tveit and sister to Lewis T. Fosse mentioned above. Susan was born on 12 September 1842 on the Tveit farm in Feios, Sogn, Norway, a small valley on the south side of the Sognefjord opposite Leikanger. She was christened Synneve Torkilsdatter on 8 October 1842 in the Rinde stavkirke. She

---

Michael P. Palmer, "Palmer List of Merchant Vessels," *GeoCities* (2001), Hammonia (1855); web page archived at *OoCities* (www.oocities.org/mppraetorius). Search for *Hammonia* (1855).

[6] *History of Ottawa County, Michigan* (Chicago: H. R. Page & Co., 1882), page 33.

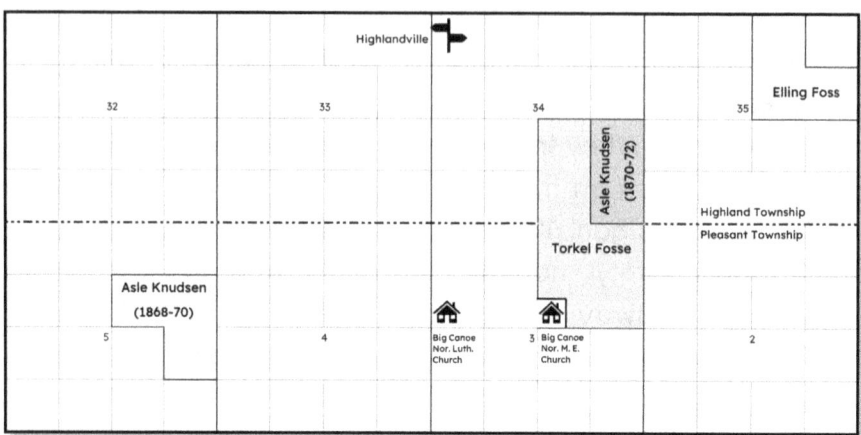

Map of Knudsen, Fosse, and Foss farms

emigrated to America with her parents in 1856,[7] after which she went by the name Susan.

After their wedding, Asle and Susan lived with her parents until 1869, when Asle purchased 120 acres in Section 5 of Pleasant Township in Winneshiek County.[8] In the 1870 agricultural census, we learn that 60 of the 120 acres were under cultivation, and the remaining 60 acres were unimproved. We also discover that Asle owned two horses, four cattle, and five pigs; he primarily grew wheat but also oats, corn, barley, potatoes, and hay.[9]

---

[7] Leikanger Parish (Sogn og Fjordane County, Norway), Leikanger Ministerialbok nr. 8 (1852–1868), folio 243, entry 39; digital images, *Digitalarkivet* (media.digitalarkivet.no).

[8] Winneshiek County, Iowa, Deed Book R, page 603, Simon Thompson to Asle Knudsen, 15 December 1868, S½ of NE¼ and NE¼ of SE¼, Section 5, Pleasant Township, 120 acres, $1,000; Recorder's Office, Winneshiek County Courthouse, Decorah. Simon Thompson was married to Susan's maternal aunt, Sigrid Anfindsdatter.

[9] 1870 U.S. Census, Winneshiek County, Iowa, agricultural schedule, Pleasant Township, Locust Lane Post Office, page 1, "Asla Knudsen."

INTRODUCTION

Two years later, in the winter of 1871, Asle sold the farm in Section 5 back to Simon Thompson[10] and bought 80 acres from his father-in-law, Torkel Fosse, in Section 34 of Highland Township, Winneshiek County.[11] Asle later sold this farm to his brother-in-law, Lewis T. Fosse.[12]

---

[10] Winneshiek County, Deed Book U, page 296, Asle Knudson to Simon Thompson, 27 December 1870, S½ of NE¼ and NE¼ of SE¼, Section 5, Pleasant Township, 120 acres, $1,000.

[11] Winneshiek County, Deed Book W, page 355, Torkel Torkelsen to Asle Knudsen, 30 January 1872, E½ of SE¼, Section 34, Highland Township, 80 acres, $700.

[12] Winneshiek County, Deed Book 27, page 426, Asle Knudson to Lewis T. Fosse, 9 July 1875, E½ of SE¼, Section 34, Highland Township, 80 acres, $1,000. Even though Asle stopped farming in the fall of 1872, this sale was not recorded until 1875.

Asle's Pastoral Appointments			
From	To	Years	Appointment
1872	1873	1	Grand Meadow and Plainview
1873	1874	1	Plainview and Belvidere
1874	1878	4	Washington Prairie and Big Canoe
1878	1881	3	Newburg and South Fork
1881	1882	1	Plainview, Red Wing, and Belvidere
1882	1883	1	Plainview, Belvidere, and Grand Meadow
1883	1884	1	Saint Paul
1884	1890	6	Presiding Elder, Saint Paul District
1890	1896	6	Presiding Elder, Red River Valley District
1896	1897	1	Eidsvold
1897	1898	1	Deer Park
1898	1903	5	Minneapolis
1903	1904	1	Diamond Bluff
1904	1906	2	North Minneapolis and Diamond Bluff
1906	1907	1	Presiding Elder, Chicago District
1907	1908	--	Financial Secretary, Preachers' Aid Society
1908	1910	2	North Minneapolis
1910	1912	2	Palmer, Glenville, and Lake Mills
1912	1920	8	Lake Mills
1920	1929	9	Lake Mills and Albert Lea
1931	1933	2	Lake Mills

Compiled from *Minutes of the Annual Conferences of the Methodist Episcopal Church*, 1872–1932.

Haugeanism to Methodism

When Asle arrived in America, he found the religious landscape far different from Norway's. Norway had a state church, the Church of Norway, which was Lutheran. Only pastors who were ordained by the state could preach and conduct worship services. During the early nineteenth century, a grassroots reform movement had taken shape within the state church. As linguist and historian Einar Haugen explains:

> The major differences may be characterized in terms of the opposition between "high church" and "low church." The high-church group emphasized the church as an institution, with properly trained ministers in charge, with religious education of the children and the laity along firmly orthodox lines according to the teachings of the Lutheran Church in Norway, and with relatively elaborate church buildings in which the service followed closely the Norwegian Lutheran ritual. The low-church group emphasized personal conversion and public confession, preferred lay preachers who were "called" by the spirit, and regarded abstinence from pleasure and worldly things like dancing, drinking, and card playing as more important than having the right theological doctrine; they preferred plain churches with a minimum of ritual and surplices. The leaders of the high-church group were usually pastors trained in the Norwegian state church, while the leaders of the low-church group were

laymen inspired by the teachings of the great Norwegian religious reformer Hans Nielsen Hauge (1771-1824).[1]

Historian Theodore Blegen further explains that Haugeanism in Norway "was superimposed upon the formal establishment of the state church. It was an informal gathering devoted to evangelism and edification, leaving to the state such matters as churches, pastors' salaries, and the symbols of organized religion."[2] The Haugeans attended services in the state church, were married in the state church, and had their children baptized there. Afterward, they gathered in their homes for meetings.

Asle had come under Haugean influence from an early age. His uncle Hermund, who raised him from age six, was a Haugean lay preacher who held meetings in his home. The Ål *bygdebok* (farm history book) characterizes Asle as an ardent follower of Hauge.[3]

As a young man attending the agricultural school in Lier, Asle appears to have lived on the Gifstad farm. He mentions Siri and Sicilia Gifstad as positive religious influences. It was during this time that Asle experienced a spiritual awakening.[4] This could be what Asle refers to when he states that the Gifstads "did much... to lead me to piety."

In America, new arrivals were free to choose from many denominations. There were Norwegian-language

---

[1] Einar Haugen, *The Norwegians in America*, Localized History Series (New York: Teachers College Press, Columbia University, 1967), page 21.

[2] Theodore C. Blegen, *Norwegian Migration to America: The American Transition* (Northfield, Minnesota: Norwegian-American Historical Association, 1940), page 101.

[3] Warberg, *Aal Bygdesoga,* volume 9, pages 131-132.

[4] A. E. Strand, comp. and ed., *A History of the Norwegians of Illinois* (Chicago: John Anderson Publishing Co., 1905), page 389.

congregations devoted to Baptist, Episcopalian, Lutheran, and Methodist teachings. In the Big Canoe area, there were two Norwegian-language congregations, one Lutheran and one Methodist, a quarter mile from each other. As an ardent Haugean, Asle would have been drawn to the Methodist congregation.

Methodism shared many similarities with Haugeanism. Like Haugeanism, Methodism stressed the importance of spiritual awakening and valued lay preaching. Methodist churches were plain and unadorned. Their services lacked ritual, consisting only of preaching, singing, and Bible readings. They eschewed drinking and smoking and favored simple clothing.[5]

On a Sunday evening in January 1867,[6] Asle and Susan attended a meeting at the Big Canoe Norwegian Methodist Church. Pastor Arne Johnson was preaching that night when they and seven others converted to Methodism.

Years later, on the occasion of Arne Johnson's 85th birthday, a celebration was held in Chicago. Asle could not attend, but he wrote a letter that was read aloud at the gathering and is worth quoting at length:

> *Pastor Arne Johnson is, for me, a great and dear name and will not be forgotten by me as long as I live and have my memory, and I thank God for his existence on Earth. May he live among us for a long time.*
>
> *It will be 53 years on the third of June this summer since I first met this small, handsome, and well-built man, and for the first time, he shook my hand, looked me kindly in the*

---

[5] *The Doctrines and Discipline of the Methodist Episcopal Church, 1876* (New York: Nelson & Phillips, 1876), pages 36, 375–376.

[6] Schevenius, "Asle Knudsen," *Evangelisk Tidende*, 26 October 1939, relates that this occurred in 1868. Asle, in his diary, places this in 1867 as does Haagensen in *Norsk-Danske Methodismes Historie*.

face, and asked if I "loved Jesus." But he got no answer then.

Johnson was then presiding elder over the Norwegian District of Minnesota and Iowa and pastor of the church in Newburg, Minnesota, and when he came to Big Canoe, Iowa, on his quarterly tour, he held meetings every evening for over two weeks and the revival power became great so that it affected me strongly. Johnson, filled with the power of the Holy Spirit, preached so that people fell on their knees and cried out for mercy and forgiveness.

On the 25th of January, 1867, in the evening, Johnson preached on John 14:9,[7] and that evening, I and eight others found Peace with God, and among them was my wife, and now I am the only one left of the nine; the others have gone home in triumph to God. The 12th of February in 1867, my wife and I were admitted as members on trial, and 15 months later, he admitted us as members in full association.

He was our pastor, and to tell the truth, I was a bad member. He had more trouble with me than all the others put together, and if Johnson had not had the grace and great wisdom to engage and deal with me, I would not have become what I am, by the grace of God, today. His fatherly and long-suffering guidance was that which came to my aid in my youth and ignorance.[8]

---

[7] "Jesus saith unto him, Have I been so long time with you, and yet hast thou not known me, Philip? he that hath seen me hath seen the Father; and how sayest thou then, Shew us the Father?" (King James Version).

[8] H. P. Bergh, "Pastor Arne Johnsons 85de Fødselsdag" [Pastor Arne Johnson's 85th Birthday], *Den Kristelige Talsmand*, 24 April 1919, page 9; Gale Family Library, Minnesota Historical Society, Saint Paul.

INTRODUCTION

When recalling that evening in January 1867, Pastor Arne Johnson said that he had never experienced anything so marvelous either before or since.[9]

The Big Canoe congregation immediately became aware of Asle's gift and encouraged him to prepare for the ministry.[10] In 1870, he was licensed as a lay preacher, his first step towards becoming a fully ordained Methodist minister. A lay preacher was allowed to preach but could not conduct worship services. Asle thus began to preach at the Big Canoe church while continuing his day job as a farmer.

By joining the Big Canoe congregation, Asle became a member of the Scandinavian District of the Minnesota Conference of the Methodist Episcopal Church, which consisted primarily of rural churches in Scandinavian-speaking areas.

For administrative purposes, the Methodist Episcopal Church was organized into conferences, and each conference was organized into districts overseen by a presiding elder (now known as the district superintendent). The congregations in each district were further organized into 'charges,' which could be either a single congregation or a circuit of two or more congregations.

Each conference held an annual meeting known as the Annual Conference. This was a business meeting for the traveling preachers, and it was at this meeting that the preachers were appointed to their charge for the upcoming

---

[9] James Sanaker, "Pastor Arne Johnsons Minde" [In Memory of Pastor Arne Johnson], *Evangelisk Tidende*, 22 June 1922, page 7; Gale Family Library, Minnesota Historical Society, Saint Paul.
[10] "Asle Knudsen femogotti Aar" [Asle Knudsen's Fiftieth Year], *Evangelisk Tidende*, 7 February 1929, page 5.

year. The districts held quarterly meetings attended by all the preachers and lay representatives from each congregation.[11]

At the Scandinavian District meeting on 9 September 1871, Asle was examined by Presiding Elder C. F. Lindquist and received a local license. In addition to preaching, a local preacher could conduct services and perform all the duties of an ordained minister, excluding the sacraments. Local preachers served a single congregation, did not receive an allowance or housing, and were required to attend district meetings.

Asle's local license was renewed at the quarterly district meeting on 7 September 1872. Subsequently, Presiding Elder John H. Johnson prevailed upon Asle to supply the Grand Meadow and Plainview circuit and thus begin his career as a traveling preacher.

Asle attended his first Annual Conference in October 1873. At this Conference, Bishop Stephen M. Merrill ordained him deacon. He could now perform baptisms and marriages. He performed his first baptism the following month in the Belvidere schoolhouse and his first marriage the subsequent month, also in the Belvidere schoolhouse.

Two years later, on 19 September 1875, Asle was ordained elder by Bishop Issac W. Wiley. Deacons were required to serve as traveling preachers for two years before they could become elders. Since Asle was one month shy of this requirement, he was ordained under missionary rules, which allowed the Conference to waive the requirement if it was deemed necessary. Asle was now fully ordained and could administer the sacrament of Communion.

---

[11] A. Haagensen, *Den Norsk-Danske Methodismes Historie, Paa begge Sider havet* [The History of Norwegian-Danish Methodism on Both Sides of the Ocean] (1894; facsimile reprint, Scholar Select, no date), page 50.

Early Pastorates

At the 1872 Annual Conference, the Scandinavian District was divided into Norwegian and Swedish Districts.[1] The new Norwegian District had nine charges but only four traveling preachers to serve them.[2] Consequently, the Grand Meadow and Plainview circuit in southeastern Minnesota was left unassigned. Presiding Elder John H. Johnson called upon Asle to serve this charge, which included a congregation with a church and parsonage near the town of Grand Meadow in Mower County[3] and a congregation located in the area between Millville and Plainview in Wabasha County, some 50 miles distant.

That December, Asle delivered his first sermon as a full-time traveling preacher in the church near Grand Meadow. The following week, he traveled to Plainview and Millville and preached there. Years later, in a memorial to Asle, Rev. C. W. Schevenius related the following story about Asle's first visit to Millville:

> *His first sermon there was preached in a pioneer hut. Afterward, when he had crawled upstairs and gone to bed, he heard the woman of the house and a young teacher discuss the sermon.*

---

[1] Arlow W. Anderson, *The Salt of the Earth: A History of Norwegian-Danish Methodism in America* (Nashville: Parthenon Press, 1962), page 73.

[2] Haagensen, *Norsk-Danske Methodismes Historie*, page 83.

[3] This church was known locally as Bear Creek Methodist Church.

"That was a poor sermon," said the young man. "I have hardly heard a worse one. He'll never make a preacher."

Brother Knudsen lay utterly crushed. He had received his death sentence from a learned man, and he resolved never to preach again. If no more had been said, he would have been lost.

"You mustn't say that," said the housewife. "I thought he did real well, considering his age and experience. I think he'll have a great future. He will make his mark in the Church."

A sensible woman restored his confidence and saved him both for God and the Church, consider what this meant for thousands down the years.[4]

Asle served the Plainview circuit for four years, from 1872 to 1874 and 1881 to 1883. This circuit at various times included congregations in Belvidere Township, the city of Red Wing (both in Goodhue County), and Grand Meadow, all in southeast Minnesota. He also reported preaching in Weaver, a town on the Mississippi River, twenty-five miles east of Millville.

During his first tenure, Asle raised funds for and built a church in the Long Creek settlement two miles south of Millville. He also raised funds for a church in Belvidere but could not attend the dedication because he had already moved on to his next appointment.

At the Annual Conference in 1874, Asle was appointed to the Washington Prairie and Big Canoe circuit in Winneshiek County, Iowa. Washington Prairie was in Springfield Township, southeast of Decorah, and Big Canoe was in Pleasant Township, northeast of Decorah. Neither congregation had a parsonage, so Asle and his growing

---

[4] Schevenius, "Asle Knudsen," *Evangelisk Tidende*, 26 October 1939, page 3.

family lived in a rented house in Decorah. The following year, a house was purchased for use as a parsonage in Freeport, about halfway between Washington Prairie and Big Canoe.

Preaching at the Big Canoe church must have been a homecoming of sorts for Asle since it was where he was awakened, converted to Methodism, and began his career, first as a lay preacher and then as a local preacher.

But Big Canoe and Washington Prairie share an even broader significance for the history of Norwegian Methodism. Twenty-three years earlier, in 1851, Rev. Ole P. Petersen was sent to northeastern Iowa to minister to the Norwegian immigrants there. The following year, he founded the Big Canoe and Washington Prairie congregations.

Later, Rev. Petersen was sent to Norway, where he organized that country's first Methodist congregation. Petersen is considered the father of Methodism in Norway, and Washington Prairie is regarded as the mother church. The esteem in which the Methodists of Scandinavia hold the pioneer church at Washington Prairie was demonstrated by the fact that the bishop of the North European Conference traveled from Stockholm to participate in the rededication of the restored building in 1973.[5]

Architecturally, the old stone church is significant because of its "exceptionally original condition."[6] The church

---

[5] "Old Time Hymn Sings Set at Washington Prairie," *Decorah (Iowa) Journal*, 19 July 1984, page A7, column 4; digital images, *Winneshiek County Newspaper Archives* (winneshiekcounty.advantage-preservation.com).

[6] Steven L. Johnson, "National Register of Historic Places Nomination: Washington Prairie Methodist Church"; National Park Service, *National Register of Historic Places*, Digital Asset Search (npgallery.nps.gov/ NRHP).

Photo by the author

Washington Prairie Norwegian Methodist Church

"The architecture of the Washington Prairie Methodist Church is a perfect expression in stone of the stoic and simple faith of the little group which built it. It is totally without adornment, making its impact through its solidity, massiveness, and absolute symmetry."
— Marion Nelson*

* Marion John Nelson, Director, Vesterheim Norwegian-American Museum to Wm. H. Baldwin, President, Kresge Foundation, letter, 15 December 1969; digital image from Kevin Lee; original held (2006) at Decorah First United Methodist Church.

remains as it was when regular services ceased, never having been modernized. Due to its unique characteristics, the church was added to the National Register of Historic Places in 1980.

Rev. James Sanaker, who as a young man converted to Methodism and joined the Washington Prairie congregation, recalled that "Washington Prairie was probably not the easiest place to serve, for quite a few members of the congregation were both theologians and philosophers and sharp critics."[7] The Conference apparently felt that Asle was up to the task since they appointed him to Washington Prairie for a fourth year.

At that time, three years was the limit for a traveling preacher to serve at a single charge, so when Asle went to the Annual Conference in 1877, his family expected to move.[8] His son Albert remembered Asle returning home and "whispering in his ear that, in his case, an exception had been made, and they were *not* going to move."[9]

Asle's next appointment was the Newburg and South Fork circuit, which consisted of a congregation with a church and parsonage in the village of Newburg in Fillmore County, Minnesota; the South Fork congregation, which had a church near the village of Choice, about 6½ miles north of Newburg; and preaching points in Preble Township and Stringtown.

---

[7] Sanaker, "Pastor Arne Johnsons Minde," *Evangelisk Tidende*, 22 June 1922, page 7.

[8] The three-year limit was raised to five years at the General Conference in 1889 (Haagensen, *Norsk-Danske Methodismes Historie,* page 122).

[9] Elmer A. Leslie, "Albert Cornelius Knudson, the Man," in Edgar Sheffield Brightman, editor, *Personalism in Theology: A Symposium in Honor of Albert Cornelius Knudson* (Boston: Boston University Press, 1943), page 4.

Methodist meetings among the Norwegian settlers around Newburg began in 1859, first in a barn and later in the schoolhouse. The congregation was organized in 1860, and later that same year, a church was built on land donated by Hans Valder, the village's founder.[10]

Hans Valder had been a school teacher in Norway, emigrated to America in 1837, and settled in the Fox River settlement in LaSalle County, Illinois. He was a Haugean lay preacher who "went over" to the Baptist church[11] and became America's first Norwegian Baptist minister.[12] But "the salary was neither worth living nor dying for," so he left the ministry and took up farming.[13]

It was said that Mr. Valder had not attended church for many years, although his wife was an active member of the Newburg congregation. He eventually began to accompany his wife to services and, in 1879, "under Asle Knudsen's gentle guidance, returned to his former convictions."[14]

The Norwegian Methodists who lived near the village of Choice were members of the Newburg congregation until 1874, when they organized their own congregation—the

---

[10] C. F. Nilsen, "Our Church History" in *Souvenir Program of the Eightieth Anniversary of the Newburg Methodist Church*, pamphlet (By the church, 1940); Congregations Papers (P0537), box 13d, folder 4; Norwegian-American Historical Association, Northfield, Minnesota.

[11] Theodore C. Blegen, *Norwegian Migration to America, 1825-1860* (1931; reprint, New York: Arno Press and the New York Times, 1969), page 249.

[12] Olaf Morgan Norlie, *History of the Norwegian People in America* (Minneapolis: Augsburg Publishing House, 1925), pages 211-212.

[13] Hjalmar Rued Holand, *De Norske Settlementers Historie* (Ephraim, Wisconsin: Forfatterens Forlag, 1909), page 363.

[14] Andersen, *Salt of the Earth*, pages 78-79.

South Fork Norwegian Methodist Episcopal Society.[15] A small frame church was constructed that same year.[16] Today, the church, as well as the village itself, no longer exist.

In his diary, Asle mentions the "Haugen people" twice, in 1879 and again in 1881. It's unclear who he is referring to. East of Choice, in Preble Township, was a Haugean Lutheran church.[17] Perhaps a group of people living in that area attended the church in Newburg.

Stringtown refers to the village of Amherst, about four miles west and three miles north of Newburg. Edward D. Neill, in his 1882 *History of Fillmore County,* had this to say about Stringtown:

> *This village, if such it may be called, is situated ... upon the crossing of county roads and is on the south branch of [the] Root River. There is nothing there to indicate that the place is a village, except one store, a blacksmith shop, schoolhouse, and the Post-office....*
>
> *The name came from the fact that all the settlers built their houses along the road in the ravine in which the would-be village is located, thus stringing it out for some distance. For this reason, the settlers commenced calling it a "Strung out town." This was shortened by common consent to "Stringtown."* [18]

Asle was the pastor of this circuit from 1878 to 1881. Haagensen's summary of the 1881 Annual Conference reports

---

[15] Thelma Ballinger Boeder, compiler, "Planting United Methodist Roots in Minnesota, 1837-2018," PDF, unpaginated, entry for Choice Methodist Church; *Minnesota Annual Conference of the United Methodist Church.* minnesotaumc.org/files/websites/www/Planting+UM+roots+in+MN.pdf.

[16] Haagensen, *Norsk-danske Methodismes Historie*, page 84.

[17] Edward D. Neill, *History of Fillmore County* (Minneapolis: Minnesota Historical Co., 1882), pages 430-431.

[18] Ibid., pages 452, 453.

that the Newburg-South Fork circuit was self-supporting, paying all its expenses, and had been so the previous seven years.[19]

At the Annual Conference in 1883, Asle was designated Conference Treasurer for the upcoming year and appointed to the Saint Paul charge.[20] This charge included First Norwegian-Danish Methodist Church of Saint Paul, a frame church, 30 x 70 feet, with a seating capacity of 200 souls located on the corner of 13th and Broadway Streets[21] and Saint Paul Mission, which served the Norwegian community in the northwest portion of Saint Paul.

During Asle's pastorate, he organized Saint Paul Mission into a congregation and completed fundraising for their church, which was built at the corner of Matilda and Merrill Avenues.[22] This church, originally known as Second Norwegian-Danish Methodist Church, subsequently became known as the Matilda Avenue Church. Asle dedicated this church in 1885 while he was the presiding elder for the district.[23]

---

[19] Haagensen, *Norsk-Danske Methodismes Historie*, page 101.

[20] *Minutes of the Annual Conferences of the Methodist Episcopal Church*, Fall 1883 (New York: Phillips & Hunt, 1883), page 252.

[21] *St. Paul City Directory* (St. Paul: R. L. Polk & Co., 1884), page 481.

[22] Merrill Avenue has since been renamed Lawson Avenue.

[23] "Gudstienster" [Church Services], *Skaffaren (St. Paul, Minnesota)*, 12 August 1885, page 8, column 1; digital images, Minnesota Historical Society, *Minnesota Digital Newspaper Hub* (mnhs.org/newspapers).

Presiding Elder

In 1884, Asle was appointed Presiding Elder for the Saint Paul District, which at that time had 27 churches with 1,816 members located in Minnesota, western Wisconsin, Iowa, Dakota Territory, and Nebraska.[1] A Presiding Elder would preside at the quarterly district meetings, mentor the younger preachers, and act as a preacher-at-large in his district. He also had the authority to supply preachers for charges left vacant at Annual Conferences.[2]

    An example of the Presiding Elder's activities can be seen during the early years of Asle's career. Before he was ordained deacon and could perform baptisms and marriages, the Presiding Elder fulfilled these functions during his visits to Asle's congregations.

    Presiding Elders were also required to report on the status of their district at each year's Annual Conference. Topics covered included revival work, the status of the Sunday schools, new congregations organized, new churches built, repairs and improvements to churches, and charitable collections. Asle's report at the 1889 Conference is typical:

> *The spiritual condition in the district is generally good, and harmony and love prevail between the preachers and their congregations. Prayer and class meetings have been held as usual and have generally been well attended. The*

---

[1] *Minutes of the Annual Conferences*, Fall 1884, page 403.
[2] *Doctrines and Discipline*, pages 105–108.

Sunday school work is running successfully, and several new schools have been established.... The charitable collections have been received with encouraging results despite the poor harvests and hard times of the last three years.[3]

In his first report as Presiding Elder of the Saint Paul District, Asle reported that he had visited every congregation six times and preached an average of four times per week.[4] In 1889, Asle further noted that due to the size of his district, he was away from home about nine-tenths of the year.[5] One can assume that he kept up this pace of activity during his entire career as Presiding Elder.

A common theme of Asle's reports is "hard times." In his second year, he reported: "Last year's crop gave an average low yield, and although the quality was good, the work was low, and for that reason, there are hard financial times." Revival meetings that year were successful, resulting in 100 trial members joining the church. "I have visited various new places and have had letters from many more in Minnesota, Iowa, Dakota, Nebraska, and Kansas, who have desired preachers who can preach to them the gospel of life, and my earnest prayer to God is that the time must soon come when we can have men and means so that we can reach the scattered flock."[6]

---

[3] Norwegian and Danish Conference, Minutes, 1889 (Chicago: By the Conference, 1889), page 17.

[4] Norwegian and Danish Conference, Minutes, 1885, page 20. For example, church notices in the local Red Wing, Minnesota, newspaper announce that Asle preached there ten times during the years 1885 and 1886. See *Red Wing Argus,* various issues 1885–1886; digital images, *Community History Archive* (redwing.advantage-preservation.com).

[5] Norwegian and Danish Conference, Minutes, 1889, page 17.

[6] Norwegian and Danish Conference, Minutes, 1886, page 21.

The hard times continued the following year: "The harvest in most places has failed completely due to drought.... Because of the bad harvest, it will indeed be very difficult for some congregations to hire a preacher in the coming year." Not for the first time, he mentions the problem of members leaving to move further west. "As regards the prospects for the progress of our work in Saint Paul District, they are generally good, except for some rural districts where many move away. From a small congregation, in the course of the year, 11 members have moved to Idaho, and from almost every place, some have moved further north or west."[7]

In 1889, he reported:

> The constant emigration to the West, especially to the Pacific Coast, has deprived us of many of our members; even so, the total number of members has increased during the year. The future prospects are good. We have had requests from several places in Nebraska, Iowa, and Dakota to come and preach the gospel, and we will continue with our work in faith and trust in God.[8]

During this time, the Norwegian-Danish Conference experienced rapid growth. The previous decade saw the opening of the Dakota Territory for settlement. At the Annual Conference in 1890, Asle was assigned to the Red River Valley District, an extensive District covering northern Minnesota and North Dakota, a territory with few members (343) organized into eight charges but only four preachers to serve them. Asle characterized this as "pioneer work" with many opportunities.[9]

---

[7] Norwegian and Danish Conference, Minutes, 1887, page 22.
[8] Norwegian and Danish Conference, Minutes, 1889, page 17.
[9] Norwegian and Danish Conference, Minutes, 1891, page 20.

In his first report as Presiding Elder of the Red River Valley District, Asle mentions previous hard times: "Churches are badly needed in several places, … but owing to the hard times which have prevailed there for several years, nothing has been able to be done in this direction." But he also expresses hope for the future: "The crop looks set to be very good this year, and this will help our work a lot. However, the farmers are still burdened with an oppressive debt, and it will take time before they can get back on a good footing." As for himself, he says, "My time has been unceasingly occupied with visiting the various congregations and with trying to expand the business of preaching in many new places."[10]

The following year, Asle reported steady progress in church affairs but noted difficulty in attracting new members:

> *Revival meetings have been held during the year, and many conversions have taken place. Nevertheless, there has not been such a large adherence to the church. They are Christians and profess to be Christians and want to participate in the services and enjoy the privileges of the church, but at the same time, they want to be exempted from all church obligations and refrain from organically uniting with us. This spirit of independence is strong in many places and has kept many from uniting with the church. We hope, however, that the fallacy of such a position will soon become apparent, and there is then greater hope for an increase in the number of members.*
>
> *The opportunities for expanding the work are good. Over the past year, we have received calls from new places to come and preach the gospel to them. To some, we have been able to go, but to others, we have not been able to reach.*

---

[10] Norwegian and Danish Conference, Minutes, 1891, pages 20–21.

> *However, to be able to make any permanent extension of the work, we must have more men and more money. Some of the preachers have three or four places under their charge, and to admit more under these circumstances is next to impossible.*[11]

In 1893, the District gained three new charges: one at Henning, Minnesota, and two in North Dakota at Enderlin and Valley City.[12] A man named Mathias Olsen was an early settler in Valley City. A carpenter, he built many of the buildings in the town, including a structure known as the "Academy of Music," which had two storefronts downstairs and a large hall upstairs where shows and musicals were held.[13]

Evangelisk Tidende published the following story about Mathias Olsen and the beginning of the Norwegian Methodist Church in Valley City:

> *Mrs. Mathias Olsen died. Mrs. Olsen had a niece in Duluth whom Mr. Olsen now wrote to with a request that she would come and take care of the house for him. She came, and after a while, there were questions about marriage.*
>
> *"No," said she, "I cannot live here. I love God and belong to the Methodist Church, and where there are no children of God, I cannot settle down."*
>
> *"But we have a hall," said Mr. Olsen, "send for a Methodist preacher, and be a Methodist if you will."*
>
> *She did, and the one who came was none other than Pastor Asle Knudsen. Soon, souls were saved, Mr. Olsen himself was saved, and a congregation was organized.*[14]

---

[11] Norwegian and Danish Conference, Minutes, 1892, pages 18-19.

[12] Norwegian and Danish Conference, Minutes, 1893, page 23.

[13] *Barnes County History: Barnes County, North Dakota* (Barnes County Historical Society, 1976), page 181.

[14] "En snartur af redaktøren [A quick tour by the editor]: Valley City, N. Dak.," *Evangelisk Tidende*, 7 June 1923, page 2.

In 1895, Asle reported "with pleasure that the Sunday school work has successfully been initiated over the entire district" and that "the congregations are increasingly including the children's religious education. I believe that there have never been so many children for weekly classes at the pastors' homes, and this makes me happy because the youth are the hope of our church's future." He points out that "in many places, where it is not possible to have regular pastoral care, the Presiding Elder must be both Pastor and Elder."[15]

During his twelve years as Presiding Elder of the Saint Paul and Red River Valley Districts, Asle and his family lived at 696 Sims Street in Saint Paul. From there, he reported traveling 175,500 miles: 157,400 by train, 3,600 by horse during the first three years, and 14,500 by team in the remaining nine years.

As Presiding Elder of the Saint Paul District, he dedicated seven churches: Minneapolis, Saint Paul, Blooming Grove, and Scandia Grove in Minnesota; Des Moines and Missouri Valley in Iowa; and Omaha in Nebraska. As Presiding Elder of the Red River Valley District, he organized a congregation in Valley City, North Dakota and dedicated three churches: Tordenskjold, Stephen, and Warren, all in Minnesota.

---

[15] Norwegian and Danish Conference, Minutes, 1895, page 21.

Minnesota United Methodist Church (UMC) Archives

First Norwegian-Danish Methodist Church
S. 9th Street and 13th Avenue S., Minneapolis

Asle, in his capacity as presiding elder of the district, dedicated this church on 11 September 1887. At that year's Conference he reported that "with its high tower, beautiful style and decoration, this church is probably the most beautiful Norwegian-Danish Methodist church in America."

At the end of his final report as Presiding Elder of the Red River Valley District, Asle wrote:

> *This concludes my sixth year as Presiding Elder of this District. Throughout this time, I have done what I could to advance the Master's cause, and He has been good to me. My health has not always been what I could have wished for. Last spring, I was very unwell for several weeks. However, through anxieties, labors, and difficulties, many of which He alone knows, He has stayed with me, and I am grateful to Him for that. However, I feel the urge to rest, and I hope the Conference will give me a year of freedom from active service.*[16]

---

[16] Norwegian and Danish Conference, Minutes, 1896, page 21.

Later Pastorates

The 1896 Conference did not grant Asle's request. Instead, it appointed him to the Eidsvold congregation in Leon Township, Goodhue County, Minnesota, a small congregation with only 12 members.[1] It must have been a welcome change of pace for Asle after serving 12 continuous years as Presiding Elder. The Eidsvold congregation had a church building built in 1893 but no parsonage, so Asle commuted to Eidsvold from his home in Saint Paul. Asle served this congregation for one year.

Asle's next appointment was Deer Park, Wisconsin. This charge included a congregation with a church in the town of Deer Park and a congregation in nearby Forest, Wisconsin. The Deer Park congregation had a parsonage, so Asle and his family moved there.

Deer Park was the largest rural congregation in the district—only the congregations in Minneapolis and Saint Paul were larger. The 1943 Norwegian-Danish Conference yearbook has brief histories of the churches that were active at the time. Of the Deer Park Church, it states:

> *This church has had almost a century of glorious history, rich in religious experience. Camp meetings have been one of her outstanding activities down through the years. To those meetings, thousands came to hear the word of God*

---

[1] *Minutes of the Annual Conferences*, Fall 1896, page 298; Fall 1897, page 610.

expounded by some of the most powerful preachers of our Conference. Her influence has been profound, at times dominating the life of the community.[2]

At the Fall 1898 Annual Conference, Asle was appointed to Minneapolis, thus beginning his long association with the Minneapolis congregations. At this time, the Norwegian-Danish Conference had one church in Minneapolis, the large brick church on the southern edge of downtown at 9th Street and 13th Avenue called First Norwegian-Danish Methodist Church.[3] This congregation had 180 members, four local preachers, and a Sunday school with over 100 pupils.[4]

In March 1900, Asle suffered a "stroke of heart paralysis" during a Sunday evening service. He was taken to his home, where he recovered. The only information we have about this incident is from an article in *Minneapolis Tidende*, which reported that he was out of danger the next day.[5]

Asle served this congregation for five years until the fall of 1903, by which time it had grown to 228 members, six local preachers, and 160 children in Sunday school.[6] The Knudsen family lived at 1822 11th Avenue South in Minneapolis during this time.[7]

---

[2] Norwegian-Danish Conference, *Journal and Year Book* (Chicago: By the Conference,1943), page 119. This was the last yearbook published before the Conference was dissolved.

[3] Norwegian and Danish Conference, Minutes, 1887, page 22.

[4] *Minutes of the Annual Conferences*, Fall 1898, page 534.

[5] *Minneapolis Tidende*, 25 March 1900, page 10, column 3; digital images, Minnesota Historical Society, *Minnesota Digital Newspaper Hub* (mnhs.org/newspapers).

[6] *Minutes of the Annual Conferences*, Fall 1903, page 453.

[7] *Davison's Minneapolis City Directory* (Minneapolis: Minneapolis Directory Co., 1899), page 733; (1901), page 765

INTRODUCTION

The Minneapolis congregation fostered two daughter congregations. One congregation was in the northern part of the city. It was known as North Minneapolis and later as Bethlehem Methodist. The other congregation was in Columbia Heights, a village northeast of Minneapolis.

North Minneapolis began as small meetings served by local preachers from First Minneapolis Church. In October 1901, a congregation was organized with ten members transferred from the mother church. Services were held in a rented hall.[8]

In 1905, the congregation decided to build a church and purchased a lot for that purpose on Emerson Avenue at 30th Avenue. An inaugural service for the finished church was held on the morning of the 3rd of June, 1906. In the afternoon, there was a ceremony during which Asle laid the cornerstone.[9] In a handwritten history of the congregation, Asle was happy to report that the congregation now had 67 members, two local preachers, a Sunday school, a choir, a youth group, and a women's auxiliary, of which his wife, Susan, was the President.[10]

---

[8] H. P. Bergh, *Femtiaarsskrift Udgivet ianledningaf* [sic] *Den norske-danske Methodismes Femtiaarsjublæum, 1901* (Chicago: Den norsk-danske Boghandel, 1901), page 49.

[9] "Hjørnesten nedlagt: En Festdag for Bethlehem norsk-danske Methodistmenighed" [Cornerstone Laid: A Day of Rejoicing for the Bethlehem Norwegian-Danish Methodist Congregation], *Minneapolis Tidende*, 8 June 1906, page 10, column 5.

[10] Asle Knudsen, "Menighedens Begyndelse" [The Congregation's Beginning], manuscript (1906), 4 pages; Congregations Papers (P0537), box 11, folder 21; Norwegian-American Historical Association, Northfield, Minnesota. A copy of this manuscript was placed inside the cornerstone.

Minnesota Conference UMC Archives

Bethlehem Methodist Church, North Minneapolis

Asle was pastor of North Minneapolis for two years, from 1904 to 1906, and another two years, from 1908 to 1910. He is considered to be the spiritual father of this congregation.[11]

Columbia Heights began as a preaching point referred to in the 1901 Minutes as Minneapolis Northeast.[12] In 1904, a Sunday school was organized, and two years later, a small church was built on the border between Columbia Heights and Minneapolis. Gospel services were held there occasionally by preachers from Bethlehem Church in North Minneapolis.[13]

---

[11] L. C. Knudson, "Velkomstfest" [Welcome Party], *Den Kristelige Talsmand,* 13 Nov 1919, page 9, column 3.

[12] *Minutes of the Annual Conferences,* Fall 1901, page 321.

[13] Norwegian-Danish Conference, *Journal and Year Book,* 1943, page 136.

Introduction

Between Asle's appointments to Minneapolis First Church and North Minneapolis, he was appointed to Diamond Bluff, Millville, and Red Wing for a year. Millville, formerly known as Plainview, and Red Wing were charges Asle had served before. Diamond Bluff is a village in Pierce County, Wisconsin, across the Mississippi River and slightly upstream from Red Wing. The church there was located 1½ miles northeast of the village. The members of this congregation were primarily immigrants from Denmark, so the church was locally known as the Danish Church. The Diamond Bluff congregation was organized in 1877 and served by pastors from Red Wing in its early years. It is likely Asle preached there during his previous appointment to Red Wing in 1844.

Asle continued serving the Diamond Bluff congregation for the following two years in addition to his duties in North Minneapolis.

At the 1906 Annual Conference, Asle was appointed Presiding Elder for the Chicago District. An article in *Minneapolis Tidende* emphasized the significance of this assignment:

> *Pastor Knudsen, who, despite his 63 years of age, still possesses the strength and energy required for this important post, was unanimously elected presiding elder for the Chicago District and must now exchange his idyllic calling in North Minneapolis for the largest field of work in the Conference. In Chicago, the Norwegian-Danish Methodists have no less than eight congregations. The district also serves Michigan, Illinois, and a large part of Wisconsin, approximately 40 congregations in all.*[14]

He served in Chicago as Presiding Elder for one year "when an accident made it necessary for him to take less

---

[14] *Minneapolis Tidende*, 5 October 1906, page 10, column 1.

taxing work."[15] Asle was not given a preaching appointment for the following year but instead was assigned the post of Financial Secretary for the Preachers' Aid Fund. After a year of recovery, Asle was again appointed to North Minneapolis for another two years.

At the Annual Conference in 1910, Asle requested retirement from active service, which was granted with an expression of thanks for many years of faithful service.[16] He was then 66 years old and probably felt he could not continue traveling. He was appointed to Lake Mills, Iowa, where he served for the next 21 years, commuting there from his home in Minneapolis.

During his first two years at Lake Mills, he was also appointed to Palmer and Glenville. Palmer was formerly known as Blooming Grove, a church Asle dedicated in 1885 when he was the Presiding Elder of the Saint Paul District. When the church building was moved, the name changed also since it was no longer in Blooming Grove Township. Little is known about Glenville.

For the last 12 years at Lake Mills, Asle's appointment included Albert Lea, Minnesota. Conveniently, Albert Lea was where he had to change trains on his way to Lake Mills.

---

[15] Leslie, "Albert Cornelius Knudson, the Man," page 2.

[16] *Kristelig Tidende*, 7 October 1910, page 316, column 1; digital images, National Library of Norway, *Nasjonalbiblioteket,* Newspaper collection (nb.no/search?mediatype=aviser).

Retirement

In the fall of 1928, at 84 years of age, Asle announced his intention to retire from active service with the hope that the Conference could find a successor. However, the congregation at Lake Mills was reluctant to accept.[1] In any case, the Conference appointed him to Lake Mills for another year.[2]

In March 1929, just two months after his 85th birthday, Asle was struck by a taxicab while on his way to Lake Mills. His son had driven him to the Great Northern station in Minneapolis. While walking between the car and the depot, the taxi hit him hard enough to knock him down; the wheel ran over his leg and stopped just short of his head! Asle got up and, despite his injury, insisted on continuing his journey.[3]

When he arrived in Lake Mills, his leg was so sore and swollen that it forced him to stay in bed. The next afternoon, members of his congregation gathered at the home where he was staying and "enjoyed a sermon preached by the Reverend gentleman while seated in bed."

Asle preached a farewell sermon on 20 October 1929 to a packed church. The *Lake Mills Graphic* reported that

---

[1] "Rev. A. Knudsen Resigns Pastorate in Lake Mills," *Lake Mills (Iowa) Graphic*, 12 September 1928, page 4, column 4; digital images, *Lake Mills Public Library* (lakemills.advantage-preservation.com).

[2] Norwegian and Danish Conference, Minutes, 1928, page 20.

[3] Information in this and the following paragraph is from "Rev. A. Knudsen Met with Accident," *Lake Mills Graphic,* 20 March 1929, p. 1, col. 6.

"Rev. Knudsen preached a very touching farewell sermon and ... stated that it was with deep regret that he found it necessary to resign the pastorate, but his advanced age made it necessary."[4]

He left that November for a trip to California and spent the winter of 1929-1930 there. During the summer of 1930, Asle, who by this time had become the oldest living Norwegian Methodist minister in the world, supplied First Church in Minneapolis for three months while the congregation's pastor was traveling in Norway.[5]

Asle also spent the following winter (1930-1931) in California. He stayed with his sister, Rina, in the Tokay Colony near Lodi from Christmas until the end of March and could "have stayed even longer on a friendly invitation."[6] Since the appointed pastor for the Tokay congregation lived 120 miles away in Cupertino, California, and the rail connection to Tokay was difficult, the appointed pastor could only serve Tokay part-time. Asle was happy to fill in and reported preaching in the Tokay church every week for two and a half months. In their appointments for 1931-1932, the Western Conference listed Asle as supplying Tokay, but by then, Asle had returned to Minneapolis. Instead, the Norwegian-Danish Conference, at their annual meeting that fall, asked Asle to supply Lake Mills for two more years, although not on a full-time basis, as the *Lake Mills Graphic* reported in May 1933:

> *The Rev. Asle Knudsen ... resumed his preaching here Sunday at the Norwegian Methodist church after an*

---

[4] "Rev. Knudsen Completes Service," *Lake Mills Graphic*, 23 October 1929, page 1, column 1.

[5] Norwegian and Danish Conference, Minutes, 1930, page 26. Also: Asle Knudsen Diary, MS (1844-1937), page 18.

[6] Asle Knudsen, "Minder fra Reisen" [Memories from the Journey], *Evangelisk Tidende*, 30 April 1931, page 7.

absence of several months. A large crowd was out to greet him. The Rev. Mr. Knudsen has been coming to Lake Mills for more than 25 years to serve the local congregation. He makes his home at Minneapolis. During the winter months, he has been traveling In California, Oregon, and Washington.[7]

On Sunday, August 27, 1933, after 21 years of service, Asle preached his final farewell sermon in Lake Mills.[8]

During his retirement, Asle continued to be active; he was pastor emeritus at First Norwegian-Danish Church in Minneapolis,[9] he would fill in at other area churches as needed, and he continued to attend the Annual Conferences. He attended various church events, such as the 70th anniversary of the Norwegian-Danish Methodist Church in Forest City, Iowa, on October 17-18, 1936, during which he gave a sermon at a memorial service by the grave of his old friend, Rev. A. O. Ulland (formerly known as A. Olsen) who was Forest City's first pastor.[10]

As he had throughout his career, Asle continued officiating at weddings and funerals for family, friends, and former parishioners. During his retirement, he was able to celebrate the golden wedding anniversaries of couples he had married. There were two instances we know of: in 1935, he attended an anniversary in Hendricks, Minnesota, for a

---

[7] "From California," *Lake Mills Graphic,* 3 May 1933, page 1, column 6.

[8] "Rev. A. Knudsen Resigns After Service of 21 Years," *Lake Mills Graphic,* 23 August 1933, page 1, column 5.

[9] "Rev. Asle Knudsen Notes 94th Year; Active as Emeritus," *Minneapolis Star,* 20 January 1938, page 11, column 2; digital images, *Newspapers.com.*

[10] "Scandinavian Methodist Church 70th Anniversary Program Sunday," *Forest City (Iowa) Summit*, 15 October 1936, page 7, column 1; digital images, Winnebago Historical Society, newspaper archive (forestcity.advantage-preservation.com).

couple he had married 50 years prior when he was the minister at the Belvidere church,[11] and in 1936, he attended a celebration for Pastor E. T. Schollert and wife, a couple that Asle had married in 1886 in Saint Paul.[12]

On Asle's 90th birthday, three of his former congregations held a reception in his honor at First Norwegian Danish Methodist Church in Minneapolis. In an interview in the *Minneapolis Tribune*, Asle remarked, "Even now, I could preach twice a Sunday. I have always been healthy. I can hear pretty well, see very well, and haven't any rheumatism."[13]

He also reflected upon pioneer times:

> *The ministers these days don't know what the older preachers had to go through. Then we had few churches; the country was wild. The ministers went out into new territory where roads were few and the oxen had to take the place of the automobile.*
>
> *Now, too, the attitude of the church is different. Denominations have come to know each other and to recognize each other. It used to be that every time different denominations got together, they would argue over the various doctrines.*

A similar celebration was held for Asle's 94th birthday. At that time, he said he could see no reason why he couldn't live to be 100. "As long as I can think clearly, I want to preach

---

[11] *Reform* (Eau Claire, Wisconsin), 23 May 1935, page 1, column 1; digital images, Waldemar Ager Association, *Waldemar Ager Museum* (rescarta.apps.uwec.edu/Ager-Web).

[12] *Reform,* 7 May 1936, page 1, column 3.

[13] Information in this paragraph as well as the following quote is from "Pastor, 90 on Friday, Will Be Honor [sic] Guest of Three Congregations at Dinner Celebration," *Minneapolis Tribune,* 17 January 1934, page 3; digital images, *Newspapers.com*.

the teachings of Christ," he said.[14] However, this was not to be. He fell ill the following September and was confined to his home. His son Albert recounts that, during his final year, a steady stream of letters and postcards went out from his sick room.[15]

He celebrated his 95th birthday at home, receiving congratulatory telegrams from around the world. Despite his illness, he could enjoy coffee with those who came to congratulate him, and he gave a short speech.[16]

Asle passed away shortly before midnight on Friday, 29 September 1939, at his home on Portland Avenue. The physician who signed his death certificate indicated the cause of death as coronary sclerosis, a hardening of the arteries caused by atheroma, a build-up of plaque on the arteries.[17]

A memorial service was held on Monday, 2 October, at Simpson Methodist Church in Minneapolis. Several hundred people attended the service, including many fellow pastors from both the Norwegian-Danish and English-speaking conferences. Pastor Asbjorn Smedstad observed: "It was a touching sight to see the long procession that passed in front of the coffin to cast its last glance at the body of one so loved by all."[18]

---

[14] "Pastor Marks 94th Birthday, Looks Forward to Being 100," *Minneapolis Tribune*, 20 January 1938, page 15, column 7.

[15] Albert C. Knudsen, "Father" in "Asle and Susan Knudsen: A Tribute," memorial booklet ([1940]), page 8.

[16] A. Kristensen Hagen, "Amerikabrev" [America Letter], *Kristelig Tidende*, 12 May 1939, page 304.

[17] Minnesota Department of Health, death certificate, number 22195 (1939), informant was Albert C. Knudsen, son of deceased; certified copy (1984).

[18] Asbjorn Smedstad, "Omkring Asle Knudsens Minde" [Remembering Asle Knudsen], *Evangelisk Tidende*, 26 October 1939, page 8.

Courtesy of Hennepin County Library

Asle Knudsen on his 94th birthday

This portrait, by a *Minneapolis Tribune* staff photographer, was apparently taken in Asle's home at 3812 Portland Avenue. It was published in the 20 January 1938 issue of the paper.

INTRODUCTION

After the service, Asle was laid to rest in Forest Cemetery, now known as Forest Lawn Memorial Park, located on the outskirts of Saint Paul.[19] His wife, Susan, three of their children, Oscar, Henry, and Charles, and Susan's father, Torkel T. Fosse, are also buried there.

The amount of space devoted to Asle's memorial in *Evangelisk Tidende* attests to the measure of esteem in which he was held. The issue dedicated its first two pages and part of a third to Asle, which included a tribute written by his son, Albert, a memorial by Rev C. W. Schevenius (both in English), and an obituary by Rev. Asbjorn Smedstad, written in Norwegian.[20]

In addition to his pastoral duties, Asle fulfilled many other roles during his career. He was the financial agent for the Preachers' Aid Fund from its beginning in 1896 until 1918 and its treasurer from 1896 to 1930.[21] He was the first financial agent for the Elim Home for the Aged, established in 1913.[22] He also served as president of the Conference Trustees and was chairman of the Conference Board of Home Missions and Church Extension "for a generation."[23]

Asle participated in organizations and events outside the Methodist church. One writer noted that whenever there was a large gathering of Norwegians in Minneapolis, Asle would probably be there.[24]

---

[19] "Rites Monday for Knudsen," *Minneapolis Star,* 1 October 1939, page 58, column 2. This cemetery is located at 1800 Edgerton Street in Maplewood, Minnesota.

[20] *Evangelisk Tidende,* 26 October 1939, pages 1-3, 8.

[21] Andersen, *Salt of the Earth,* page 278.

[22] Ibid., page 176.

[23] Schevenius, "Asle Knudsen," page 2.

[24] "Pastor Asle Knudsen død," *Reform*, 5 October 1939, page 1.

He was a member of the Hallinglag of America. A *lag* is an organization for immigrants from a particular district in Norway (in this case, Hallingdal) and their descendants. He served on the Resolution Committee in 1913.[25] In the March 1923 issue of *Hallingen*, the lag's monthly publication, the editor marveled that, despite his many years in America, Asle could still speak pure Halling dialect at the annual *stevne* (reunion).[26]

The Norwegian-language newspapers reported his attendance at South Minneapolis Temperance Association meetings. On one occasion in 1899, he gave a lecture, and at meetings in 1936 and 1937, he delivered the closing prayer.[27] We don't know if Asle was a member of this organization. Still, as a lifelong teetotaler, he would have supported their cause.[28]

He was a popular speaker, being asked to talk about "old times" on several occasions. In 1920, Asle spoke at the Hallinglag stevne, where his topic was "Hallingdal Half a Hundred Years Ago."[29]

He probably addressed his largest audience when he spoke at the 1925 Norse-American Centennial celebration at the Minnesota State Fairgrounds in Saint Paul. Despite being limited to 15 minutes:

---

[25] "Hallinglaget: Talrigt Fremmøde til Hallinglagets sjette aarlige Stævne" [Large Attendance at the Hallinglag's Sixth Annual Convention], *Minneapolis Tidende*, 12 June 1913, page 12, column 5.

[26] "Norsk-amerikanske præster af Hallingæt" [Norwegian-American Pastors of Halling Descent], *Hallingen*, March 1923, page 15.

[27] *Reform*, 18 April 1899, page 3, column 3; *Nordisk Tidende*, 5 March 1936, page 13, column 1; *Reform*, 13 May 1937, page 2, column 3.

[28] Carl G. O. Hansen, *My Minneapolis* (Minneapolis: Standard Press, 1956), pages 84–85.

[29] "Fraa pastor Asle Knutson til Hallinglaget" [From Pastor Asle Knudsen to the Hallinglag], *Hallingen*, 15 September 1920, page 775.

> *Monday Forenoon*
> JUNE EIGHTH, 1925
> ## NORSE SESSION
> HIPPODROME
> *Nine-Thirty O'Clock*
> WALDEMAR AGER, ORDSTYRER
> INTRODURETJ AV LAURA BRATAGER
>
> SANG — — — — — — — *Concordia College Choir*
> PROF. HERMAN W. MONSON, LEDER
>
> FEMTEN-MINUT-TALER
>
> DET NORSKE FOLK — — — — — — *L. Oftedal*
> FÆDRENEARVEN — — — — — *Prof. O. E. Rølvaag*
> SANG — — — — — — — — *A. J. Bøe*
> GLIMT FRA NYBYGGERLIVET — — — — *Past. Asle Knutsen*
> ET BLIK PAA NORDMÆNDENES HISTORIE I AMERIKA
> *Past. L. M. Gimmestad*
> SANG — — — — — — *Concordia College Choir*
> NORDMANDSFORBUNDET — — — — — *W. Morgenstierne*
> BRODERSKAPSFORENINGER — — — — — *L. Stavnheim*
> SANG — — — — — — — — *Alvin Snesrud*
> NORSKE HJEM — — — — — — *Past. T. O. Tolo*
> PRESTEHJEMMETS PLADS I VORT FOLKELIV — *Ola Johann Saervold*
> SANG — — — — — — *Concordia College Choir*
> INTRODUKTION AV ÆTLINGER AV SLUPPEFOLKET

Norwegian-American Historical Association

1925 Norse-American Centennial program

On Monday morning, June 8, 1925, each speaker was limited to 15 minutes. Asle's topic was "Glimpses of Settler Life."

> *Pastor Asle Knudsen of Minneapolis delivered one of the most successful speeches during the festivities on Monday morning in the great Hippodrome to an enthusiastic gathering. His subject was 'Settler Life,' and he painted in broad strokes and with lively colors both the serious and tragicomic situations that met the newcomer, especially as they behaved 60 years ago. We thought it was almost a miracle that a man of 81 years could keep the huge gathering interested from his first word to the last, a new proof of the word of God, which says: 'Even in old age, the fresh shoots sprout.'* [30]

Several writers have attested that Asle was a compelling speaker and preacher. Pastor Ole Røhrstaff once stated: "Those who know Pastor Knudsen know that he can sow his words to suit the occasion."[31] An anecdote from Asle's son, Albert, illustrates this point:

> *I remember particularly his speaking four or five years ago on a very hot day at the funeral of a popular young man. A thousand people or more were crowded into the chapel. Many of them probably had little, if any, religious interest. Yet this veteran of more than ninety summers arose and, in about twenty minutes, delivered one of the most fitting and helpful addresses I have ever heard on such an occasion.*[32]

---

[30] "Fra Pastor Asle Knudsen," *Evangelisk Tidende*, 16 July 1925, page 8, column 1. One source estimates the attendance at this event was 8,000 people. See "Hundreaarsfesten" [Centenary celebration], *Scandinaven*, 12 June 1925, page 7; *Nasjonalbiblioteket*.

[31] O. Røhrstaff, "Indtryk fra Aarsmødet" [Impressions from the Annual Meeting] *Den Kristelige Talsmand*, 3 October 1918, page 8.

[32] Albert Knudson, "Father," pages 7–8.

After Asle preached at a camp meeting near Hillsboro, North Dakota, in 1918, Rev. H. M. Holm, who was the pastor there, had this to say:

> *Very few preachers have such a winning disposition and peculiar ability to win friends among young and old, rich and poor, learned and unlearned, indeed all classes of men, as Pastor Knudsen. And his sermons! What a joy to sit and listen to them! Simple truths presented in such a way that they are awakening, edifying, and, at the same time, worthy of being tested in the light of modern thinking. Despite his advanced age, Pastor Knudsen's thoughts are clear and logical.... He preaches the Gospel of Jesus Christ in a dignified manner and at the same time with a feeling and sincerity that sets the very innermost strings of the human heart in motion.*[33]

And, after a district preachers' meeting in Crookston, Minnesota, Rev. Holm reported:

> *The veteran, Pastor Asle Knudson, was to speak in the evening. Everyone knows Pastor Knudson as a noble, gracious man. His fine, heartfelt presentation touched the tenderest strings in the heart of everyone in the audience....*
>
> *His speech, well-arranged, was illuminated with fine illustrations from Real Life. Pathos and Humor alternated but without a trace of excessiveness. Everything was so warm, so beautiful, so moving. It's too bad that no such man can live this life again.*[34]

---

[33] H. M. Holm, "Korrespondance fra Hillsboro, N. D.," *Den Kristelige Talsmand,* 3 July 1919, page 7, column 1.

[34] H. M. Holm, "Referat for Red River Valley Distrikts Prestemøde afhold i Crookston, Minn., 24–28 April 1918" [Minutes of the Red River Valley District Preachers Meeting held at Crookston, Minn.], *Den Kristelige Talsmand*, 23 May 1918, page 7.

Asle's Diary

Preface to Asle's Diary

In the year 1895, Rev. Asle Knudsen sat down to write the story of his life. Writing longhand in Norwegian, he made annual entries until 1937, two years before his death.

After his death, this document's precise provenance is unknown. Ultimately, the diary made its way into the possession of his granddaughter, Dorothy Petersen Swaney, who had it translated into English in 1977.[1] The translator she hired, whose identity is unknown, refused to finish it because it included things Asle wrote when he was discouraged.[2] It is unknown if anyone completed the translation, so what we have may be incomplete. The original Norwegian-language diary has been lost.

The translation is a typewritten document 18 pages long with parenthetical insertions by the translator and hand-written notes by Dorothy. I have divided the diary into chapters corresponding to Asle's pastoral appointments. Chapter titles have been added, but the subtitles remain the same as in the translation.

Long blocks of text have been broken into smaller paragraphs, and commas have been added where necessary to make it easier to read. Dorothy's handwritten notes and comments, as well as parenthetical comments added by the

---

[1] Stan Petersen (a nephew of Dorothy Petersen Swaney) to Jim Larson, email, 4 March 2019, "RE: Family Tree DNA."

[2] Bob Swaney (son of Dorothy Petersen Swaney) to Stan Petersen, email, 4 March 2019, "Re: Asle Knudsen Diary." Both Stan and Bob are grand-children of Stella (Knudsen) Petersen, Asle's daughter.

translator, have been footnoted. Abbreviations have been spelled out. Some of the bishop's names were misspelled and, in one case, omitted. The correct names have been added in square editorial brackets [ ]. Also, state names after place names have been added in square brackets. In one instance, the text repeats itself for a couple of paragraphs. The duplicate text has been omitted and is indicated by ellipses (…).

    Asle provides a set of statistics for each year that he was a traveling preacher, which includes a detailed accounting of the money he collected for various benevolent societies. The first time this happens (1874), I included all the information as it appears in the diary and expanded the abbreviations used in the diary to their full names. In subsequent years, I have summarized the data with an editorial comment such as [benevolent societies].

    I first became aware of this document's existence when Sue Daigle, a great-granddaughter of Asle, posted extracts from it on her *Facebook* page. Sue was kind enough to send me a copy. Later, in a conversation with Stan Petersen, it was discovered that his copy had additional handwritten notes by Dorothy that were not in Sue's copy. All of the notes from both copies are incorporated into this work.

JML

Asle's Relatives in Winneshiek County

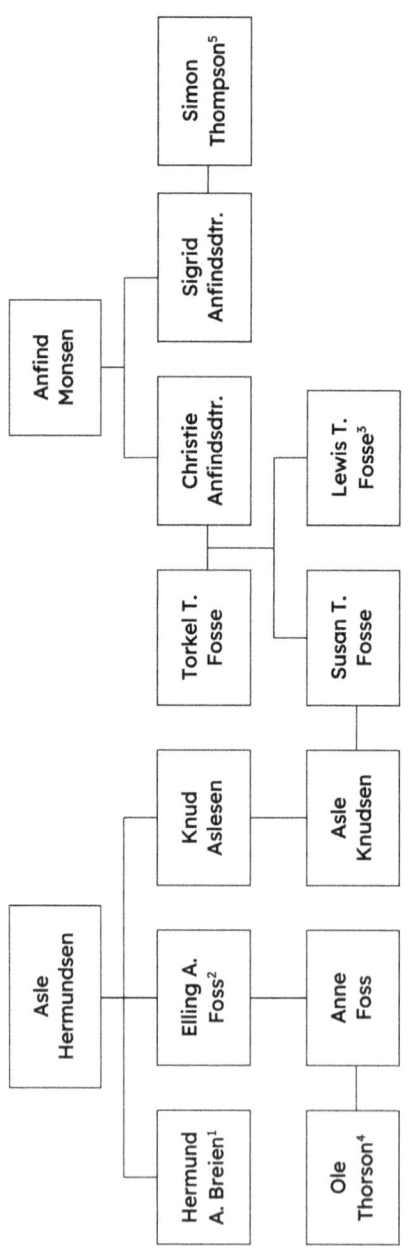

1. Uncle Hermund raised Asle from the age of 12. Asle lived with Uncle Hermund from 1856–1865.
2. Uncle Elling emigrated to America in 1850 and offered Asle a place to stay if he should decide to come to America.
3. Lewis T. Foss gave Asle a ride from Lansing, Iowa, to Uncle Elling's farm when Asle arrived in 1865. Asle would later marry Lewis' sister, Susan.
4. Asle worked for Ole Thorson during his first summer in America.
5. Simon Thompson sold a farm to Asle in 1896.

Early Years

The 19th of January 1844, I, Asle Knudsen, was born into this world, of parents Knud Aslesen Nygaard and Birgit Knudsdatter Flaaten, in Aals Parish (now Hols Parish) in Hallingdal, Norway.[1] My dear mother died when I was six years old, and my dear father was left with three children: I was the only son, sister Eli the oldest, and Astrid younger than I. One year, I was a herdsboy for Gutorm Tufte in Ustedalen.[2] At 12 years of age, I went to live with my father's brother, Herman Breen.[3] My father was married a second time to Guri Olsdatter Tufto in Kunslen[4] and had four daughters with her, so I now have three half-sisters living (January 28, 1895). Father died the winter of 1888 in his 73rd year.[5]

---

[1] Citations for birth, marriage and death events are in the "Lineage of Asle Knudsen" in the Appendix. The modern spelling for these parishes is Ål and Hol.

[2] Ustedalen is the name of a *grend* (a rural neighborhood or group of farms) near the modern-day town of Geilo.

[3] Asle's uncle's name is spelled Hermund in the Norwegian records. This translation uses the anglicized spelling of his name throughout. The modern spelling of the Breen farm is Breie.

[4] The correct 1865 spelling was Qvislen, the modern spelling is Kvisla. This is a grend between Geilo and the village of Hol.

[5] According to the church records, Knud Aslesen died on 18 November 1885. See Hol Parish (Buskerud, Norway), Hol Ministerialbok nr.2, folio 355, entry 15; digital images, National Archives of Norway, *Digitalarkivet* (media.digitalarkivet.no), parish registers.

At my Uncle Herman's, I served as a herdsboy for four years, and in May 1860, I was confirmed by Pastor Kjelstrup[6] in Aals Church in Hallingdal. I moved that same fall to Drammen with my Uncle Herman. We lived a year at Utenga near Lier, and then I went to Gifstad's in Lier, where I stayed for about two years to learn farming.[7] Siri and Sicilia Gifstad were very God-fearing and did much for me to lead me to piety.[8] So, I lived in Drammen two or three years and then with Uncle Herman near Thorrud in Skougar for two years. These two years, I was a manager on the farm for Uncle Herman and had it very good. He and his wife, Ingeborg, were very pious and did everything possible to get me to go the Lord's Way.

Overseas to America

1865—The 12th of May, we sailed from Christiania[9] for the land of America, and after three days on the North Sea, we stepped ashore at Hull, England. After a day's stop there, we continued our journey by railroad over England to Liverpool and stayed there three days. The 17th of May, we went out to see the big, wide city of Liverpool. Andrew Johnsen and Peter Linam were my traveling companions, and we had a

---

[6] Frederik C. A. Kjelstrup was Pastor of Ål Parish from 1851 until 1867. See Thor Warberg, *Nye Ål bygdebok* (aal-bygdebok.no/111001-.htm), Prestgarden, gnr. 111, bnr. 1-, entry 5648.

[7] Asle attended the agricultural school in Lier from 1862 to 1864. Lars Reinton and Sigurd S. Reinton, *Folk og Fortid i Hol*, volume 2, *Frå 1815 til Vår Tid* (Oslo: Grøndahl & Søn, 1943), page 68.

[8] Rolf Fladby, in *Liers historie*, volume 2, *Gårdshistorie* (Lier Bygdeboknemnd, 1963), page 284, states that the Gifstad farm was owned by Herman Christiansen and that he had eight children, among whom were two daughters; Siri and "Sille."

[9] Present-day Oslo.

wonderful day. The 20th of May, we went aboard the steamer *Hamilton*[10] and were 11 days on the Atlantic Ocean. We had a terrible storm that lasted one night, but all went well, and we landed in Quebec, Canada, the 2nd of June.[11]

We stayed there a day and then continued over land to Breden on Lake Michigan, and there we took a steamboat to Milwaukee, [Wisconsin]. Arriving there late in the evening, we were taken to a hotel and were supposed to sleep there, but what a terrible experience we had with bedbugs, which I was not familiar with.

The next day, we separated as companions, and my journey was supposed to be to Prairie du Chien, [Wisconsin], but instead, I came to La Crosse, [Wisconsin], at midnight and the next day to Lansing, [Iowa], by steamboat. I slept under the open skies at night and bought breakfast at the tailor's, as they called him. Then I got a ride with Lewis Fosse to my Uncle Elling's[12], but oh, how tired I was on that trip, and oh so glad I was safely arrived in this great land; but I didn't see any spit-broiled hogs with knife and fork standing out of their backs—which they spoke of in Norway.[13]

---

[10] This was the *Hammonia,* which had been renamed *Belgian* the previous year.

[11] Passenger List, SS *Belgian*, page 6, entry 887, Asle Knudsen; "Passenger Lists: Quebec 1865-1921," digital image, *Library and Archives Canada,* (collectionscanada.gc.ca).

[12] Elling Aslesen was Asle's paternal uncle and went by the name of Elling Foss in America. He emigrated in 1850 and bought a farm in Highland Township, Winneshiek County, Iowa. Lewis Fosse (no relation) lived on a neighboring farm and was a brother of Susan Fosse, Asle's future wife.

[13] Asle later wrote, in a letter to *Hallingen,* that he "came to Decorah, Iowa, just as the soldiers were returning home from the [Civil War]. The many sick and wounded made a deep and lasting impression on me" (*Hallingen*, January 1917, page 30).

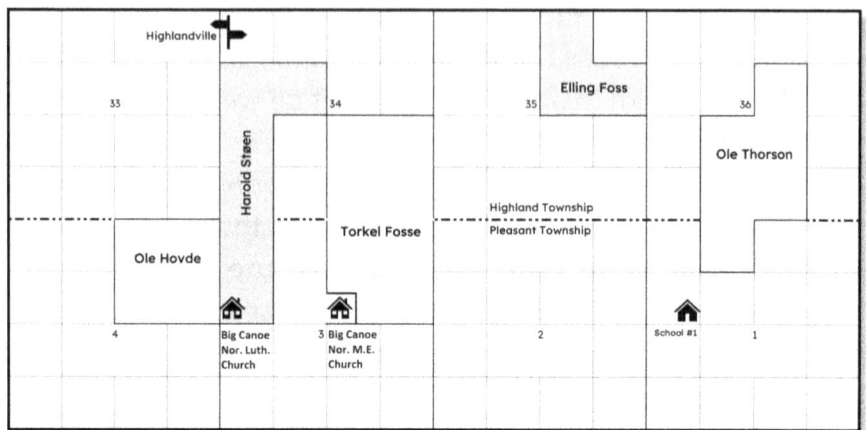

Map of nearby farms in the Big Canoe area

Out to Work

The 5th of July, I began the summer work at Ole Thorson's, haying and harvesting, stacking and threshing, all heavy work.[14] In the fall, I was at Ole Dummerud's for two months and worked hard husking corn. That summer, I made $140 and bought a pair of horses of Ole Dummerud, but that was a poor deal because they weren't trained well.

The first winter I was in America was spent in English School, for a time at Aase schoolhouse[15], and at Harold Stoen's.[16] An Irish teacher was the first one, and the next one

---

[14] Ole Thorson was married to Asle's cousin Anne Foss, step-daughter of his uncle Elling Foss.

[15] Anders Aase was one of the earliest settlers in the Big Canoe area. The location of this schoolhouse has not been determined.

[16] Harald Halstensen Støen (1831-1910) emigrated from Nes in Hallingdal in 1850 on board the bark *Drafna*, on the same voyage as Asle's uncle Elling Foss. His family is listed immediately before Elling's family in the *Drafna* passenger list. "New York Passenger Lists, 1820-1891," digital images, *FamilySearch* (familysearch.org);

was Sever Ellingson, my cousin.[17] I stayed part-time with Elling and then with Mr. Ole Hovde during the school period The summer I spent at Aase, I got $25 a month salary for 7 months and had a good job as manager of the work. I drove often to Decorah and Lansing, and on these trips, I took a heavy cold which developed into a sickness.

Entering Matrimony

The 27th of November, 1866, I married Susan Torkelsen Fosse of Winneshiek County, Iowa.[18] She was born in Feiaas, Sogne, Norway, September 12th, 1842, of parents Torkel Fosse and Christina Anfinson Twedt,[19] and came with her parents to America when she was 12 years old. She was confirmed by Elder Clausen[20] at Spring Grove, [Minnesota].[21] We were married at the courthouse in Decorah by Judge Willett. My wife was then 24 years old and healthy and beautiful as a rose. She weighed 170 pounds. Shortly after we were married, I became sick with pneumonia, and we then moved in with my wife's parents.

---

citing National Archives and Records Administration microfilm publication M237, roll 091, list 850.

[17] Sever Ellingson was a stepson of Elling Foss.

[18] They were married in the Winneshiek County Courthouse.

[19] The modern spellings are Feios, Sogn, and Tveit.

[20] Here Asle uses Methodist terminology to refer to Clausen, a Lutheran pastor. In Methodism, Elder is a title given to an fully ordained minister, someone who is not a lay preacher or a Deacon. In Lutheranism, all ministers are ordained and are referred to simply as Pastor.

[21] Susan was confirmed 26 September 1858 in the Ostre Skolehuus [East Schoolhouse] in the Big Canoe Settlement by Pastor F. C. Clausen of Spring Grove, Minnesota. See Big Canoe Lutheran Church, Record Book 1 (1857–1893), page 219, entry 21, "Synneva Torkelsd"; Evangelical Lutheran Church in America microfilm #44.

Glory to God!

1867—In January, meetings began in the church at Big Canoe. The Pastor was Arne Johnson, E. Endreson was also there,[22] and during these meetings, my wife and I found peace with God the same evening. That evening, Johnson preached on John 14:9.[23] That was a wonderful evening that will be remembered to eternity. We went in as candidates the next month in church and as full members a year later, with A. Johnson, Pastor.

The 10th of December, 1867, while we lived in a little room with my father-in-law, our first-born son, Charles Theodore, was born into this world. He weighed 10 pounds and caused his mother great pain at his coming. He was baptized by A. Johnson and was very sick as a small child.

The 8th of February, 1868, I took out my first citizenship papers[24] ... My cousin, Kittel Ellingson, was with me. Three years later, I got my second citizenship papers[25], but I learned that they had not been legally made since it had been done only by the clerk without the District Judge, and so on the 26th of October, 1876, I got my present official

---

[22] Arne Johnson was the pastor of the Big Canoe congregation from 1867–1870; Endre Endresen was the pastor from 1870–1872 (*Minutes of the Annual Conferences of the Methodist Episcopal Church*, New York: [various publishers], 1866–1871).

[23] "Jesus saith unto him, Have I been so long time with you, and yet hast thou not known me, Philip? he that hath seen me hath seen the Father; and how sayest thou then, Shew us the Father?"

[24] Winneshiek County, Iowa, District Court, Naturalization Record, book 2, page 99, "Aslay Knutson"; Recorder's Office, Winneshiek County Courthouse, Decorah.

[25] Winneshiek County Naturalization Records, Second Papers, book 5, page 93, "Asle Knutson," 10 October 1870.

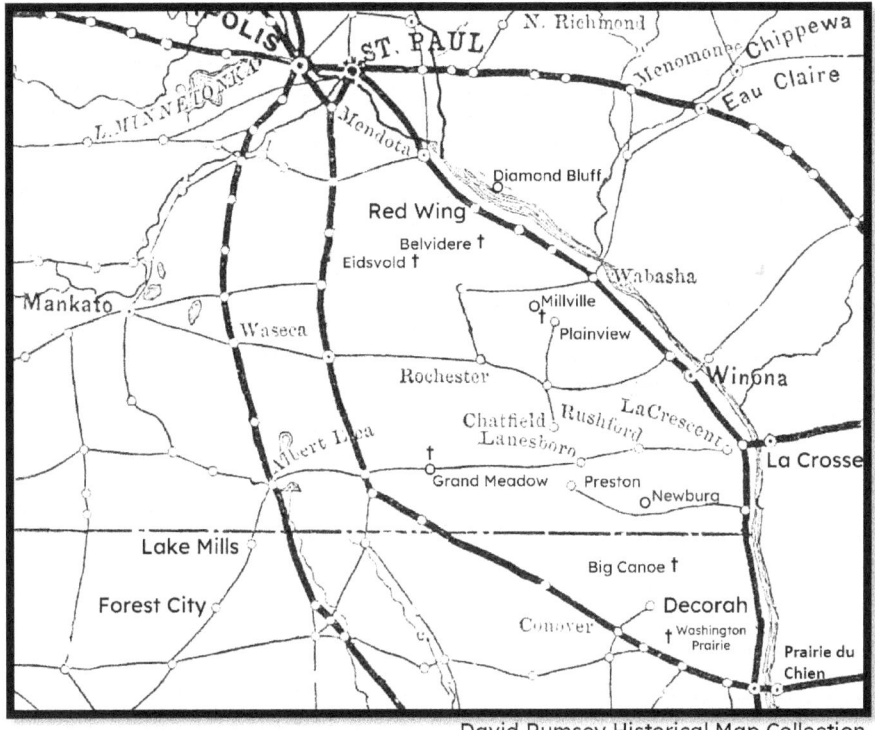

Railroad map of southeast Minnesota, circa 1885

citizenship paper with R. Nobel, Judge, at the courthouse in Decorah.[26]

1869—In the spring we moved to the farm which we bought from Simon Thompson.[27] Our daughter, Tina Alvina, was born in Simon's house the 22nd of June, 1869, and was baptized by A. Johnson. We had this farm two years, and there we worked and almost wore ourselves out. We sold it

---

[26] Ibid., book 6, page 279, "Asle Knudson."
[27] Simon Thompson was married to Susan's maternal aunt, Sigrid Anfindsdatter.

after two years and lost a lot of money.[28] In the winter of 1871, we moved to my father-in-law's and bought 80 acres from him for $700. In the summer we cleared about 20 acres and got it plowed and paid $500 down.

In 1870, I got a lay preacher's license when E. Endreson was our Pastor.

1871—The 7th of March, our son Henry Bethuel was born in the same room in which Charles was born, and he was baptized by E. Endreson. The 9th of September, I was examined as a local preacher at Big Canoe by Presiding Elder C. F. Lindquist and then received a local license.

---

[28] The price of wheat, Asle's main crop, rose dramatically after the end of the Civil War and peaked at $1.43 per bushel in 1867. After that, the price began to drop and reached a low of $.85 in 1869–1870. This was probably why Asle says he lost money on the farm. See Thorstein B. Veblen, "The Price of Wheat Since 1867," *Journal of Political Economy*, 1 (December 1892), chart 1, between pages 70–71; PDF, *The University of Chicago Press: Journals* (journals.uchicago.edu/doi/epdf/ 10.1086/250116).

Grand Meadow and Plainview

1872—September 7th, my local license was renewed at the quarterly conference in Newburg, [Minnesota], A. Johnson, Presiding Elder pro tem, and G. Gabrielsen, Sec'y. That same fall, we sold our cattle and hay and all to get ready to move to supply a congregation. The 7th of November, we left with our children Tina and Henry. Charlie was left at his grandfather's house.[1] Our means of travel was a small black horse by the name of Charly, which we bought from Rev. A. Johnson, and a poor little buggy. Torkel Fosse drove our household goods.

After two days of travel, we came to Grand Meadow, cold and hungry. We stayed with Ole Sorbon,[2] and the following day, we moved into the parsonage that stood next to the little church. We didn't have any carpet to lay down, and it was pretty simple, but all clean and pretty and cozy in the home.

---

[1] Charlie was almost 5 years old, old enough to stay with his grandparents. Tina was 3 ½ and Henry was 6 months old.

[2] Ole Sorbon was one of the early settlers in the Bear Creek community and would have been Asle's nearest neighbor. The church and parsonage were located on the northeast corner of the Sorbon farm. See Franklyn Curtiss-Wedge, *History of Mower County, Minnesota* (Chicago: H.C. Cooper, Jr. & Co., 1911), page 360. Also:
An Illustrated Historical Atlas of the State of Minnesota (Chicago: A.T. Andreas, 1874), page 140; digital images, Minnesota Historical Society, *Minnesota Reflections* (reflections.mndigital.org/catalog/mhs:1192).

When Sunday came, I had my first sermon on Second Peter 3:18.[3] On Tuesday I went to Plainview and had my first sermon there at the home of H. Nelson, "Hold fast to that which you have lest someone take your Crown."[4] Tuesday night, I stayed with Mr. Martin Grove and preached at the home of C. Christe on "I am the Bread of Life."[5]

A short while before Christmas, I went on horseback from Plainview to Belvidere and back, stopping overnight with Olin O. It was a very hard trip, which I will not easily forget.[6] The Sunday before Christmas, we had our quarterly meeting in Plainview. J. H. Johnson, presiding elder, was there, and K. Knudsen from Belvidere.[7] It was very cold. On Monday, we went to Grand Meadow, 50 miles, by team, in 45-degree temperature. When we got home, we were almost

---

[3] "But grow in grace, and in the knowledge of our Lord and Saviour Jesus Christ. To him be glory both now and for ever."

[4] Halvor Nelson, a.k.a. Oliver Nelson, lived north of Plainview in Highland Township and was one of the area's earliest settlers. *History of Wabasha County* (Chicago: H. H. Hill & Co., 1884), pages 942-943.

[5] Martin A. Grove was a farmer and a prominent member of the community. He was a trustee of the church and served as county commissioner for fourteen years. See *History of Wabasha County*, pages 775, 1168-1169; also "Five Civil War Veterans ... ," *(Sioux Falls, South Dakota) Argus-Leader*, 14 May 1927, page 18. C. Christe was probably Christopher Christophersen, a neighbor of Martin Grove. On the 1874 map of Wabasha County, there is a C. Christopherson located about a mile from the Methodist church (*Illustrated Historical Atlas of the State of Minnesota*, page 102). Both men had farms in the Long Creek settlement two miles southeast of Millville.

[6] Belvidere is a township in Goodhue County, Minnesota, about 30 miles northwest of Plainview, a day's journey on horseback. The fact that he had to stop overnight indicates that the weather must have been terrible.

[7] Knud Knudsen was a local preacher in Belvidere. See Franklyn Curtiss-Wedge, *History of Goodhue County, Minnesota* (Chicago: H. C. Cooper, Jr. & Co.,1909), page 416.

frozen stiff. We were four in the company, myself, J. H. Johnson, K. Utigaard, and J. Jacobson.[8] Oh, what a memorable time. I went home for Christmas, but my horse had to be left behind, and I had to walk from Grand Meadow to Long Creek,[9] where I stayed until New Year's Day and had a wonderful day. God was with us in his great mercy, and many sinners were saved.

1873—The 7th, 8th, and 9th of January were memorable storm days. When I got back to Grand Meadow the stable was not to be found. The house was half snowed in and almost invisible with the snow drifted around it. My wife had been brought from the house on the 8th of January. She had to dress herself in trousers and struggle through the snow up to her armpits for half a mile. I found her at Engebret Sorbon's in good condition.[10] People froze to death in that storm.[11]

The 23rd of January, our son Albert Cornelius was born in our simple parsonage in Grand Meadow. Old Mother

---

[8] John H. Johnson was the Presiding Elder for the District; Knut Utigaard was a layman; John Jacobson had converted to Methodism in Grand Meadow in 1871 and was made an exhorter in Plainview by Asle. See A. Haagensen, *Den Norsk-Danske Methodismes Historie, Paa begge Sider havet* [The History of Norwegian-Danish Methodism on Both Sides of the Ocean] (1894; facsimile reprint, Scholar Select), pages 83–84. He became a travelling preacher in 1874. See *Minutes of the Annual Conferences*, 1874, page 121.

[9] Long Creek was a settlement in Oakwood Township southeast of Millville. Asle uses the names Millville and Long Creek interchangeably to refer to the same location.

[10] Engebrit Sorbon was the father of Ole Sorbon.

[11] This storm was known as the Great Blizzard of 1873. One researcher has documented 84 deaths statewide. See Carolyn Mankell Sowinski, *The Great Storm: Minnesota's Victims in the Blizzard of January 7, 1873* (Amazon.com: Kindle Direct Publishing, 2022), page 3.

Sorbon helped us greatly.[12] Albert was baptized by J. H. Johnson, Presiding Elder. The 24th of February, I had my first funeral at Weaver, [Minnesota], for a young man, Gunder Halverson, 22 years old. Tuesday, the 10th of June, I went by horse to Forest City, [Iowa], camp meeting, and when I got there, the 12th, the meeting had begun. Haagensen, A. Johnsen, J. H. Johnsen and I were there. Bedbugs tried to eat us up at night, and we had to fight them. I heard a lady pray, "O Lord, send a revival down to this house!" A man ran after a dog right during a sermon and hit him with a long pole, and then there was a lot of barking.

Tuesday, the 25th of June, I drove with my wife to a camp meeting in Newburg, which began the 26th. There we saw for the first time the Rev. N. Christopherson and Holland. After the camp meeting, we gathered in the church in Newburg the 2nd of July for a District Pastors meeting. There was J. H. Johnsen, Presiding Elder, A. Johnsen, N. Christophersen, H. Holland, A. Olsen, E. Endresen, A. Olufsen, B. Hansen, A. Knudsen, A. Haagensen, and it was reported that this man had gone 7 years to Wittenberg School—can one do worse with justification?[13]

My first year was now soon over and the Conference met in Anoka, Minnesota—Bishop S. M. Merrill presided. The 4th of October 1873, I was received on trial in Minnesota

---

[12] This is probably Engebrit's wife Kari Olsdatter.

[13] Andrew Haagensen was a minister, hymn writer, and author of an 1894 history of Norwegian-Danish Methodism. He was Presiding Elder of the Norwegian District of the Wisconsin Conference for seven years, from 1869 to 1876. During this time, he was also a director of the seminary in Evanston, Illinois, and joint editor of *Missionæren*, a Norwegian-Danish Methodist monthly. As editor, he defended Methodism from attacks by the Norwegian Lutheran press. See Arlo W. Andersen, *The Salt of the Earth: History of Norwegian-Danish Methodism in America* (Nashville: Parthenon Press, 1962), pages 69–72.

Conference as <u>Oscar</u> Knudsen—the Presiding Elder had "changed" my first name![14] The 5th of October, I was ordained deacon by Bishop Merrill. My salary for the year had been $200 from the Mission and $275 from the congregation. I had collected $96 for missions, subscribed $500 for the Long Creek church, had gone by horse and buggy at least 3,000 miles, and preached 155 times. There were 8 candidates and 72 full members; one local preacher; one member died, 7 children were baptized by J. H. Johnsen; the church in Grand Meadow was worth $900 and the parsonage $800.[15] Our district numbered 518 full members and 102 candidates.

---

[14] In the *Annual Minutes* for that year, Asle's name is spelled "Asker" (*Minutes of the Annual Conferences*, 1873, page 125).

[15] Preachers were required to report these statistics for their respective charges at each Annual Conference.

Family Members Asle Joined in Marriage in 1874

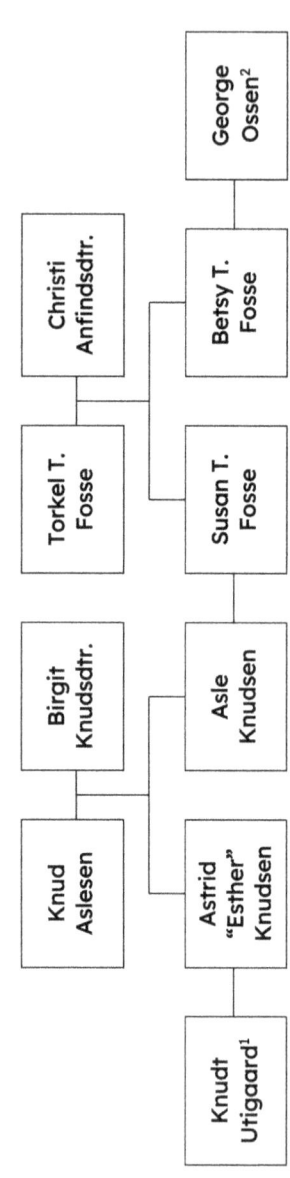

Marriages performed by Asle Knudsen in 1874:

1. Knud Utigaard married Asle's sister, Astrid (who went by the name Esther in America), on the 25th of May in Oakwood Township, Wabasha County, Minnesota.
2. George Ossen married Asle's sister-in-law, Betsy Fosse, on the 25th of June in the Big Canoe Norwegian Methodist Church, Winneshiek County, Iowa.

Plainview and Belvidere

On the 7th of October 1873, my name was announced in the Conference as being appointed to Plainview and Belvidere, and I was supposed to move to Plainview. A parsonage was to be built there—and it was built too—but so late that there was already frost and the plaster froze, and my wife became very sick, so she was as if dead for 20 minutes, but came out of it again; but she has never been strong since then. The 26th of October, I gave my inaugural sermon on the text 2 Peter, 1 & 2. Our meeting house was an old schoolhouse. The previous night, I stayed with R. E. Olsen and had a fine conversation which benefited me through life.

The 12th of November, I had my first baptism of a child in the old schoolhouse in Belvidere. The child was the daughter of Charlie Olsen and his wife. She had three names, which are the following: Carrie Amelia Margaretha.[1] In the same schoolhouse, I had the honor of marrying the first couple whom I had ever brought together in marriage—Andrew Johnsen and the oldest daughter of Herman Hansen,

---

[1] Belvidere Norwegian Methodist Church, Record Book 1, page 35, "Karen Emlia Margretta föd den 19 Octtober 1873 af foreldrene Charly og Thea Olsen. Döbt den 16 November 1873" [Karen Emilia Margretta born the 19th October 1873 of parents Charly and Thea Olsen, baptized the 16th November 1873], signed "A. Knudsen"; Minnesota Conference UMC Archives, "Belvidere Norwegian-Danish Methodist Episcopal Church, 1858–1922," box 1: book 1.

in Belvidere.² The 24th of November 1873, my ordination papers were recorded in Red Wing, Goodhue County, Minnesota.

The 25th of November, the decision was made to build a church in Belvidere, and we got subscriptions for $500 the first day, but the location of the church was not established, and there was no little debate regarding it; but then the place was chosen where the church now stands on Mrs. Larsen's land. It was very tiring traveling between Plainview and Belvidere. The parsonage was in Plainview, but the church was built in Millville and was dedicated by J. H. Johnsen the 14th June, 1874, assisted by A. Olsen and E. Endresen.³ Johnsen preached on Matthew 5:13 and 14.⁴ The church in Belvidere was built during the summer but was not ready until our Conference. During the winter, I toured in Iowa and collected money for the church at Millville.

We had a camp meeting on Herman Hansen's land in Belvidere, which began the 18th of June—it was a blessed gathering. J. H. Johnsen, presiding elder, J. Jacobsen, B. Hansen, and E. Endresen were there. Rev. John Jacobsen lost his horse there in the pasture. Rev. B. Hansen preached to a full house. Three members were accepted into full

---

² Belvidere Methodist Church, Record Book 1, page 100, "Andrew Johnsen fra Pierce County, Wisconsin og Helina D. Hansen fra Goodhue County, Minnesota Eghevielser i Belvidere Den 9 Dec. 1873" [Andrew Johnsen from Pierce County, Wisconsin and Helina D. Hansen from Goodhue County, Minnesota, married in Belvidere the 9th of December 1873], signed "A. Knudsen."

³ The parsonage was built in the southwest part of Highland Township near Plainview (*History of Wabasha County*, page 915). The church was seven miles away in the southwest part of Oakwood Township near Millville.

⁴ "Ye are the salt of the earth: but if the salt have lost his savour, wherewith shall it be salted? it is thenceforth good for nothing, but to be cast out, and to be trodden under foot of men. Ye are the light of the world. A city that is set on an hill cannot be hid."

membership and five came in on probation at the camp meeting. On the 25th of June, my wife and I traveled to Washington Prairie, [Iowa], where a camp meeting began on the 27th. Many Pastors were there, and it was a good meeting. Eighteen were accepted on probation.

After the camp meeting, our District meeting of Ministers began with preachers J. H. Johnsen, O. L. Hansen, A. Olsen, E. Endresen, A. Knudsen, B. Hansen, J. Jacobsen, N. Christophersen, L. A. Larsen and B. Johnsen. At the meeting, the ministers were so lively that Elder J. H. Johnsen stamped on the floor and asked T. Olsen to sit down. The discussion was regarding secret societies.[5] We took a trip to Hartland, [Wisconsin], that summer, and I preached for the first time in that church, which was only half ready.

The 23rd of September, our Annual Conference was held in Saint Paul's First Church, and Bishop E. R. Ames presided. My salary that year had been $150 from the Mission and $350 from the congregation, a total of $500. We had collected for the Mission, $74; Church Extension, $7.50; Tract Society, $2.00; Sunday School Union, $2.00; Freedmen's Aid Society, $1.00; Board of Education, $1.25; Bishop's Salary, $7.50; [Conference Claimants], $8.50; a sum of $101.75; money raised for the building $800.[6] I traveled by horse and buggy over 2,000 miles, reported 2 local preachers, 3 had died, 13 children were baptized, and I had married 3 couples—Andrew Johnson, Knudt Utigaard, and George

---

[5] The question of secret societies was not decided until the Annual Conference of 1881 which "resolved; 1. that we will not receive anyone into our conference who will not separate himself from secret societies, and 2. that we also call upon everyone who desires to join our church to first withdraw from secret societies" (Andersen, *Salt of the Earth*, page 108).

[6] Another aspect of the preacher's job was to collect donations for various Methodist benevolent societies.

Ossen.[7] Members on probation—4; full members—84. On the 14th of June, the church at Long Creek, or Millville, was dedicated by presiding elder J. H. Johnsen. He spoke on David's Psalm 27, 4th verse.[8] The ministers A. Olsen and E. Endresen were there also, and we had a good time.

---

[7] For Andrew Johnson, see note 2 above; Knud Utigaard married Asle's sister, Astrid (who went by the name Esther in America), on the 25th of May in Oakwood Township (Wabasha County Marriage Register, unknown volume, page 237) and George Ossen married Asle's sister-in-law, Betsy Fosse, on the 25th of June in the Big Canoe Norwegian Methodist Church (Winneshiek County Marriage Register, book B, page 246).

[8] "One *thing* have I desired of the LORD, that will I seek after; that I may dwell in the house of the LORD all the days of my life, to behold the beauty of the LORD, and to enquire in his temple."

Washington Prairie and Big Canoe

On Wednesday, the 30th of September, 1874, my name was approved for Washington Prairie and Big Canoe. I was frightened of moving on to another place from this one that I was used to. We left Plainview in our little horse and buggy, and Arne Nelson took a load for us. My first sermon was not preached by me but by Jesus Christ!! We rented a stone house from an old lady, Pige Olia, who was a fine person.[1] We lived there 8 months and paid $10 a month in house rent. In the first quarter, 12 were taken in on trial and 5 in full membership. The 25th of December, 1874, the young people of Washington Prairie surprised us in Decorah. In the spring, they bought a house and lot in Freeport, and they built a barn, which cost $900, all of which was paid for by the Conference. In the summer of 1875, I went to Grantsburg, [Wisconsin], to a camp meeting, which began the 11th of June and ended the 16th. The ministers present were J. H. Johnson, Presiding Elder, N. Christophersen, E. Endresen, J. Jacobsen, B. Hansen, and A. Knudsen. Then we went by team to Deer Park [Wisconsin], where we dedicated a church on Sunday, June

---

[1] This house was in the city of Decorah. See Washington Prairie Norwegian Methodist Church (Springfield Township, Winneshiek County, Iowa), Record Book (1851-1902), unpaginated, Historical Record: 2nd page; "Norwegian Methodist Episcopal Church – Springfield Twp," WC 0226, Folder #3; Winneshiek County Historical Society, Decorah, Iowa.

20th. We were there four days and then went by team to New Centerville, [Wisconsin], and began a camp meeting on the 23rd of June with a number of ministers—J. H. Johnson, H. Holland, —?—, Endresen, A. Knudsen.

    The fellowship preaching began the 30th of June in the church in New Centerville, and five of the ministers from Wisconsin were there with us. Important issues came up. I then went home to Decorah—a railroad had been built from Canoe to Decorah.[2] The 30th of March, I had the funeral sermon for old Knud Opdahl, who died the 27th of March.[3] There were five deaths in the congregation that year; 5 children were baptized, and 6 were married. My salary from the congregation was $500, nothing from Missions—we were self-supporting. Given to [benevolent societies] $105. Two churches were worth $4,000, one parsonage $650. Full Members 120, on probation 4. The parsonage in Freeport had been bought and a barn built, which cost altogether the sum of $900, all of which we paid. That same year, we had trouble in the church over T. Simonson and he was finally put out of the church.

    1875—September 15th, our conference was held in Red Wing, Minnesota; Bishop Wiley presided. On the 18th, I was accepted in full membership in the Minnesota Conference, and September 19th, I was ordained Elder by Bishop Wiley

---

[2] A branch line of the Chicago, Milwaukee, and St. Paul Railway was completed from Conover to Decorah in September 1869, providing a connection to McGregor on the Mississippi River. This was the only railroad line serving Decorah at that time. This appears to be an error in the translation, as there never was a railroad from Decorah to Canoe. See W. E. Alexander, *History of Winneshiek and Allamakee Counties, Iowa* (Sioux City, Iowa: Western Publishing Co., 1882), pages 218–219.

[3] Knud Opdahl was one of the founding members of the Washington Prairie congregation (Haagensen, *Norsk-Dansk Methodismes Historie*, page 19).

under the missionary rules. During the Conference session, I stayed with B. E. Olin. One night, I was locked out, and I got in by crawling through a hole over the door and went upstairs and no one knew anything about it. Thursday, September 21st, we got our appointments, and I was sent to Washington Prairie for the second time, and we lived in Freeport. The house was roomy, on a large lot with a good barn. We bought a cow which we got from Mr. Sanaker.[4] The 27th of October, our daughter Rose Adella was born in the parsonage in Freeport and was baptized by J. H. Johnsen. That Christmas, we got a present from the friends in Freeport of a silver castor stand.

The 20th of April, there was a joint preachers' meeting in Chicago, and I was there a week and stayed with O. B. Jacobs. I bought a lot of cloth and went home with a full trunk. The 9th of June, 1876, a camp meeting began near Swan Lake, [Minnesota], and I went there…. After we were through, we traveled to Lake Elizabeth, [Minnesota], and a camp meeting began the 16th of June and it was so very cold we nearly froze stiff. Then we went to Newburg to a camp meeting which started the 23rd of June and lasted until the 28th or 29th, followed by a district preachers meeting attended by J. H. Johnsen, N. Christophersen, C. Christophersen, A. Olsen, E. [Arvesen], A. Knudsen, O. L. Hansen, L. A. Larsen, O. Jacobsen, J. Jacobsen.

The Annual Conference was held the 20th of September, [1876], in Minneapolis, the bishop was Thomas Bowman. It was at this conference that we had a wonderful missionary sermon by N. Christophersen. At this conference, I was appointed Deacon, 2nd class, and we were divided into

---

[4] This was probably Christian O. Sanaker, a shoemaker in the Freeport area and a trustee of the Washington Prairie church. His sons, James and Otto, both became Methodist ministers.

two districts: the Iowa district with A. Olsen, Presiding Elder, and the Minnesota district with N. Christophersen, Presiding Elder. The 26th of September, 1876, appointments were read for those there from the Iowa district and the Minnesota district, and I was sent for the 3rd time to Washington Prairie. My salary had been for the past year $500, collected for [benevolent societies] a total of $72.30; two churches were worth $2,000, the parsonage was worth $650, no one died, 12 children baptized, 5 were married; preached 170 times, traveled 1,800 miles by horse; members on probation 12, full members 123. Our district had a total of 694 in full membership and 112 on probation.

We had a blessed time during the winter. During the summer of 1877, I went to a camp meeting at Corn Prairie,[5] and we had a camp meeting at Washington Prairie with many pastors in attendance. There was a lot of trouble with those who wanted to remove Samuel Stend, but it was, as a whole, a good Conference.

On June 1, 1877, our son Tyrel Oscar was born in the parsonage in Freeport, and he was baptized by A. Olsen, Presiding Elder. Oscar cried more than any of our other children. During that Conference year, 1 had died, 16 children were baptized, 5 were married, 12 members on probation, and 119 full members. My salary for that year was $450; collected for [benevolent societies] $68.75; traveled by horse 1,500 miles, preached 140 times. The Iowa part of the district had 4,493 full members and 76 on probation, the Minnesota part had 523 full members and 129 on probation.

---

[5] I have not been able to determine a location for Corn Prairie. This may be a reference to Coon Prairie in western Wisconsin, where there was a Norwegian Methodist church known to have held camp meetings. See *History of Vernon County, Wisconsin* (Springfield, Illinois: Union Publishing Co., 1884), page 690.

October 10th, 1877, our Conference began in Faribault, Minnesota, with Bishop Andrews presiding. For the 4th time, I was sent to Washington Prairie and lived in Freeport. On the 19th of October at noon, ten big wagons loaded with people—the whole congregation from Washington Prairie—surprised us, and we got $20 as a gift.[6] The young people from Big Canoe surprised us during the winter and we had a good time in our meetings.

---

[6] A correspondent in Freeport wrote about this event in a letter to *Den Christelige Talsmand:* "The Washington Prairie congregation, on the 19th, paid their pastor and wife a surprise visit arranged by the Sisters, and a recurrence of their previously shown goodwill toward their pastor. Mrs. Omlie handed Mrs. Knudsen, the pastor's wife, as a gift, $18 in cash and a number of other items. After a pleasant meal with friends and a time spent in conversation, prayer and song, the friends returned home, happy and satisfied that they came" (*Den Christelige Talsmand*, 30 October 1877, page 3, column 4).

Courtesy of the author

Asle Knudsen, circa 1875

Studio portrait mounted on card stock and probably taken while Asle was appointed to Washington Prairie and Big Canoe. This style was very popular in the 1870s and was used as a calling card.

Newburg and South Fork

September 18th, 1878, our Annual Conference was held in Rochester, [Minnesota], led by Bishop Foster, and I stayed at the home of merchant Nelsen. D. A. McCabe was there and talked on Church Extension. It was overwhelming what he brought to the conference, and a whole day was given to it. From this conference, I was sent to Newburg and arrived there with my family to live on October 17th. I was very frightened because I had heard that they were looking forward to my coming. The 26th of October, I preached my first sermon in the Newburg church on the text John 21:16-17.[1] The church was filled with people and good times.

That winter, I was busy with a lot of meetings in different places, and many were the Praises to God. During that year, we took in 35 into the church, mostly young people. The 29th of December, our daughter Stella Charlotte was born in the parsonage and was baptized by A. Olsen. The 16th of December, on a stormy evening, there was a surprise for us by the people of South Fork.

The 14th of January, 1879, we were surprised by the older people of Newburg. There were over 100 people there.

---

[1] "He saith to him again the second time, Simon, son of Jonas, lovest thou me? He saith unto him, Yea, Lord; thou knowest that I love thee. He saith unto him, Feed my sheep. He saith unto him the third time, Simon, son of Jonas, lovest thou me? Peter was grieved because he said unto him the third time, Lovest thou me? And he said unto him, Lord, thou knowest all things; thou knowest that I love thee. Jesus saith unto him, Feed my sheep."

March 7th, 1879, the Haugen area surprised us, and we got a gift of $15. We had a camp meeting in Chesborg, Wisconsin, and I went and had a good time. Then we had a camp meeting in Newburg and this was a blessed meeting—God was in power there. My salary—not from Missions but from the congregation—had been $500, collected for [benevolent societies] $95; baptized 14 children; married 6 couples; traveled 1,200 miles by horse and buggy; members accepted—26 on probation, 94 full members.

Sent to Newburg the Second Time

1879, Conference in Winona, [Minnesota], the first of October, Bishop J. T. [Peck] presided. We had a young people's meeting one morning that was quite an outstanding conference. The Lord was there, and I was, on the 6th of October, sent back to Newburg. Pastor H. A. Helgeson, who was then at Freeport, and I were together at Conference, and he was very sick.[2] In the fall a new barn was built at Newburg that cost $150. The 19th of December, there was another surprise party for us by the people of Stringtown, and they gave us $24. The 27th of December, the people of South Fork had a surprise party for us, and we got $11.50. The 27th of January, 1880, there was a surprise in Newburg, and they gave us a feather down blanket and $18. Mother was sick with a fever then and was in bed for several weeks, but we had a blessed time all through that winter. Three camp meetings were held that summer. My salary that year was $500 from

---

[2] Due to his illness, Hans A. Helgeson resigned after this Conference and died less than two years later at the age of 37 (Haagensen, *Norsk-Danske Methodismes Historie*, page 90).

the congregation; members on probation 16, full members 103; children baptized 12; died 2; 7 married. The Iowa district had 97 members on probation, and the Minnesota Conference had 56, for a total of 153; the Iowa District had 602 full members, and the Minnesota Conference had 527, for a total of 1,129. In 4 years, 30 deaths reported, 614 children baptized. I collected for [benevolent societies] $105.

Sent to Newburg the Third Time

P. Jensen was Presiding Elder for Saint Paul District. The 13th of September, 1880, there was a Norwegian-Danish Conference organized in Racine, Wisconsin, by Bishop Harris.[3] The winter was cold and stormy; had a good time. The 9th of February, we were surprised by the Haugen people and got $14; the 6th of May surprised by Newburg and got $19; the 22nd of May surprised by the people of South Fork and got $25. My salary was $550; collected for [benevolent societies] $125. 18 children baptized, 8 married; on probation 13, full members 105. Our daughter Anzonettie was born on August 21st, 1881, in the parsonage in Newburg. Mama was very sick for a long time. So ended my third year.

---

[3] This was the first meeting of the newly formed Northwest Norwegian Conference, later renamed the Norwegian and Danish Conference. (Andersen, *Salt of the Earth,* pages 82–85).

Courtesy of *(Rochester, Minnesota) Post Bulletin*

Oakwood Methodist Church, 1881

This church lies two miles south of Millville in the Long Creek area of Oakwood Township in Wabasha County, Minnesota. It was variously referred to as the Plainview Church, the Millville Church, and the Long Creek Church. In 1944, the name was changed to Oakwood Methodist. Today, it is the Hilltop Fellowship Church, a non-denominational society.

Plainview, Belvidere, Red Wing, and Grand Meadow

The 1st of September, 1881, our Annual Conference was held in Chicago in the church on West Indiana Street, Bishop Foss presided there. On the 6th of September my name was read for appointment to Plainview, Belvidere, and Red Wing.[1] I traveled there alone as mamma was sick in bed, and she was sick for several weeks. She got better and later came, but then she got sick again, and we didn't think she was going to get well. We lived in the parsonage in Plainview until spring, and then we rented a house from Ivar Andersen and moved to Millville and I had lots of driving to do. That year, I got $150 from Missions and $475 from the congregation, making $625; we had 4 members on probation, 104 full members; collected for [benevolent societies $86]; baptized 10 children, married 4; 4 died.

1882 – The 28th of October Conference was held in Saint Paul—Bishop S. M. Merrill presided. I was appointed to Millville, Belvidere, Red Wing, and Grand Meadow. That was a traveling circuit.[2] I got $120 from Missions, and my whole salary was $550 that year, and I reported 2 members on probation and 90 full members; I baptized 14 children and

---

[1] This is the same circuit that Asle was appointed to in 1873 with the addition of the congregation in Red Wing in Goodhue County.

[2] The distance between Grand Meadow and Red Wing is 78 miles by road.

married 2 or 3 couples. Collected for [benevolent societies $122]. That was an extremely cold winter; the temperature was 30 to 35 degrees below zero some mornings. Our son Cyrus was born on March 17th and died on April 22nd, and was buried in the Millville cemetery on the 24th of April, 1883.[3]

1883 – The 19th of September, our Annual Conference was held in Racine, and Bishop Andrews presided. I was appointed Conference Treasurer; my name was approved for Saint Paul and I moved. My first sermon was on Sunday, the 14th of October, 1883, on John 21:16-17[4] and in the evening on Matthew 12:50.[5] (Here, he lists the texts for his sermons for the following year.) My salary had been $600 and our house. I had baptized 20 children, married 8 couples, collected for Missions $150, taken into the church on probation 40, and many were in full membership. My wife had 2 operations that year, and all the children were sick with scarlet fever. That was a very trying year, but we got much help from the congregation.

---

[3] Today, this is known as the Oakwood Cemetery, located behind the Hilltop Fellowship Church (the former Methodist church) on County Road 2, two miles south of Millville.

[4] "He saith to him again the second time, Simon, son of Jonas, lovest thou me? He saith unto him, Yea, Lord; thou knowest that I love thee. He saith unto him, Feed my sheep. He saith unto him the third time, Simon, son of Jonas, lovest thou me? Peter was grieved because he said unto him the third time, Lovest thou me? And he said unto him, Lord, thou knowest all things; thou knowest that I love thee. Jesus saith unto him, Feed my sheep."

[5] "For whosoever shall do the will of my Father which is in heaven, the same is my brother, and sister, and mother."

Saint Paul District

1884—On September 17th, our Conference was held in Forest City, Iowa, Bishop Foster was there, and on Monday the 22nd of September, I was appointed Presiding Elder for Saint Paul District, a complete surprise to me! We rented a house at 198 Glencoe Street and moved there on October 1, 1884. (Here, he lists his itinerary from October 4th to January 25th.)

In this first year as District Superintendent, I had preached 154 times, traveled by train 9,266 miles and by horse 902 miles, married 6 couples and baptized 25 children; dedicated a church in Blooming Grove, [Minnesota], on July 5, 1885—the pastor was B. E. Olin—a basement in Minneapolis dedicated the 19th of July, 1885;[1] a church in Saint Paul dedicated the 9th of August, 1885;[2] a parsonage in Forest City built.

September 10, 1885, our Conference was held in Cambridge, Wisconsin, under Bishop Bowman. This was my second year as Superintendent. I had traveled that year

---

[1] This church, at S. 9th Street and 13th Avenue S., was known as First Norwegian-Danish Methodist Church of Minneapolis. It was still incomplete, so the dedication service was held in the basement. See "Dedication of the Norwegian Methodist Episcopal Church," *Minneapolis Daily Tribune*, 20 July 1885, page 5, column 1; digital images, Minnesota Historical Society, *Minnesota Digital Newspaper Hub* (mnhs.org/newspapers).

[2] This was the Matilda Avenue Church. See "Gudstienster" [Church Services], *Skaffaren*, 12 August 1885, page 8, column 1.

8,560 miles by railroad and 1,200 miles by horse, dedicated a church in Skandia Grove, [Minnesota], the 22nd of August, 1886, baptized 49 children and married ten couples, preached 200 times.

September 16, 1886, our Conference was held in Minneapolis with Bishop Merrill presiding. This was my 3rd year as Superintendent. I traveled that year 12,000 miles by railroad and 1,500 miles by horse; dedicated a church in Des Moines, Iowa, on October 24, 1886, and one in Minneapolis the 11th of September 1887.[3] I had preached 195 times, baptized 45 children, and married 3 couples.

September 21, 1887. Conference was held in Chicago First Church with Bishop Fowler presiding. I got $460 from Missions, $600 from the District, extra income $162, travel expense $188; dedicated a church in Omaha, Nebraska, on August 12th, 1888; a parsonage was built in Brighton, [Minnesota]. Our son, Oscar, died the 30th of January 1887,[4] when I was snowbound by a storm for two days, but I got home, and we had the burial.[5] That year, I baptized 39 children, married 5 couples, and preached 225 times; travelled 12,000 miles by railroad and 1,500 by team.

September 18, 1888. Conference was held in Saint Paul, Bishop Hurst presiding. I dedicated a church in Missouri Valley, [Iowa], the 12th of July, 1889. Our son, Henry, died the 25th of October, 1888, of scarlet fever—very sick for three weeks.[6] From Missions that year, I got $440, from the District

---

[3] The church in Minneapolis is the same one that was dedicated in 1884 when it was still incomplete.

[4] It should be noted that the date of death on Oscar's death certificate is 31 January.

[5] Oscar was 9 years old when he died. He is buried in Forest Lawn Memorial Park, Maplewood (Saint Paul), Minnesota.

[6] Henry was 17 years old when he died and is also buried in Forest Lawn Memorial Park.

$639, and gifts of $218; I baptized 47 children, married 5 couples, travel expense $197; traveled by railroad 13,000 miles and by team 1,400 miles.

September 12, 1889. Conference was held in Racine, Wisconsin, Bishop Fitzgerald presiding. I received $440 from Missions, $660 from the District, gifts of $179, traveling expenses $155. I traveled 14,000 miles by railroad and 1,600 miles by team. I baptized 40 children, married 6 couples, preached 250 times. That made a total of six years as Superintendent of the Saint Paul District.

Red River Valley District

September 11, 1890. Conference met in La Crosse, Wisconsin, Bishop Fowler presiding. I was appointed as [Red] River Valley District Superintendent.[1] The Missions payment was $550, the District $355, gifts $150, travel expenses $50. I baptized 31 children, married 4 couples, traveled 10,000 miles by railroad and 2,000 by team. I preached 150 times, dedicated a church at [Tordenskjold][2] on July 5, 1891.

September 9, 1891. Conference was held at First Church, Chicago, Bishop Merrill presiding. I received $550 from Missions, $366 from the District, gifts of $184.… I traveled 15,000 miles by railroad, 2,000 by team; I baptized 32 children, married 4 couples; two parsonages were built—at Halstad, [Minnesota], and Fergus Falls, [Minnesota]; travel expenses $50.

October 22, 1892. Conference was held in Duluth with Bishop Goodsell presiding. My Missions payment was $550, the District $333, extra $236. I baptized 15 children, married 2 couples, traveled 16,000 miles by railroad and 1,400 by team;

---

[1] The translation reads "Rock" River Valley, but that is incorrect. Asle was appointed superintendent of the Red River Valley District (*Minutes of the Annual Conferences*, Fall 1890, page 292).

[2] The name of this church was left blank by the translator. In Asle's Presiding Elder's report for that year, he identifies this church as Tordenskjold, 12 miles east of Fergus Falls, in Ottertail County, Minnesota (Norwegian and Danish Conference, Minutes, 1891, page 20).

dedicated a church in Stevens Point, [Minnesota], December 27th, 1892.

Sept 21, 1893. Conference was held in Maplewood Church, Chicago, Bishop [Ninde] presiding. The Missions payment was $550, from the District $367, extra $113; I baptized 20 children, married 8 couples, travelled 15,000 miles by railroad and 1,500 by team; travel expense $40.

September 13, 1894. Conference was in Minneapolis, Bishop Foss presiding. The Missions paid $480, the District $398, extras $152; I baptized 32 children, married 2 couples, travel expense $30. I traveled 17,000 miles by railroad and 1,600 by team.

September 4, 1895. Conference was held in Milwaukee, Bishop Merrill presiding. I had been paid $480 from Missions, $550 from the District, extras $152; I baptized 32 children, married 1 couple, traveled 16,000 miles by railroad, 1,500 by team, dedicated a church in Warren, [Minnesota], on the 22nd of December 1895.

Eidsvold, Deer Park, Minneapolis, Diamond Bluff, Chicago, and Lake Mills

September 10, 1896, Conference held in Hillsboro, [North Dakota], Bishop Warren presiding. I was sent to Eidsvold, Minn., with $700 from Missions and $100 salary[1]; baptized 3 children and married 2 couples.

September 9, 1897, Conference was held in Forest City with Bishop [Vincent] presiding. I was assigned to Deer Park, Wisconsin, with $50 from Missions and $450 from the congregation. I took in 17 members on probation and 17 in full membership; I baptized 15 children and married 5 couples; they had two surprise parties for us.

August 31, 1898, Conference was held in Racine, Wisconsin, Bishop Joyce presiding. I was appointed to Minneapolis (lived at 1822 11th Ave. South),[2] salary $900, extras $75, house rent $180, received 26 into full membership and 31 on probation; baptized 19 children, married 4 couples; the total of church debt $500.

August 31, 1899. Conference was held in Minneapolis, Bishop Foss presiding. My salary was $900, extras $150,

---

[1] The word "salary" is handwritten, presumably by Dorothy Petersen Swaney, in a space the translator left blank.

[2] This was First Norwegian-Danish Methodist Church, which Asle dedicated in 1886 while he was Presiding Elder of the Saint Paul District.

house rent $180, received 40 on probation and 41 into full membership, baptized 21 children, married 8 couples, 21 buried, and our total church debt $1,200. Revival that year.

September 6, 1900, Conference held in Milwaukee, Bishop [Mallalieu] presiding. My salary $1,000, gifts $100, house rent $240, received 33 on probation and 33 into full membership, baptized 16 children, married 14 couples, buried 12, fixed up the church basement $500.

September 5, 1901, Conference held in Saint Paul, Bishop Fowler presiding. My salary in Minneapolis $1,000; received 23 on probation and 25 into full membership; baptized 11 children, married 5 couples, 14 buried. That summer, I was in Norway for 3 months, where I was born.[3] Olin preached for me.

September 4, 1902, Conference held in Chicago, Maplewood Church, Bishop Merrill presiding. This was my 5th year in Minneapolis with a salary of $1,000. I received 32 on probation and 25 into full membership; 15 children were baptized and 10 couples married; 16 buried.

September 3, 1903, Conference was held in Racine, Bishop Goodsell presiding. I was appointed to Diamond Bluff,[4] [Wisconsin], Red Wing, and Millville, salary $1,000; baptized 15 children, married 13 couples, took in 35 members.

September 25, 1904, Conference was held in Duluth, Bishop McDowell presiding. I was appointed to North Minneapolis[5] and Diamond Bluff. My salary was $260 from

---

[3] Asle wrote about this trip in a letter to *Hallingen*. A translation of this letter can be found in the appendix.

[4] Diamond Bluff is located in Pierce County, Wisconsin, across the Mississippi River from Red Wing, Minnesota. The church was 1½ miles northeast of the village. See "History Sites—Diamond Bluff," *Pierce County Historical Association* (piercecountyhistorical.org/history-sites-diamond-bluff).

[5] This congregation was also known as Bethlehem Methodist.

the congregation, $216 from Missions, total $480. I baptized 20 children, married 4 couples, traveled many hundred miles. No funerals.

September 7, 1905, conference in Minneapolis, Bishop Spellmeyer presiding. My salary $300 and $300 from Missions for a total of $600. I baptized 8 children, married 6 couples, traveled many hundred miles, collected money for a church in North Minneapolis, and laid the cornerstone [on] Pentecost.

September 19, 1906. Conference was held in Chicago with Bishop [Berry] presiding. I was appointed Superintendent of the Chicago District and moved to Chicago in October. My salary from the District was $1,155, house allowance $420; I baptized 4 children, married 3 couples, traveled about 10,000 miles, dedicated a church in North Minneapolis in June.

August 29, 1907. Conference in Forest City, Bishop Goodsell presiding. I was appointed Financial Secretary for the Preachers' Aid Society. I baptized 4 children, married 4 couples, traveled thousands of miles. My total earnings were $1,371.50.

September 17, 1908. Conference held in Saint Paul, Bishop Wilson presiding. I was appointed to North Minneapolis with $700 in salary. Baptized 8 children, married 9 couples … and the debt was paid.[6]

---

[6] A handwritten note by Swaney indicates that Asle lived at 2116 Fremont Avenue North in Minneapolis at this time.

> A. Knudsen.
> RES. 2116 FREMONT AVE. N.
> Pastor at
> Bethlehem Norw.-Dan. M. E. Church.
> 30TH AND EMERSON AVER. N.
>
> 4
> Minneapolis, Minn. 190
>
> Saa deres Prædikant Kan staa og
> Prædike ud. — Maa da Heren velsig=
> ne denne menighed med god
> og Stadig fremgang! — Søndag-
> Skolen er i god og Stadig vext
> Hans Nordby er Superintendent Samt
> Ungdoms forening er i god og
> Stadig virksamhed med J. L.
> Odegaard som bestyrer — Lokal
> Prædikanter ere John Halstad og
> Sofus Norlaman Formænen ere
> J. L. Odegaard og Oluf Andersen
> Klasseledere ere Iver Hagen og John
> L. Odegaard — Sang Korets Leder er
> Carl J. Svensen Organist Bertha Svensen
> Kvindeforengen med Rev. Mrs. Knudsen
> President Mrs. P. Christen Kasere Mrs. John
> Halstad Sekreter —, Maa da Heren
> velsigne alt arbeide i en hver
> gren af Christi Kirke! og da
> Serskilt i denne menighed!
> Er Deres Ringe Tjeners Bøn!
> Asle Knudsen Pastor!

Norwegian-American Historical Association

A page from Asle's handwritten history of Bethlehem Church

September 8, 1909. Conference held in Duluth, Bishop [McIntyre] presiding. Appointed again to North Minneapolis, salary $700. Baptized 15 children, married 10 couples, had a good time that year, decorated the church at a cost of $300, paid by faith!

September 7, 1910. Conference at First and Emmanuel, Chicago, Ill. Total salary $700; baptized 15 children, 12 marriages. Here, I took my retirement and supplied Palmer, Glenville, and Lake Mills (Iowa). Got $105 from the Pension Fund.

A. Knudsen

Afterword

After 1910 the journal continues for an additional 27 years until 1937. From this point forward, for each year, Asle lists the date and place of the Annual Conference and the name of the presiding bishop. He reports his salary, how many children he baptized, and how many couples he married.

The only comments he makes are that in 1930, he visited California and on August 27, 1933, he stopped traveling to Lake Mills.

Letters to the Editor

Preface to the Letters to the Editor

The following letters are from issues of *Den Kristelige Talsmand* [The Christian Advocate] and its successor publication *Evangelisk Tidende* [The Evangelical Times]. The *Talsmand* was published by the Norwegian-Danish Conference of the Methodist Episcopal Church and reached a regional audience in the Midwestern United States. In 1922, it combined with two other regional papers to form *Evangelisk Tidende*, which served all Norwegian-Danish Methodism nationwide. Except where noted, these letters were originally published in Dano-Norwegian[1] and have been translated by the author.

Digital images of the issues from 1918 to 1923 can be found online at the *HathiTrust Digital Library* (catalog.hathitrust.org/Record/100074208) and *Google Books*. Bound originals from 1913-1917 and 1924-1933 were examined by the author in the Gale Family Library at the Minnesota Historical Society in Saint Paul. The years 1913-1914 are unbound and incomplete. Scattered issues from 1877-1914 were examined on microfilm in the Preus Library at Luther College in Decorah, Iowa.

---

[1] Dano-Norwegian was the official written language of Denmark and Norway in the nineteenth century. It is best described as Danish with some distinctive Norwegian words added. See Einar Haugen, *Norwegian English Dictionary* (Madison, Wisconsin: University of Wisconsin Press, 1967), Introduction: pages 22-23 for an authoritative discussion of this topic.

The editors of the papers were:[2]

Den Kristelige Talsmand

Rasmus F. Wilhelmsen	1908-1914
Carl A. Andersen	1914-1919
Rasmus F. Wilhelmsen	1919-1920
Peter M. Peterson	1920-1922

Evangelisk Tidende

Peter M. Peterson	1922-1925
Hans K. Madsen	1925-1926
Carl A. Andersen	1926-1930
John M. Beckstrøm	1930-1933
Sigbjørn Fosdal	1933-1934

---

[2] Arlo W. Andersen, *The Salt of the Earth: History of Norwegian-Danish Methodism in America* (Nashville: Parthenon Press, 1962), pages 212, 240, 263, 264. Arlo Andersen, the author of *Salt of the Earth*, was a son of Carl A. Andersen, one of the editors listed above.

Den Kristelige Talsmand
January 8, 1914

Des Moines and Lake Mills, Iowa

Dear Editor!

The thought occurred to me to let the *Talsmand's* readers hear a little from Des Moines and Lake Mills, Iowa. After all, Des Moines is the capital of Iowa, and it is growing very quickly. It now has almost one hundred thousand inhabitants.

It has been 29 years this month since I had the joy and honor of organizing our congregation there. They have a beautiful church and no debt on it, and next to the church is the parsonage, on which there is a debt, but since the house is now rented out, the debt will soon be paid. Our congregation there is not large, and since there is no Mission money for the place, it was arranged that I should temporarily serve the congregation by preaching every 3rd Sunday. On the other Sundays, when I am not there, our dear brother, Christ Nelsen, the local preacher and Sunday school superintendent, preaches. It turns out that everyone likes him. We recently had a surprise party for him, and there were many cheerful friends who participated.

On Christmas Eve, the Sunday school had a *juletræfest*,[1] which was very successful. The children knew their parts well and celebrated with us around the beautiful trees with their delicious decorations, and after the trees had been picked, everyone happily went home.

---

[1] An after-Christmas party during which the tree is re-lighted and candies, etc. are taken from the tree and eaten.

Lake Mills is located 15 miles north of Forest City. Our congregation has a beautiful church with a bell in the tower. We have now brought in electric lighting, and a platform for the choir has been built. The church has been painted twice on the outside, and all debts have been paid. I travel there and preach twice every 3rd Sunday; the meetings are well attended. We now have a good Sunday school, and Brother Dakken is superintendent.

On Christmas Eve, we had a Christmas party for the Sunday school. The children did excellently, and we had excellent singing. The tree was well endowed with decorations and fruits, and after we had harvested, we went home happy, richer than when we came.

May the Lord bless the friends in Des Moines and Lake Mills, which is our constant prayer, and may the Lord's blessing be great to all our congregations in the Conference!

Yours in Christ,
A. Knudsen

* * *

Den Kristelige Talsmand
January 15, 1914

Some Encouraging Words

A committee appointed by the Annual Conference last fall to determine the site for an old-age home chose me as temporary Finance Agent for the home, as it was decided it should be in Minneapolis or its vicinity.

To get something started as soon as possible, I got Pastor Beckstrøm to promise to come to his congregation in

Deer Park, Wisconsin, on Sunday, the 21st of December, the Sunday before Christmas. The weather was nice, and many people came to the church. It was encouraging to see Pastor C. Christophersen and his wife in the church, as well as many others, old and young. But I couldn't embrace some of the old ones, who, in recent years, had been called home from strife to eternal rest.[2]

So, back to the point, and that was to collect money for the retirement home. Pastor Beckstrøm and I explained the nursing home's case as well as we could, and the congregation also gave as well as they could so that $298 was secured, mostly in cash, and more will come from some who could not be there that day. Brother John Thompson lives there in Deer Park and takes good care of the money. He is the treasurer, and money can be sent to him.

Yes, the people of Deer Park have set a good example by taking such a strong part in this important work and great cause. Others will probably do the same.

Greetings and a happy New Year from your humble servant.

A. Knudsen

---

[2] Beckstrøm was Deer Park's appointed pastor at the time and Christoffersen was a retired pastor who lived there. See *Minutes of the Annual Conferences of the Methodist Episcopal Church*, Fall 1913 (New York: Methodist Book Concern, 1913), pages 499-500.

Den Kristelige Talsmand
March 19, 1914

A Question and the Answer to It

What is the Norwegian-Danish Methodist Preachers' Aid Fund, and who manages it?

It was organized at our Annual Conference in 1890 and was incorporated in 1896, and the papers were recorded in Saint Paul, Ramsey County, Minnesota. Its purpose is to collect funds through gifts of money, land, lots, or houses, as well as bequests; in short, gifts, large or small, are gratefully received. The money is lent out at interest and secured by a first mortgage. The interest can then be used each year as the Annual Conference decides.

As long as there are adequate funds, those who are in need can get help. Those who are entitled to help from this fund are old, retired preachers or their widows, or sick preachers with families, even if they are not old. When their health is broken, and there is a lack of food and clothing, they are entitled to receive help as members of the Annual Conference.

The rules have recently changed so that only those who have served congregations within the Annual Conference for a period of 15 years or longer are entitled to help from the fund.

The fund is managed by a board of nine trustees, and these trustees are elected by the Annual Conference. They are in three groups, so three must be elected each year. The current council is Pastors R. P. Petersen, J. A. Jacobsen, and E. T. Schollert for one year; Pastors O. L. Hansen, H. Danielsen, and O. H. Wilson for two years; and Pastors J. C. Tollefsen, M. L. Kjelstad, and A. Knudsen for three years. These nine trustees have their meeting every year and elect their board.

J. C. Tollefsen is chairman; E. T. Schollert, secretary and A. Knudsen, treasurer and agent. This board submits its report each year to the Annual Conference, which accepts or rejects it.

Many people have the misunderstanding that this money must be used to build a home for old preachers' families, but that is not the case. We want these faithful witnesses of the Lord and their families to live where it pleases them best, either in California or some other state in the East or West. Because if you were forced to live in a place you didn't like, you would die of boredom, and we want these pioneers to live long, prosper well, and reap a rich harvest from their work. This aid fund will then become a permanent aid so that those in need, wherever they live, receive help from it.

I am glad to say that our people, in general, are very willing to sacrifice for this good cause. Yes, our people are very good at being involved and supporting everything that is good. I believe that the people are not yet tired but will continue to be fruitful in every good deed they reap in due time.

Remember this good and serious matter in your prayers and continue to extend your helping hands either by sending a letter with enclosed money or, when I come and see you, by giving a pledge or cash to the preachers' aid. We now have $6,600 in cash and bequests for a similar amount, but what is that among so many? To ask for money for such a blessed thing as this is a great privilege, and to give to such a good cause is an equally great and good privilege. Therefore, take this opportunity now and give. I don't think a day goes by without me talking to someone about helping the fund.

Den Kristelige Talsmand
June 14, 1917

A Pleasant Journey to the East

When my congregations, which I serve, were kind enough to give me some time off this summer, I decided to go to Boston to join my son and his wife[3] on their trip to their summer residence in the Thousand Islands on the St. Lawrence River.

The journey began on Thursday evening, the 31st of May, and ended in Boston, Massachusetts, on Saturday evening, the 2nd of June, at 7, so in 48 hours, we covered over 1,600 miles. We traveled through the beautiful city of Detroit, Michigan, and the great city of Buffalo, New York. When we traveled in the state of Indiana, we saw all the farms fenced with split rails, and I was vividly reminded of settler life in Iowa and Minnesota. And, as we traveled in New York State, there were really old-fashioned stone fences around almost every piece of land; even in the state of Massachusetts, they have a lot of that kind of fence.

Yesterday, Sunday, I attended four meetings. In the evening, we were in the Norwegian-Danish Methodist church,[4] where Pastor Carlsen is the minister. They have a very tasteful church and a lovely congregation, and this was the first time I preached in Boston. My son, who was with me, spoke afterward in English. It was also a great joy to greet the Pastor and his family and become acquainted with so

---

[3] Albert C. and Mathilde Knudsen. By this time, Albert had changed the spelling of his last name from *-sen* to *-son*.

[4] This church was in the Roxbury neighborhood of Boston and was listed in the *Minutes* as the Roxbury Norwegian-Danish Church (*Minutes of the Annual Conferences*, Spring 1917, page 131).

many kind children of God, members of this good congregation. I also had the pleasure of greeting Pastor A. M. Hansen of Buffalo, New York; Pastor J. P. Ingerslew of Berlin, New Hampshire; and Mrs. O. Nielsen of Perth Amboy, New Jersey. All of these had been at the Epworth League Convention together and had had a good and blessed time.[5] Many more had been present at the meeting but had returned home.

Our friends here are dedicated folks. Most members have a long way to go to church; it takes over an hour on the tram for the vast majority of them. But despite this, they are present at the meetings. God bless the work among our countrymen here. More later from the east.

Regards, yours,
A. Knudsen

---

[5] The Epworth League was a Methodist young adult association for people aged 18 to 35. Its modern equivalent is the United Methodist Youth Fellowship.

Den Kristelige Talsmand
June 21, 1917

A little more about the East

Dear Brother Andersen[6] and *Talsmanden's* readers!

Boston is a historic city. About its greatest attractions, I shall write something later. Will now give a short summary of the solemn graduation, which took place on 6th June.[7] The Tremont Temple was packed, with at least 2,500 people gathered.[8] The huge organ droned out its mighty notes with the help of the masterful organist. Bishop Edwin H. Hughes of the Methodist Church delivered a very blessed sermon or address for the occasion. Diplomas were then awarded to 393 students who graduated from the various departments of Boston University, and out of these, there were 53 from the theological department who will, therefore, become Methodist preachers. Seeing the crowd of men and women of all nationalities who will soon go forth to all parts of the country—and many other countries—was an uplifting sight. It was no less inspiring to see the love shown between teachers and students, and it was wonderful to see parents standing and embracing their sons and daughters who were now to go out into the world and try their luck.

On Sunday, I will be in Concord.

---

[6] Carl A. Andersen was editor of *Den Kristelige Talsmand* from 1914-1917 (Andersen, *Salt of the Earth*, page 212).

[7] At the time, Asle's son Albert was a professor at Boston University School of Theology.

[8] The Tremont Temple is an historic Baptist church in downtown Boston.

Den Kristelige Talsmand
June 27, 1918

A Visit to Devils Lake, North Dakota

Pastor J. Lorentz of Grand Forks, North Dakota, serves our congregation at Crary, near Devils Lake, and sent me an invitation to attend the tent meetings, which were scheduled to be held from June 3rd through the 9th.

An attractive tent was set up on Mathias Lee's farm. We had two meetings every day, and the Lord blessed the Word to strengthen the faith and awaken those who slumber. Thank God for his power, which is palpably known among us.

It was 22 years since I was in those parts, and many of those there then had now died or moved away. But we have some nice friends there who stand together and love God and each other, and it was a real joy for me to meet them.

I would like to say a big thank you to all the friends and especially to Melvin Larsen for the lovely drives we had. Also, thanks to Mother Larsen for the excellent and tasty hospitality that you gave us. May you all live well in the Lord. So, thank you, Brother Lorentz, for all the good you showed me. May the Lord continue to give you great progress in the good work you are doing in this place.

On my way through, I visited Pastor Holm in Hillsboro, North Dakota, which was very encouraging. Thank you, Brother and family.

Greetings to all,
A. Knudsen

> In the same issue of *Evangelisk Tidende,* Pastor Lorenz wrote:
>
> *At the clergy meeting in Crookston, I urged Brother A. Knudsen to come to Crary and help us with a series of meetings we had planned. He readily complied with the invitation. The friends at Crary and Devils Lake were, as could reasonably be expected, very happy at the opportunity to once more see and hear the distinguished pioneer, veteran and father....*
>
> *Thank you, Brother Knudsen, for coming. The friends do not often expect to have the joy of seeing Brother Knudsen among them at a tent meeting.*

* * *

Den Kristelige Talsmand
November 21, 1918

At our last Conference in Chicago in September, I resigned my appointment as financial agent for the Norwegian-Danish Methodist Preachers' Aid Fund. Pastor H. K. Madsen was then elected financial agent, and Pastor E. T. Schollert secretary and assistant agent. I would like to express my heartfelt thanks to the many who have listened to my prayers and requests for help with the fund and have given to it with willingness and joy. May God give you many blessings in return. I am very happy that our dear Brother, Pastor Madsen, was chosen as financial agent. He understands the matter of collecting money—*that* he has clearly demonstrated. The Lord will bless you, Brother Madsen, in this necessary and good work.

For the information of those who have made a pledge or would give gifts to this good cause, send everything to any of the association's officials: Rev. H. K. Madsen, Rev. E. T. Schollert, or Rev. A. Knudsen.

So, a friendly greeting to all friends of the Preachers' Aid Fund.

Your brother in the Lord,
A. Knudsen

* * *

Den Kristelige Talsmand
January 9, 1919

A Little from Columbia Heights

Columbia Heights is located in the northeast part of Minneapolis.[9] There, we have a small church and a lovely congregation. Pastor S. A. Norlemann has served there and built up their congregation during his six years there. But last fall, he was transferred to Chicago, and that was a big loss for Columbia Heights, and the place was unsupplied. It then fell to me to take care of the charge temporarily until something better could be arranged. I have so little time, as I also manage Lake Mills, Iowa, and Colfax, Wisconsin, but

---

[9] Columbia Heights was a village adjacent to Minneapolis. It incorporated as a city in 1921.

everywhere I go, they are so kind and not demanding, grateful for the little that can be given and done.

Columbia Heights Sunday School had its juletræfest last night, and it was a delightful party from start to finish. Sister Hansen[10] had arranged everything, and it all went well. It was a magnificent program with music, songs, and speeches from young and old. After the gifts were distributed, we happily made our way home.

Brother H. P. Norby will now join and help with the Sunday school work. Sister Hansen has faithfully worked for many years, and she has reaped great fruit and will see the fruit of her work in heaven. We also have a good Epworth League, of which Brother Norby is president. Now, I must finish, or this epistle will be too long.

I would ask all who have the spirit of prayer to pray that the Lord's blessing and strength may always be given to us as we need it. A Happy New Year!

Yours in the Lord,
Asle Knudsen

---

[10] Possibly Mrs. Jens Hansen, one of the founding members of the congregation. See Norwegian-Danish Conference, *Journal and Year Book* (Chicago: By the Conference, 1943), page 136.

Den Kristelige Talsmand
January 9, 1919

Juletræfest in Lake Mills, Iowa

Thursday evening, December 27th, was a happy time for our Sunday school and congregation in Lake Mills. The Christmas tree was very beautifully decorated. The children performed their program magnificently, so it was a pleasure for us older people to watch and listen. Our Sunday school workers, Mr. O. E. Dakken, N. L. Thoe, Ed Petersen, and Miss Mable Petersen, deserve praise and thanks for what they do for the children. They will receive their reward from God for all their work. Among the many who got Christmas presents, the most fortunate was me, and I say many thanks for the monetary gifts from the congregation and from outside friends who were there and participated.

Happy New Year to all friends everywhere.

* * *

Den Kristelige Talsmand
January 16, 1919

Dear Editor,

We wish you and your family a blessed and happy New Year! Think of the opportunity you have to preach to many through the good *Talsmand*.

If I live until the 19th of January 1919, I will be in my 75th year. I am happy and thank God for the good health I have.

Den Kristelige Talsmand
July 3, 1919

From Columbia Heights, Minneapolis, Minnesota

It is very rare that there is a report from this place, so I would like to ask for some column space.

In the last Conference year, I served this congregation together with Brother H. O. Bakke, but now that I am traveling to be with my son this summer, I have handed over all responsibility and service to Brother Bakke.

On Wednesday evening, the 18th of June, the congregation prepared a very beautiful farewell party for me. It was a rich program of music and song, and several gave beautiful speeches. The last speaker on the program was Mr. H. P. Norby, who, at the same time, on behalf of the assembly, handed me a considerable sum of money, for which I was very grateful. It came out very well, and I say many thanks for all your kindness and encouragement. The Lord bless you all. That will be my prayer.

For over two months, my address will now become: Murray Island, The Thousand Islands, New York.

Most brotherly,
A. Knudsen

Den Kristelige Talsmand
July 10, 1919

Some Travel Reports

On Saturday evening, June 21, 1919, I traveled from Minneapolis to Lake Mills, Iowa, and on Sunday, the 22nd, I had the pleasure of preaching to a large gathering. And the Lord blessed His Word so that we could feel and experience that the gospel of Christ is a power of God for salvation for everyone who believes. From Lake Mills, I traveled to Davenport, Iowa, and from there to Chicago. When I got to La Salle Station, Pastor S. A. Norlemann met me, and we had a very pleasant time together until 10 in the morning when I boarded a train to go to Clayton, New York, which is the terminus of the railroad for the Thousand Islands. From there, it is only four miles by boat over to Murray Island, where I will now live with my son. We are going to fish here, and his wife is an excellent cook, so we are going to eat well. It's so chilly here now. We have to light the oven every morning to warm up the room.

With kind regards to all friends,
Rev. A. Knudsen

Den Kristelige Talsmand
July 17, 1919

From the St. Lawrence River, New York

The water level is very high this summer, but the fish are biting well—late and early. Yes, it is fun to pull up the big fish of various kinds, and when the butcher has them ready for the kitchen and a good cook, Mrs. A. C. Knudsen, has prepared them by frying or boiling them, and the dishes are ready on the dining room table, then we eat, and it tastes excellent, so we thank God for the good fish which our dear God and Father has placed in the river and the sea for us humans. The weather here is very nice, and many people come here to live on these many hundreds of islands, which are mostly covered with stones and pine forests. We have services every Sunday in churches on the largest islands, and the Lord is with us and blesses his Word.

Kind regards to the *Talsmand's* readers and mainly to the editor and family.

Your humble servant,
A. Knudsen

Den Kristelige Talsmand
November 6, 1919

Dear Brother Wilhelmsen,[11]

Congratulations on the editor's chair, and many blessings on your very important post, which the church has put you in. Thank you for our pleasant time together in the Twin Cities during your stay here.

Greetings from friends in Lake Mills, Iowa. As you know, I have now begun my 10th year as pastor of our friendly congregation there. When I was there last time, the congregation had a lovely welcome party in the form of a surprise, and it was, in fact, a real surprise for me.

Brother N. L. Thoe asked me to go with him to Brother Dakken's, and, without knowing it, I met a crowd of people shouting: "Welcome again—the tenth year." Everyone smiled and happily rejoiced and encouraged me. The evening was spent in a very constructive way. The women took care of their part so that there were excellent refreshments. Then I was handed a very welcome gift of money, for which we would like to say many thanks. May the Lord bless us in this Conference year.

Brotherly greetings from yours in Christ,
A. Knudsen

---

[11] Rasmus F. Wilhelmsen was editor of *Den Kristelige Talsmand* from 1919-1920 (Andersen, *Salt of the Earth*, page 212).

Den Kristelige Talsmand
July 15, 1920

A Brief Travel Letter

Traveling at this time of year is very cheerful when the grass and trees are in full bloom, so that their scent fills the air.

The journey from Minneapolis to Davenport, Iowa, is 350 miles. Happily, one could see how everything that the farmers had sown in the ground grew in abundance, both in the west and in the east, and it seems there will be a rich harvest.

I stopped for a few days in Davenport to see my daughter and her family. Mr. H. Petersen, my daughter's husband,[12] took me around to visit three towns: Rock Island and Moline, Illinois, and Davenport. These three cities lie side by side so that they form a three-leaf clover and are very active in business affairs. In Moline, there is a Swedish Methodist church with a strong congregation, but in the other two cities, there is no Scandinavian Methodist church.

On Wednesday morning, June 30, I traveled to Chicago, 180 miles. Pastor Munson met me at the station and kindly took me over to *Den Kristelige Talsmand's* office, and there I found the editor, Pastor Wilhelmsen, at his desk. He immediately put down his pen and spent a pleasant time talking to us.

From there, we went up to Evanston, Illinois, to greet Pastor A. Johnsen, but he had gone to visit his daughter in Stoughton, Wisconsin. However, we did get to greet Mother

---

[12] Asle's daughter Stella was married to Hans Petersen.

Mrs. Pastor Haagensen.[13] She is in her 80s but fresh and fiery as she has always been. We had a very entertaining conversation about pioneer times and God's gracious guidance for advancing his cause in this country.

From Evanston, went back to Chicago and had a good night's rest in Pastor Munson's cozy home.

On Thursday morning, July 1st, the journey continued from Chicago to Clayton, New York, and now we are at the St. Lawrence River, ready to go by boat four miles out to the island. My son, his wife, and I will spend a few weeks there. More another time.

Kind regards from an old friend,
A. Knudsen

* * *

Den Kristelige Talsmand
July 22, 1920

A Few Words from the 1,000 Islands

It has been very rainy and cold here in these parts, but now we expect dry and warmer weather. The water level is much lower this year, 23 inches lower than last year, so, for those who have big boats, it is probably difficult to get in and out of the boat houses, as the water is so shallow. A lot of people are living on these islands this summer. Large hotels, which have not been in use for five years, have now opened,

---

[13] Julia Haagensen was the wife of Pastor Anders "Andrew" Haagensen.

and several hundred stay at these hotels. They will probably find out how much it costs to be guests there.

Here we have very good fishing waters. The fish are biting, and the fish we catch are big and fat, and you can catch as much as you want and eat as much as you want, and it tastes pleasant after it is prepared by a good cook. Yes, it's really good to live here in the summer, but in the winter, almost no one lives here because it's too cold.

Someone has asked about what the mail delivery is like. Yes, we get mail 3 to 4 times every day. There are also shops here on the islands so that you can buy all kinds of food. The milkman comes around with his milk boat every day, but it would taste a little better if it were a little richer. To my taste, it is very thin.

As for Sundays and meetings, there are churches and meeting places for services. In particular, there is an island that a generous man donated for use as a meeting place for worship called the Crescent Island. There is a half-bay inside the island and an entrance with deep water for large and small boats to enter, and this bay is surrounded by a vertical rock wall about 20 feet high. There is room for over 50 boats and a place on the beach for the minister to stand and preach by a stone that the Lord has put there. And then we all sit in our boats, and the songs and the music have a wonderful reverberation off the water and rocks surrounding the place. We gather there every Sunday afternoon at 4:00.

Kind regards from me,
A. Knudsen

Den Kristelige Talsmand
September 2, 1920

The holiday is over

Dear Brother R. F. Wilhelmsen,

It's now seven weeks since we arrived at this remarkable Murray Island, and in two days, I'll be traveling back to my old home in Minneapolis.

It has been very pleasant to be with my son and daughter-in-law in their beautiful summer home, and it has been fun to pull up the fish. The biggest one I pulled up with my hook and line was 36 inches long and weighed 8 pounds—it was a pickerel.

The *Talsmand* has come regularly, which I have been pleased with. Would you please change my address to 3812 Portland Ave., Minneapolis, Minnesota?

A kind greeting to you and the *Talsmand's* friends,

A. Knudsen

Den Kristelige Talsmand
November 25, 1920

My good Brother Editor,

Having just now sat and read our dear journal *Talsmanden*, I feel like expressing my joy at the contents of the paper.

I would like to ask for space for some lines to send a friendly greeting to my many friends in the Lord who live in the cities and the countryside, scattered over this great, rich, blessed land of America.

I have great reason to be very happy and thank God, who surprises me with the health and strength to still be able to work in the Lord's vineyard. Yes, my desire is to be in the Lord's house to preach the Lord's pleasant words about salvation in Jesus.

After I preached twice last Sunday in Lake Mills, Iowa, I went to Father and Mother Thoe's, where I stopped. Then, in a little while, Brother Nels Thoe,[14] who lives in the nearest house, came and said: "Come to our home for a while." And when we got there, we found that there were four rooms—quite large rooms—that were fully occupied, and everyone was smiling, happy to be able to surprise me entirely without the slightest hint. So now we met for the third time that day. We listened to many fine songs, and so many spoke so much encouragement that I must mention some of them: N. L. Thoe, Mr. O. E. Dakken, M. O. Bakken, C. E. Colby, Mr. Holland, Mr. Anderson, and others. Then, at last, Father L. N. Thoe spoke,

---

[14] Nels L. Thoe was a prominent businessman in Lake Mills and one of the Norwegian Methodist Church's strongest supporters. See "Townsmen Pay Tribute to Late Nels L. Thoe," *Lake Mills (Iowa) Graphic*, 13 May 1936, page 1; also, Norwegian and Danish Annual Conference, Minutes (Chicago: By the Conference, 1936), page 37.

and after his speech, he presented the pastor with a handsome sum of money, which was gratefully received.

It was now the women's turn, and it was with pleasure that we could sit and watch how good they were, the older and younger, at serving the large gathering. Mrs. O. E. Dakken said, "This is a reception for your eleventh year serving us here in Lake Mills, and my prayer is that it will be the best year we have together."

So, will you all send a prayer to God for me, who is so old?

With kind request, do not forget to send money to the Preachers' Aid Fund, and a receipt will be given.

Brotherly greetings,
A. Knudsen

Den Kristelige Talsmand
June 9, 1921

Dear Brother Pastor P. M. Peterson,[15]

A few words to you and the *Talsmand's* readers, if it so please the editor.

I came here to Enderlin from Minneapolis yesterday and will go home tomorrow. All the fields are very beautiful and green here in North Dakota.

My work has also succeeded today, which I am very happy about. I have had a will written for a kind Sister; 83 years old. It was for $2,600 and distributed as follows: to the Norwegian-Danish Methodists' Aid Fund, $1,000; to Elim Old Home in Minneapolis, $1,000; to the Norwegian-Danish Theological School in Evanston, $300; and to the work of the internal mission in the Norwegian-Danish Conference, $300. It was so kind and wise of her to give to these good and necessary causes, and we anticipate someone else will follow the example of our Sister here in Enderlin.

Just received a $50 pledge to the Norwegian and Danish Methodist Preachers' Aid Fund from our kind brother, G. G. of Romness, North Dakota.

The *Talsmand* is pleasant and well talked about everywhere.

Kindest greetings,
A. Knudsen

---

[15] Peter M. Peterson was editor of *Den Kristelige Talsmand* from 1920–1922 (Andersen, *Salt of the Earth*, page 212).

Den Kristelige Talsmand
June 30, 1921

A Camp Meeting in Old Times

This was from 1872 to about 1892.

We had our largest and strongest rural congregations here in the West: Minnesota, Iowa, and the Dakotas, and, as a standing rule, each presiding elder's district had from three to five camp meetings, which were held in the month of June, and the preachers in the districts came along to preach at these meetings.

The month of June was chosen to accommodate the farmers who, after they had sown their wheat and oats, had free time before the slaughtering and harvesting. Their fields were not so large back then, and they had far fewer cows, pigs, and chickens to take care of than they do now.

When the time came for the camp meeting, each family came prepared with a tent that was set up on the campsite. Wagons with tents, food, and clothes came from the neighboring congregations so that when all the tents were up, one could count 50 to 60 of them, more or less. At that time, there were no large tents to hold meetings in. Therefore, we had to make seats under the shady trees around the pulpit and the altar.

Now that everything was ready, the meeting began with the presiding elder of the district being the self-appointed chairman. The program was usually as follows: at 5:30 AM, the bell rings, and at 6:00, you gather for a prayer meeting, which lasts one hour; then you eat breakfast in your tents and have your family devotion until 9:00, then one gathers for Bible reading and prayer with song; 10:30 is the sermon, and then, in the afternoon at 3:00, another sermon as well as personal testimony of spiritual experience; then

Library of Congress

1819 Engraving of a Methodist camp meeting

prayer meeting and witness meeting as well as Bible study at 7:00 to 8:00 when the evening sermon begins, after which you are allowed to come forward and gather around the altar and pray with other God-seeking souls. And so, one kept on for a week or more, and there were spiritual awakenings and joyful singing so that there was life in the camp.

I remember that, at one such meeting, 56 people were converted to God and praised the Lord for salvation in Christ. As a rule, God's awakening power was present at the camp meetings, no doubt, because there was harmonious prayer and faith in God. And when I start thinking about it, it's like Brother P. M. Petersen says: It warms the heart with the glow of grace, just as it warms up that which is dull and stiff.

Well, now my epistle is too long, but our dear editor has every right to cut off, take off, or completely reject as he pleases.

Den Kristelige Talsmand
November 3, 1921

Dear Editor, Pastor P. M. P.,

It is my desire to get some lines into the *Talsmand*, and I know you are so kind as to provide space.

Now that I have come home after being in the hospital for about five weeks and having undergone a serious operation, I thank the Lord with all my heart for His great mercy and help to me, as unworthy as I am.[16]

I would like to send my kind regards and thanks to the members of this year's Conference for the telegram that they sent to me, expressing sympathy and comfort. Thank you, brothers.

And then, I would like to express my gratitude to the many friends who came to the hospital to greet me and spoke comforting and encouraging words. It was like a healing salve on the wounds. When I sit and think of the many who brought me roses so that my room was always filled with beautiful and precious flowers that came from afar and near, I find the words to express my humble thanks simply and straightforwardly. The hospital board itself was amazed at the beautiful flowers and the many kind friends I had who brought them in. Yes, I did not know I had so many friends. The Lord bless you all.

And as for me, I'm out of pain, and everything's fine. Only my strength is lacking. I now take small walks every day

---

[16] A handwritten note by Dorothy Petersen Swaney in Stan Petersen's copy of the diary indicates that Asle had his appendix removed. An editor's note in the October 5th issue of the *Talsmand* states: "Pastor Asle Knudsen underwent a difficult operation last week and was therefore absent from the Conference. However, he is improving. May God raise him up and make him strong again."

and have the happy hope of being completely healed. Dr. Fred Olsen was a blessed doctor to me, and God must have the credit for everything, for God heard your Christian prayers for me.

Your humble brother,
Asle Knudsen

* * *

Den Kristelige Talsmand
December 1, 1921

Dear Editor,

Last Sunday, the 13th of November, I was in Lake Mills for the first time after spending five weeks in the hospital. It was a real pleasure for me to meet with the friends, and we had a good, blessed time at church. I stopped at Nels Thoe's. He has a big house, but on Monday evening, their house wasn't big enough, as the whole congregation and many more came to surprise the pastor with a demonstration of affection. And it was a very uplifting evening; songs, prayers, and speeches alternately—and nice refreshments. And as we used to say, "When it rains on the pastor, it drips on the sexton." But this time, the pastor got both the rain and the drops, so there was nothing for the sexton. The pastor got the whole purse, and he was happy and says many thanks to everyone.

Yours in Christ,
A. Knudsen

Evangelisk Tidende
November 16, 1922

From Old Fields

Coming home from Deer Park, Wisconsin, where I spent a few days visiting as a guest of Pastor Folkestad, I will be allowed to send a greeting of thanks to the pastor and his family, as well as congregation members and old friends. I will long remember the Sunday that was spent with you in your beautiful church, listening to the delightful songs and the preaching of the word.

It was heartwarming to be in Forest, Wisconsin, and to meet acquaintances there and see their friendly church, which is now fully finished with a finely equipped basement and modern heater. All is in good order and without being in any debt, so it is well done for that congregation.

We had dinner with our good old friend, Andersen, and were greeted by his old mother-in-law, Mrs. Hedemark[17], who is now nearly one hundred and two years old, and she was able to have a good conversation and walk around her room. She was very happy that we visited, and we were happy to see her.

On Monday, Pastor Folkestad took me around in his car, north and south and east and west, so that I could greet and talk and eat and drink in friends' homes. It made my old heart glad to hear how happy the friends were with the pastor and his family, and that they had so much good to say about his congregations.

---

[17] Andrus G. Anderson was a farmer near Forest. He was married to Emelia Hedemark, whose mother was Mrs. Sofie Hedemark.

Courtesy of Trinity Methodist Church

Trinity Methodist Church, Deer Park, 1910.

On Tuesday, the pastor took his car, and four of us drove to Minneapolis, where we met our dear Bishop Bast from Denmark[18] and heard him speak in his warm, powerful way. A large assembly was gathered in First Norwegian-

---

[18] Anton Bast, a Dane, was the first Scandinavian minister to serve as a Methodist bishop. He was the bishop for Northern Europe.

Danish Methodist Church, Minneapolis, and about $1,600 was collected for the mission of helping the needy in Europe.[19]

So, many thanks to all of you at Deer Park, and not least to the pastor, who showed me so much kindness and so undeserved.

Yours in Christ,
A. Knudsen

* * *

Evangelisk Tidende
December 21, 1922

It's not often that you, Mr. Editor, hear from this beautiful little town, Lake Mills. That is why I will now send a few lines if you would be so kind as to make room in our dear publication.

Last Sunday, the 3rd of December, I was in Lake Mills and preached two times. The weather was fine, and many came to our church, so the congregation was large both morning and evening.

After the meeting, the whole crowd stealthily went over to Brother and Sister Dakken's home and filled three or four rooms. So, when Brother Nels Thoe and I came in, everyone was smiling and happy that the pastor was now the ignorant man and knew nothing about the beautiful event. It

---

[19] In November 1922, Bishop Bast visited America to raise funds for the European mission. At this meeting, three men, a Dane, a Norwegian, and a Swede, were chosen to speak to the three language groups. Asle was the Norwegian speaker ("Biskop Basts Besøg" [Bishop Bast's Visit], *Minneapolis Tidende*, 9 November 1922, page 14, col. 1).

was all about holding a jubilant party for me on the grounds that it was 50 years since I was installed as a preacher in the Methodist community. The evening was spent in a very solemn manner, with singing and several speeches, and the last one who gave a lecture handed me a good sum of money given by the dear friends who had gathered.

Then the women came with very tasteful, good refreshments.

So, we all went our way happy. Thank you, dear friends, for what you have done for me!

Your poor servant,
Asle Knudsen

* * *

Evangelisk Tidende
January 18, 1923

Portland, Oregon

Dear Editor,

May I wish you and your family a happy new year, and may there be many bright, happy days for you this 1923.

Thank you very much for the picture and the article in *Evangelisk Tidende;* maybe it would be interesting for *Tidende's* readers to hear a little from Portland and the journey here.

On December 15, we boarded the Great Northern R.R. in Minneapolis. It was very cold and rather much snow as we traveled through Montana. At Spokane Falls, there was 18 inches of snow, which they said was something that did not happen often in those places.

By stopping for a few hours in Spokane, I was able to greet District Superintendent Pastor Field and family, as well as some other friends.

After visiting my relative, Mrs. Garberg, in Cheney,[20] the journey continued toward Portland, and on Wednesday morning, we entered the city, which now numbers 260,000 inhabitants. The city encompasses a wide area across hills and valleys. Many of our countrymen live here, carrying on large and good businesses. There is no snow here. The air is mild. There is no dust or dirt in the streets because it sprinkles here every day, more or less—a gift from above to all the city's inhabitants.

It has been a great encouragement to me to meet with the pioneer preacher, Pastor Larson, who has worked faithfully in these parts and all over the West for many years.[21] I also had the pleasure of meeting Pastor Scarvie and Pastor Storaker, and was well received in their homes and churches.[22]

---

[20] Lorensa (Kittleson) Garberg (1877-1960) was Asle's first cousin once removed. Their common ancestor was Asle's maternal grandfather, Knut Andressen (1784-1857). Cheney is a city near Spokane.

[21] Dr. C. J. Larsen organized the first Norwegian Methodist congregation on the West Coast in Oakland, California. He organized many more congregations, including San Francisco, Portland, Seattle, Spokane, and Tacoma and is considered the founder of the Western Norwegian and Danish Conference. See Martin T. Larson, editor, *Memorial Journal of Western Norwegian-Danish Methodism* (By the Conference, 1944), page 3.

[22] Scarvie was pastor of First Church, Portland, and Storaker was pastor of Vancouver Avenue Church.

At the vigil service, I had the pleasure of listening to Mrs. Pastor Scarvie,[23] who spoke so powerfully and inspiringly about the missionary matter.

On New Year's Eve, we were in Pastor Storaker's church, which was packed with people.

Pastor H. O. Jacobsen[24] has been so kind as to drive me around to seek out old friends and acquaintances. I preached in Jacobsen's church once and visited their lovely and beautiful home.

Monday, I travel to the beautiful land of California.

Sincerely,
A. Knudsen

After Asle's visit, Pastor Elias Gjerding of Portland wrote:

Recently we have also had a visit from Pastor Asle Knudsen and it made my heart glad to meet him again after so many years, as well as to sit down in the church and hear the old giant preach with life and vigor.

— Evangelisk Tidende, 1 February 1923.

---

[23] Pastor Scarvie was married to the former Annie Marie Landswick.

[24] Rev. Hans O. Jacobson was pastor of the Mt. Scott Church of the Nazarene. See *Polk's Portland City Directory, 1923* (Portland: R. L. Polk & Co., 1923), page 244. He later joined the Western Norwegian-Danish Conference and served as Conference Evangelist and, ultimately, was pastor of Emanuel Church, Seattle, for many years.

Evangelisk Tidende
February 15, 1923

San Francisco

The journey here from Portland was magnificent, as the weather was clear so that you could see the great high mountains and the deep valleys, which made the trip seem not so long.

On arrival here in this magnificent city, one meets Pastor Haver and his capable wife, who had prepared space in their own house for this old wanderer. Then, one gets to meet many friends who, with willing hands, stand ready to help a stranger. As a newcomer, it feels good to be in safe hands. Brother A. Ipson[25] has not spared his car but used it early and late, yes, all day long, to take us out. Some days, the machine has traveled 200 miles, and we have seen magnificent things throughout the countryside, in this vast city of San Francisco, and over in Oakland which is said to be growing as fast as its neighbor.

Have been to Stockton and greeted Brother Smeland[26] and his friendly family. We were also in the Tokay colony, stopping at my sister's for a week.[27] We were twice at the cozy old age home in Tokay and then got to preach twice in Pastor Ellefsen's church,[28] where several of the old people were present. Brother and Sister Carlsen now manage the old home, and they certainly have a lot to do; they have 700

---

[25] Andrew Ipson was a former member of Bethlehem Methodist Church in Minneapolis when Asle was the pastor there.

[26] Hans G. Smeland was married to Asle's daughter-in-law, Emma Olson, widow of Asle's son, Charles T. Knudsen.

[27] This was Asle's half-sister, Rina.

[28] P. M. Ellefsen was the pastor of the Tokay church, which was located across the road from the old age home.

chickens, many cows, some sheep, etc. The old people are doing well and are very satisfied.

In San Francisco, I met with Pastors R. P. Peterson, H. S. Haver, and C. N. Hauge, as well as many of the church members, and attended several church meetings. The last meeting was with the women's association, and they not only provided refreshments but also handed me a heavy money roll, for which I hereby thank them.

It was also a real pleasure to be a guest at Pastor Engebretsen's in Oakland last Sunday and be a part of their friendly church, greet so many of our countrymen, and listen to the excellent choir. Thank you, Pastor Engebretsen and friends, for what you did for me in that regard!

It was uplifting to attend the clergy meeting today in the great city, which our District Superintendent, Pastor R. P. Peterson, so magnificently presented.

Brother C. Tobson took us one day out to Stanford University. There, we saw the most magnificent temple to be found in this land.[29] More later.

Sincerely,
Asle Knudsen

---

[29] Stanford Memorial Church, the university's architectural crown jewel, is an interdenominational church with seating for 1,200 people.

Evangelisk Tidende
March 15, 1923

Los Angeles

Evangelisk Tidende, of which you are the editor, is very well mentioned, and I have not heard the slightest remark against the magazine's content or management, and we are glad of that.

On February 2nd, I arrived in Los Angeles, and Pastor M. L. Olsen met me at the station with his wife and took me by machine to his home. Since then, they have not gotten rid of me, so here I am and will be until I return to Minneapolis.

On the way from San Francisco, I stopped in the town of Santa Cruz, where my sister, Mrs. McDonald, lives.[30] There, I had the occasion to travel out into a forest to see some of the big trees. I myself measured one, and it was 58 feet around the trunk and was said to be 310 feet tall. The city of Santa Cruz has 12,000 inhabitants and is a fine place.

This city, Los Angeles, is growing at such a fast rate that one thinks and predicts that it will be like Chicago or New York in just a few years.

It has been a real pleasure to visit places and villages around here, as well as go on mountain trips. When I was in Pasadena, I visited our good friends Mr. Dahl and Mr. Rohr and their families and, at the same time, took a trip to Mt. Lowe. Oh, that was great. Have visited the cities of Hemet, San Bernardino, Colton, Riverside, Burbank, Santa Ana, San Diego, Long Beach, and San Pedro, and have found acquaintances and relatives in almost every place.

---

[30] This was Asle's youngest half-sister, Birgit, who went by the name Bertha in America and had married Charles McDonald.

Evangelisk Tidende

Veterans C. F. Eltzholtz and A. Knudsen

These two aging dignitaries were photographed by Mrs. M. L. Olsen during Pastor Knudsen's recent visit to Los Angeles, California. Pastor Eltzholtz is now 83 years old and Pastor Knudsen 80, but look how solid they look. Pastor Eltzholtz has been a little weak in the body lately and Pastor Knudsen underwent a serious operation not so long ago, but, as I said, they look great! Both of these men have been involved in our work from the very beginning and have held the highest positions of trust within the Norwegian-Danish Conference and enjoy its full esteem. May God give them much peace and joy in the evening of their lives.

— *Evangelisk Tidende*, 22 March 1923

But what has occupied my greatest attention is the church and the meetings. The Norwegian-Danish Methodist congregation here in the city is good at attending church, not only on Sunday but also during the week, and there is life and energy in the meetings. Pastor Olsen is a very good leader of the flock, and his wife is the manager of the Sunday school. It is a real pleasure to be a part of such a well-organized Sunday school. Mrs. Olsen knows how to put everything in its proper place.

Our venerable veteran, Pastor Eltzholtz, is present at Sunday school and for the sermon, as he is healthy enough, and it is a real pleasure to see him and talk to him. We have had the opportunity to be together several times.

Then, took a trip down to San Diego and got to see the sprawling city and visit my old friend, Mr. Daniel Ausland, and family, as well as being a guest with Professor A. A. Veblen[31] from Minneapolis.

On March 1, Thursday evening, Pastor M. L. Olsen and his congregation in Los Angeles had a grand celebration in honor of Pastor Storhøi and me. And it was a joy and a pleasure to see the many friends who came from far and near so that the church was packed. The evening program opened with a prayer and welcome speech by the local pastor, Olsen, and a song by the choir. Pastor Storhøi gave us a really good sermon. Mr. Rohr sang a song that he himself had composed for the occasion. There were several speeches, some in Norwegian and then in English. After the magnificent choir had sung several songs, we were all invited to go to the dining

---

[31] Andrew A. Veblen was professor of Mathematics and Physics at the University of Iowa. He organized and was first President of Valdres Samband, a bygdelag for immigrants from Valdres and was President of the Council of Bygdelags. See *Who's Who in America*, volume 13, *1924-1925* (Chicago: A. N. Marquis & Co., 1924), page 3256.

room downstairs. There were tables covered with all kinds of good dishes, and we all ate until we were satisfied. Thank you, sisters, for the delicious meal.

Friday, the 2nd of March, we said farewell to Los Angeles. Pastors C. F. Eltzholtz, M. L. Olsen, and O. A. Doublough were at the station to say goodbye. Thank you, brothers and friends, for all the goodness you showed me when I was with you.

Saturday night, I came to Salt Lake City. Sunday morning, after a good night's sleep in the hotel, we went to the Tabernacle and the Temple to learn as much as possible about what was going on. There was also a special service for us tourists. Salt Lake City is a beautiful city. The streets are very well arranged.

Then, came home to Minneapolis on March 7th. On the round trip, I have traveled 6,800 miles by rail and 1,175 miles by car, have been high and low, far and wide, so plenty of space was needed to write about it.

Kind regards to all friends,
A. Knudsen

Evangelisk Tidende
April 19, 1923

Lake Mills, Iowa

This beautiful city, Lake Mills, has two railroads: the Minneapolis & St. Louis, from Saint Paul, Minnesota, to Des Moines, Iowa, and the Chicago & North Western to Chicago, Illinois.

The population of the city and the surrounding country are mostly Norwegian and good, enterprising business people. Here in the city, there are six churches: the Norwegian Methodist Episcopal, the English-speaking Methodist, the Norwegian Lutheran Church in America, the Norwegian Synod in America, the Norwegian Lutheran Free Church, and a Catholic church. When all these churches ring their bells at once, it is a solemn sound and an invitation to worship. The people here are also good at going to the house of God.

We Norwegian Methodists have now been holding meetings every night for two weeks. And despite the cold weather and bad roads, there were still good gatherings.

Pastor H. A. Ofstie, our district superintendent, was with us for a week, and Pastor J. P. Andersen of Forest City, Iowa, came and stopped with us for a few days. We thank God that these brothers received great grace from Jesus to preach His gospel with spirit and power so that more were awakened, and some found the peace that the world cannot give.

So, we all say to you, dear brethren, thank you very much for coming to us, and we pray that you will come again.

With best regards,
Asle Knudsen.

Evangelisk Tidende
July 19, 1923

A 50th Anniversary

The 1st of July 1923 was a day of celebration for the Martell and Viking congregation in Pierce County, Wisconsin, as they could celebrate the 50th anniversary of their first church, which was dedicated by the then-presiding elder, J. H. Johnson, in the year 1873.

The first class was organized by Pastor Nils Christophersen in 1860 and was named Rock River Congregation. However, when the church was built in New Centerville, Wisconsin it was renamed New Centerville Congregation.

After a while, it was found that this church was not good for the congregation, and it was agreed to demolish it and move to a more central place, which was Martell. The church there was built under Pastor J. Lorentz's pastorate in 1902. Then, a church was built in Viking under Pastor H. P. Bergh's pastorate, so the congregation's current name is Martell and Viking Congregation.

The anniversary day, July 1, dawned cool and clear, and, as early as 10 o'clock, one car after another came, filled with people from the neighborhood and elsewhere, to take part in the festivities; the Hartland congregation was especially well represented.

At 10:30 AM, the service began in the Martell Church. This pretty and spacious church was filled to capacity. The pastor of the place, N. H. Kolberg, opened the meeting with a beautiful welcome speech, after which a hymn was sung, and Pastor John Lorentz of Virginia, Minnesota, led in prayer. Pastor Kolberg read the Word of the Lord. The choir from Hartland sang, as did the quartet from Martell. The singing was very moving. The undersigned preached, after which the Lord's Supper was distributed, and quite a number participated. The pastor informed us about the meetings, and then the morning service ended with prayer and the Lord's blessing.

Then we were invited to a delightful dinner of tasteful dishes.

The afternoon meeting began at 2 with several beautiful songs from the choir from Hartland and the quartet from Martell. Our District Superintendent, Pastor H. A. Ofstie, had now arrived and took charge of the meeting. He spoke some well-chosen words, after which there was scripture reading and prayer—Pastor John Lorentz now gave us a blessed sermon, and we experienced the presence of the Lord's spirit, which warmed our hearts. Mrs. Julius Olsen from Saint Paul, Minnesota, read a historical memoir about the beginning of the congregation when she was one of the first members and participated in the congregation's work, especially the Sunday school work. There was much information to be gained from Sister Olsen's speech and writing. C. O. Christiansen then spoke about the blessed memories he had from his time as the head of the congregation. The meeting ended with song and prayer.

At 8 in the evening, we met in the beautiful Viking Church, and there was a large crowd. District Superintendent H. A. Ofstie gave us a blessedly powerful sermon, after which Pastor Lorentz spoke encouragingly and instructively to us all. After some songs had been sung, the meeting ended with thanks to God and each other for the festive day we had together.

And herewith, we express our thanks to the many dear friends with whom we were able to be together, especially to the pastor and the congregation. May the Lord's work still go forward to victory.

Evangelisk Tidende
July 19, 1923

A visit to the Hartland Congregation[32]

By invitation, we came to Bay City, Wisconsin, July 7th by train and were met at the station by Pastor N. H. Kolberg, who took us to his pleasant home. Sunday dawned clear and warm; despite the heat, a lot of people came out, and the congregation's magnificent choir sang, resonating with those of us who listened to it.

It was encouraging to be able to greet many acquaintances. Still, I miss the old ones we got to know 50 years ago and who now rest in the beautiful cemetery.

The congregation thrives under Pastor Kolberg's service. A parsonage, good and comfortable in every way, will soon be finished; an honor, not only for the pastor and his family but also for the congregation and the neighborhood. Then, on Tuesday evening, July 10, I had the honor and pleasure of joining the congregation for an ice cream social. Seeing the crowd come together and show their great interest in collecting donations for the new parsonage was a real pleasure. About 400 people gathered at Brother Krosby's farm. Thank you, dear friends, for all the kindness you have shown me. And thanks to Mr. and Mrs. Haagensen for my stay in their home—and not to forget the pastor and his family.

Yours,
A. Knudsen

---

[32] The Hartland Church was located in Hartland Township, Pierce County, in southwestern Wisconsin.

Evangelisk Tidende
November 22, 1923

Dear Editor!

You will be kind enough to make room in our dear paper, *Evangelisk Tidende*, for a brief report from the old pastor of Lake Mills.

Our church here is not large in number, but it is a peaceful flock that stands together in loving union and, with its gifts of grace, works to advance the kingdom of God.

Sunday school is growing, and we are now looking forward to a group of 35 children, and we expect more. September 23rd was a holiday in our church as we had confirmation, and a class of four was examined in front of the congregation and received their diplomas. On the same day, members were admitted in full union to the congregation. Our church building is bright and spacious, with a durable bell in the tower, so when the time comes for the service, it rings, and the sound is heard all over the city.

They have just finished putting a new roof on the church, which cost $335, and a new cement pavement around the church, which cost $90, so it will be a total of $425, and everything is now paid. Now, the interior of the church remains to be repaired.

Last week, the congregation had a surprise, and since the poor pastor was utterly ignorant, they had their fun. So, we all had to smile. About 60 people, many outsiders, were gathered at Brother and Sister N. L. Thoe's, so their large, spacious house was almost overcrowded. Speeches were given by Mr. Lars Thoe, Mr. O. E. Dakken, as well as the town's mayor, Mr. Bakken, and more. Brother N. L. Thoe and Brother Elmer Anderson gave us many songs of great blessing to us all. The friends put together their dollars, and Sister Dakken went and picked them up, and when the sack was full, it was given to me, for which I must say thank you again. Our good women did not forget to serve us with tasty dishes.

This was now my 14th welcome party in Lake Mills. It was you, Brother P. M. Peterson, who, as the head of our Minneapolis district, sent me here 14 years ago, and here I am still.

As my article has become too long, I will end by asking all friends who are interested in us to carry us forward to God in prayer—brotherly greetings to them, the editor, and others.

Yours in Christ,
Asle Knudsen

> We congratulate Pastor Knudsen and the people of Lake Mills. It is probably the longest pastorate within our church. If all appointments were so satisfactory, it would have been easy to be the district superintendent. — Ed.

Evangelisk Tidende
January 17, 1924

Lake Mills, Iowa

We had a very good *juletræfest* here at our church last night.

It was mainly for the Sunday school. Our Sunday school has doubled in number in the last year. Almost all the children took part in the program and performed their parts with resourcefulness and dignity. Finally, the children were given presents, which they joyfully received. And the pastor got his share, for which he is thankful. I would very much like to be allowed to express my gratitude to our dear brothers and sisters who sacrificed themselves for the good work. There cannot be more kind and faithful people. They have the children's welfare at heart. May the Lord bless them with the grace to not grow weary.

Live well, dear editor, and congratulations on the New Year ahead.

Your brother in the Lord,
The same old Asle Knudsen

Evangelisk Tidende
April 17, 1924

Lake Mills, Iowa

It will perhaps be of interest to those who read *Evangelisk Tidende* to see some lines from here.

Last week, we held a series of meetings in our church every day and evening. The roads were almost impassable, so the people from the country were completely excused from coming along, but despite that, there were still large gatherings. Pastor H. A. Ofstie, our district superintendent, preached with spiritual power and conviction, and God's call was heard, even palpably experienced in the assembly, and the Word became a comfort and blessing for many who came to the meetings. Then we had real blessed singing. It was a pleasure to hear Niels L. Thoe and Elmer Anderson sing, but when Pastor Ofstie joined in, there was an echo, so they closed. The young girls' quartet was beautiful; they sing every Sunday at the church services.

Sunday was the big feast day. Elder Ofstie preached, and after the sermon, Holy Communion was administered. Forty-six came to participate, and we could learn that Christ was in us, that is the hope of glory—Yes, He is the bread of life and the source of life—who gives himself to us, with strength for the journey. And, for our English-speaking neighbors, Ofstie preached in the English church at three in the afternoon and eight in the evening and thus ended our wonderful meetings.

We say many thanks to all our friends in Lake Mills for their hospitality, attendance, and help and for making our stay among them so pleasant.

Evangelisk Tidende
November 6, 1924

It has been a long time since you have heard from us here in this fine, pleasant city of Lake Mills, Iowa, and therefore, we would like to send a few words to our dear paper *Evangelisk Tidende* (or "Talsmanden" as we call it). We have quite a few here who subscribe to our paper, and everyone is well-satisfied with the paper's content.

We have just finished continuous meetings. The weather was so nice, and God's word was preached every evening. Pastor J. P. Anderson of Forest City spoke three evenings, and also district superintendent Pastor H. A. Ofstie of Minneapolis was with us one evening, and they both gave a clear, blessed sound of the gospel trumpet.

On Monday evening, the congregation and the congregation's friends had gathered in Brother Niels Thoe's house, and I, unknowingly, sat in leisure and comfort at Edward Peterson's. Then N. L. Thoe came in with an air of authority and said, "Now you are going with me," so I had to go. There was a large gathering of good, happy people to have a fifteenth-year welcoming party for their old pastor, so this was my fifteenth welcoming party at Lake Mills. We then got to listen to many good songs, both by young and old, and then we had many good speeches and, after many had spoken, the town's Mayor stood up and spoke and handed the pastor a box of money as a gift from the group of friends. We would like to mention those who spoke, but that would take up too much space.

I am therefore very grateful to my friends for their kindness to me.

Asle Knudsen

Evangelisk Tidende
August 13, 1925

From Lake Mills, Iowa

Sunday, the 26th of July, was a day of celebration for the Norwegian-Danish Methodist congregation in Lake Mills. The church building had been under repair for over two months, and now it was finished, so it was like an inauguration celebration.

The day dawned clear and beautiful, and the church bell from our house of worship began to ring with its inviting tones. People from town and country came so that when it was time for the service to begin, all the seats in the church were occupied.

Pastor H. A. Ofstie, our district superintendent, opened the meeting with prayer and the reading of God's Word, after which the choir sang two songs.

Elder Ofstie preached in his clear and straightforward way so that we all felt joy and gladness and said to ourselves: "Lord, it is good to be here!"

The local pastor expressed his and the congregation's joy that the church now stands so beautifully renewed, both inside and out. It is an ornament for the city and an honor to the congregation.

A voluntary collection was taken, which amounted to $127.25. This shows how kind the people we have in Lake Mills are.

From the report that was read, it appeared that it cost $907.75, with material and wages, not including all the work that many of the friends had done freely, without payment.

It was a big undertaking for the small congregation as we had no help from Church Extension. But we began in prayer and faith, and now everything is done so that the church stands dressed up like a bride. Everything is paid for except $140, and we will easily take care of that.

For the information of those who ask: "What have you done with the church?" I will mention just a few among the many things that have been done. It has had compressed iron all over the roof and the inside walls and has been painted twice inside and out.

We thank everyone who has supported us with money and labor. The Lord bless you for all good things.

That was the end of the day's activities. Pastor Ofstie had preached three times, once in English and twice in Norwegian. There were always good gatherings.

The current pastor is completing his 15th year as pastor of Lake Mills. The Lord bless the friends of Lake Mills.

Asle Knudsen

Evangelisk Tidende
January 28, 1926

From Lake Mills, Iowa

On Christmas morning, we had the sermon. Many people were gathered. A Christmas offering for the school in Evanston, was taken up, and more came in than we had expected because everyone was willing to make a sacrifice.[33] And in the evening, there was a Christmas party for our Sunday school—a large, delightfully decorated tree stood in its splendor and brilliance, well-equipped with electric lights. Many gifts were distributed, and the one who got the most money and other gifts was the minister. So, with these lines, let me express my thanks many times to all the happy donors.

Between Christmas and New Year's, I took a trip to Portland, Oregon, and stopped in Seattle, Washington, on the way. Arrived in Seattle on Saturday morning, January 2, and at the station was Pastor L. C. Knudsen and Dr. J. O. Hall with his fine carriage, and it was off in a hurry to Knudsen's lovely home, where Mrs. Knudsen had prepared lunch. On Sunday the 3rd, I had the opportunity to be a guest of Pastor David Hassel in his lovely church in the morning and in Pastor J. O. Hall's church in the evening.[34] In both places, there were good gatherings and a blessed spirit. Also had the opportunity to visit district superintendent Rev. M. L. Olsen, and we are happy about the good work he is doing in the extensive

---

[33] The Norwegian-Danish Theological School in Evanston, Illinois, was founded in 1890 on the Northwestern University campus. A Christmas offering for the school was an annual tradition (Andersen, *Salt of the Earth,* pages 171–174).

[34] Rev. Hassel was the pastor at Emanuel Church and Rev. Hall was the pastor at Seattle's First Church.

district. *Evangelisk Tidende* is very well spoken of, which is encouraging for the editor to hear.

Kind regards. A little more later.

Sincerely yours always,
Asle Knudsen

* * *

Evangelisk Tidende
February 18, 1926

Portland, Oregon

Dear brother, Pastor Madsen![35]

It is a pleasure for me to be able to tell you, without flattery, that our dear church newspaper, *Evangelisk Tidende,* is very well talked about, and everyone is so happy that you are giving a sermon on the front page. Yes, we are very satisfied with our editor of *Evangelisk Tidende*. It is the language we hear everywhere we go, and it suits our taste, so we look forward to it with joy.

Ever since I came out here, it has fallen to my lot to preach every Sunday alternately in the two Norwegian-Danish Methodist churches. Reverend H. P. Nelsen is pastor of the first church, and Reverend G. Storaker is pastor of the

---

[35] Hans K. Madsen was editor of *Evangelisk Tidende* from 1925-1926. Under Madsen's stewardship, the sermon of the week was moved to the front page and "appeared faithfully" (Andersen, *Salt of the Earth*, page 263).

second church.[36] These good men are doing good work both in and outside the church.

Just now, it is so lonely and sad for these servants of the Lord, as their wives had to be taken to the hospital for surgery. We are happy to hear good reports from the hospital that the operation was satisfactory.

On January 19, it was my 82nd birthday, and on that occasion, the first church had prepared a very grand and successful party for this old man, for which we were happy and grateful.

The other night, we were in Storaker's church; they had a party for sailors, and there were 20 fine young guys from Norway. They were to go straight back with the boat *Roosevelt*. It was very encouraging to talk to these men and listen to them as they sang in both English and Norwegian. Pastor Storaker knows how to deal with these young men. Yes, now my letter is long and must come to an end this time, so more later.

Sincerely,
Asle Knudsen

---

[36] Rev. Nelsen was the pastor at Portland's First Church, Rev. Storaker was the pastor at Vancouver Avenue Church.

Evangelisk Tidende
March 18, 1926

Memories from the West Coast

There is a place called Salmon River near Vancouver, Washington, and I have visited this lovely place several times. Mr. Albert Strand and Mr. J. P. Enevoldsen live there with their families. These good people were my members in Saint Paul, Minnesota, when I served the congregation there 42 years ago. They have now each built themselves a castle on separate hills, quite close to each other. Before entering the buildings, you pass through a flower garden, and the orchard is on the other side. Several times, we had festive dinners there in a truly royal manner.

During my stay in Portland, I was so often able to attend parties, but to mention them would make my letter too long. But I would like to mention a party, which they called a farewell party, that Pastor Storaker and his capable congregation had prepared in the church the evening before I left the lovely city of Portland. In the dining room, tables were set for 100 guests, and when we were seated, all seats were occupied.

The program was magnificent: with music, song, and speeches by the local minister, Storaker; Dr. C. J. Larson, the founder of the Norwegian-Danish Methodist organization in California and on the West Coast; and Pastor E. Gjerding, minister of the English division of the Vancouver Avenue Church. Many more gave speeches, both lay and learned, but I would lack space if I were to name them all. But I must say that the last person to speak was Miss Naomi Nelsen, daughter of Pastor H. P. Nelsen, who ended her words by handing the guest of honor a lovely present, a period overcoat, from the [Epworth] League, the congregation and friends. The gift is received with warm words of thanks.

The following day, February 18, was the journey to Tacoma, Washington. Pastor Haugland, who is now minister of our church in Tacoma, met me at the station. I then lectured in his church in the evening. Then, on Friday, we went out to that lovely place, Beulah Park,[37] and got to see Rev. C. Aug. Peterson's beautiful home and eat the good dishes of the house that Mrs. Peterson had prepared for us.

Stopped in Tacoma over Sunday. I was then able to participate in the large, magnificent Sunday school and two large gatherings in the church. I stayed at the home of Brother and Sister L. T. Sæther. Heartfelt thanks to the pastor and congregation for everything good towards me. It was very nice to find so many acquaintances from places back east. Now, I must interrupt. Something more later.

Yours in Christ,
Asle Knudsen

---

[37] Beulah Park was a Methodist retreat on an island in Puget Sound. It was used for camp meetings, and an annual Epworth League retreat was held there. The town of Cove is on the same island, and the parsonage for the Cove church was built in Beulah Park.

Evangelisk Tidende
January 13, 1927

From Lake Mills, Iowa

Dear Brother Pastor C. A. Andersen,[38]

The small congregation I serve in Lake Mills would very much like to send you a friendly New Year's greeting. You became well-known to our congregation when you were our district superintendent for a few years, and you are loved by all of us. And since you now visit us every week by way of the dear *Evangelisk Tidende*, we stand closely united. You write, and we read.

The church building has been improved and refurbished, both inside and out, so you will hardly recognize the church when you come. And everything is paid for, so there is no debt on the property. Many people come to the meetings, for which we are happy and thank God. The Sunday school has grown so that it is now large and well looked after by Brothers N. L. Thoe and O. E. Dakken. They are assisted by several young girls, who are very clever and self-sacrificing teachers in the Sunday school.

Juletræfesten for the Sunday school was held on Christmas Day evening. The tree was splendidly decorated, and a large congregation listened to the delightful program. It was a very good and edifying evening; educational and spiritually strengthening, so we all went home satisfied.

So, we conclude by wishing you a happy New Year.

---

[38] Carl A. Andersen was editor of *Evangelisk Tidende* from 1926-1930 (Andersen, *Salt of the Earth*, page 263).

Evangelisk Tidende
June 30, 1927

From Lake Mills, Iowa

Dear Editor, Rev. C. A. Andersen,

Some words from this small town may be of interest to someone. Last Saturday, June 12, was an important day for the congregation. We had confirmation—a class of five was examined, and it was a real pleasure to listen to the clear, sensible answers that were given to the questions. Then we had extra fine singing and as many people as the church could accommodate, so chairs had to be brought in and placed in the aisles. The evening meeting was also well attended.

Lake Mills is located just 15 miles from Forest City, and there we have a lovely neighbor congregation and a very friendly neighbor minister, Pastor Gilbert Gilberts. Whenever we asked him to come and preach for us, he was kind and came without hesitation, and he was able to speak both Norwegian and English. May God bless you, Brother Gilberts! Please, come again!

Here, we have had a lot of rain and cold weather this spring, so we are waiting for warmer air. Yes, our God and Father is the one who controls the weather and the wind and holds the elements of nature in his hand.

Yours in Christ,
Asle Knudsen

Evangelisk Tidende
November 3, 1927

Lake Mills, Iowa

Lake Mills is a friendly and pleasant village. The majority of the inhabitants are of Norwegian descent, and many are in good businesses, both men and women. There is a magnificent sweet corn canning factory, a tomato cannery, and a number-one creamery. Of the many stores, the Union Department Store is the largest in town.[39]

Within the city limits, we have six churches, four Norwegian and two English, and all these church buildings have bells in the tower, so when they all agree to ring for church service, it is heard not only in the city but far beyond in the country. And as a rule, all these churches are well attended.

The Norwegian-Danish Methodist congregation has been served by an old minister for the last 17 years, and he has now started his 18th year. As a rule, the congregation holds a welcoming party for its minister every year, and it was done again on Monday evening, the 17th of October, and instead of going to church, people came in groups to Mr. and Mrs. N. L. Thoe's large home, which was festively decorated and every room in the house was filled to capacity. God's Word was read, prayers and speeches were made by several, and then there was lovely music and singing. Everything was intended to encourage the minister, which was accomplished both in word and deed. After the program was over, the women served a good and very tasty lunch. Brother Thoe

---

[39] Nels L. Thoe was the majority shareholder and president of the Union Department Store ("Townsmen Pay Tribute To Late Nels L. Thoe," *Lake Mills Graphic*, 13 May 1936, page 1, column 3).

then handed over a fine box containing coins of all kinds, at which the minister was surprised and grateful and expressed his gratitude to the large assembly. It was now nearly 12 o'clock, and many had several miles to travel to their homes, so we parted with happy hearts and smiling faces.

Asle Knudsen

*　*　*

Evangelisk Tidende
January 12, 1928

A Delightful Christmas Party in Lake Mills

It was a lovely Christmas day; the weather was rather cold in the morning, but in the evening, the weather was beautiful. Sunday was as follows: Sunday school at 10 am, the sermon at 11. The text was the Christmas gospel. The offering was sent to our seminary in Evanston, Illinois. (The money has been sent to Brother T. H. Loberg, the school's secretary.)

The Sunday school juletræfest was on the evening of Christmas Day. The church was almost too small to have enough room for all the people who came, and the last seat was taken, which was a joy for us to see. The children performed their program excellently, which is a great credit to those who had worked so hard at the rehearsal. The young children as well as the older ones sang, and the music was absolutely excellent, so it attracted everyone's attention and enthusiasm, and as a congregation, we express our thanks to the Sunday school management, Mrs. Mathisen, and her assistants, for a job well done.

The Christmas tree was trimmed and decorated, and all the presents were distributed, as well as candy and oranges and the undersigned was not forgotten but received a present, which came in very handy, which is why many thanks are said to all, both members and outside friends who showed their kindness by participating in the monetary gift. We live well in Lake Mills.

A Happy New Year greeting from your humble servant,
Asle Knudsen

*　*　*

Evangelisk Tidende
February 9, 1928

Pastor Asle Knudsen Thanks You

Dear Editor,

Would you be so kind as to convey, through *Evangelisk Tidende*, my personal greetings and thanks to the many who remembered me on my birthday with congratulations and gifts? There are so many friends who remembered me with cards, letters, and telegrams that I will lack the time and ability to personally answer all of them in writing, so I would like to say thank you. Yes, thank you very much for keeping this old Asle Knudsen in memory.

The Lord bless you all.

Evangelisk Tidende
October 25, 1928

From Lake Mills, Iowa

I now wish, through our dear paper *Evangelisk Tidende*, to thank the friends of Lake Mills and the surrounding area for the grand welcome party you held for me on Saturday evening, September 29, 1928.

Brother and Sister Nels L. Thoe have a large house, but that evening, nearly all the rooms were crowded, and it was indeed a festive occasion. We had lovely music and singing, and many gave speeches, and the one who spoke at the end was Brother Lars Thoe, who at the same time handed the minister a box full of money, which was a welcome gift. The women gave us all a very lovely reception.

I pray that God bless the friends in Lake Mills and those who live out in the country and then help me so that I may be of some use for edification and teaching.

Your lowly servant in the Lord's service,
Asle Knudsen

Evangelisk Tidende
May 16, 1929

From Lake Mills, Iowa

On Sunday evening, April 28, we finished a series of meetings in the Norwegian Methodist Church in Lake Mills. We will now have something reported about it in our dear paper, *Evangelisk Tidende*.

We were lucky enough to have with us our district superintendent, Pastor A. Smedstad, for a week, and God gave him great grace to preach God's Word, so we had to exclaim with Peter, "Lord, it is good for us to be here, here we will build and live."[40] Despite the bad roads, people came out in droves, and besides the beautiful singing of the congregation, we had solo and quartet singing by several of the young girls, as well as by Mr. Thoe, and Mr. Elmer Anderson and his wife. The organist, Mrs. Mathison, was always available, which we greatly appreciated.

The congregation has increased by one family, and more are expected. A friendly greeting to all the paper's readers with a request not to forget us in your prayers to God.

Your lowly brother in the Lord,
Asle Knudsen

---

[40] Matthew 17:4

Evangelisk Tidende
June 27, 1929

A visit to Hartland and Viking, Wisconsin

At the invitation of Pastor N. H. Kolberg, I left for Hartland on Friday, June 14th, and arrived at Bay City, Wisconsin, the nearest railroad station to Hartland. Pastor Kolberg met me there in his fine automobile, and we quickly came to the parsonage, where Mrs. Kolberg had arranged for the table to be covered with many good dishes and, imagine, a dish of cream alongside everything else. Then we went to the church, where I was to give a lecture at a festive function that the Ladies Aid Society had arranged, and there was a large gathering.

On Saturday the 15th, Kolberg took me around this beautiful Hartland Township and over to Salem, Wisconsin, so we got to say hello to some of the old and infirm. One of them was Mr. Christian Larson. He and his wife are among the elders in the congregation and have taken a strong stand by fundraising to build the new church. They bought the church bell, which now hangs in the church tower, and when it rings, it is heard several miles across the country. Brother Larson is now so weak that he has to keep to his bed almost constantly, and his wife and children wait on him. Then we got to see Mother Krosby. She is bright as she has always been. Then we visited Albert Krogstad; his wife is paralyzed by a stroke.

On Sunday, the people gathered for the morning service, where it fell to me to preach and then to greet the wonderful crowd of young people who have followed in their parents' footsteps to build and maintain God's church. I also got to speak to the Sunday school. Miss Olsen is the manager. Sunday afternoon, we drove to Viking, and when we got there at 3, the church was filled to capacity. Mrs. Joseph Ofstie is the Sunday school superintendent, and, as it was Children's Day, they had a program, and we must say that Mrs. Ofstie understands how to organize a very good, edifying program for the children and the adults. And then, after we had talked for a while both with the Sunday School and the adults, there was an infant baptism, and it was so solemn when Pastor Kolberg took the sweet little child in his arms and baptized the child in the name of the triune God. Finally, I had the pleasure of greeting old and young people whom I had met in previous days.

A friendly greeting to the Hartland and Viking friends.

Yours in Christ,
Asle Knudsen

* * *

Evangelisk Tidende
July 18, 1929

From Lake Mills, Iowa

On Sunday, June 30, there was a confirmation in our church in Lake Mills, Iowa. There were eight in the class, five boys and three girls. All answered loudly and clearly to every question that was put to them so that the large assembly could hear every word. The class also had some songs that they sang together, which was very uplifting. And then, our choir was kind enough to sing several songs, and our able organist, Mrs. Jennie Mathisen, gave us some pieces of music. It was truly a solemn moment in the Lord's house.

Evangelisk Tidende
November 14, 1929

From Lake Mills, Iowa and Albert Lea

Dear Brother, Pastor C. A. Andersen!

Would you be so kind as to print these few lines in our dear paper, *Evangelisk Tidende?*

On Sunday, the 20th of October, I was in Lake Mills and had my farewell service after having served the congregation for 19 years. It was a clear, sunny day. People came, and all the seats in the church were taken. We then got some inspiring songs and then a short sermon. Then Brother Mr. Nels Thoe spoke up and, in his fine way, asked for a parting offering to be taken up for the old pastor, and Mr. Edward Peterson, who for these many years has carried the offering plate around the church, was now at his post, and this time got an overflowing basket, for which we say many thanks. May the good Father bless the congregation and the many self-sacrificing friends in Lake Mills.

At the evening service, we were lucky enough to have a visit from Pastor Røhrstaff from Forest City, who came with his magnificent choir, and several other kind friends were there. Thank you for the good songs you gave us, and thank you to Pastor Røhrstaff for the good sermon. Pastor J. J. Wang is now my successor. He has the strength of youth and is mighty in both languages, which I am delighted about. The Lord bless his comings and goings among the people of Lake Mills.

Let me express my thanks to our friends in Albert Lea, Minnesota, for what they did for me on my last visit to them. Pastor J. J. Wang will now visit you. He is a good man, full of the Holy Spirit and faith.

Evangelisk Tidende
November 21, 1929

Crumbs from the Journey to the West

The journey began on Wednesday evening at 11:15 by train from Minneapolis, and we arrived in Grand Forks, North Dakota, at 8:00 the next morning. My old friend, Pastor O. Nilsen, was kind enough to meet me at the station, and we chatted for a while about things past and present. He is steadily working as the editor of *Hallingen*.[41] He has a very good talent for making the journal interesting and informative. When we left Grand Forks, we were met by a heavy snowstorm, which continued until we were well into Montana.

When we arrived in Spokane, Washington, we were met by Pastor Elvigen and his wife and district superintendent Langness. Brother Langness is big and strong, which is necessary for him to get around his large district. Pastor Elvigen has had a good start in Spokane. He and his wife work diligently, and God will bless their work.

Then we arrived in Seattle on Saturday morning, where Pastors L. C. Knudsen and R. P. Petersen were to meet us, so it was just a matter of getting into Petersen's fine automobile and driving to Knudsen's home, where his wife had set the table so that we could eat and rest.

Sunday, the 3rd of November, we were in the church in Ballard (Seattle). It is Pastor R. P. Petersen's church, and there was a large, beautiful congregation, a lovely choir, and Mrs. Petersen sang uplifting songs, and the Word of God was preached.

---

[41] *Hallingen* is a monthly publication of the Hallinglag of America.

In the evening, we were in First Church, and there we had a meeting with Pastor Andersen, a good congregation and good singing. It was also encouraging to meet Pastor Scarvie and several acquaintances. More later.

Sincerely,
Asle Knudsen

* * *

Evangelisk Tidende
November 28, 1929

Seattle, Washington

After visiting several acquaintances in Seattle, including Dr. C. W. Knudsen[42] and family, we traveled to Puyallup. My granddaughter, Synette Swenson, lives there. She is married to Dr. Fred Scheyer; he is a doctor there and has a good practice.

While stopping there for a week, I went to the city of Tacoma and visited Pastor Storaker and preached two times in his church to large congregations.

On Monday, the 11th of November, we went to Seattle and got to participate in the monthly pastor's meeting, which was gathered at the lovely home of Pastor L. C. Knudsen. Pastor C. Aug. Petersen presided at the meeting and filled his place with dignity. The pastors present were Reverend Andersen, First Church, Seattle; Reverend R. P. Petersen of Emanuel Church, Seattle; Reverend Storaker of First Church, Tacoma; Reverend Christensen of Everett; Reverend Larson

---

[42] Dr. C. W. Knudsen was the son of Pastor L. C. Knudsen.

of Olalla; Reverend Scarvie of Seattle; and several brothers and sisters.

After a good program, we had a delicious reception, which Mrs. L. C. Knudsen gave us, and we were all full, and there were probably many baskets left over. The 13th of November starts the journey to Portland, Oregon. It's clear, fine weather here.

A friendly greeting to the paper's readers. More later,

Asle Knudsen

In the same issue of *Evangelisk Tidende*, in a letter about Asle's visit to Seattle, Pastor L. C. Knudsen wrote:

We have had the pleasure of having our venerable brother, pastor Asle Knudsen, with us for a few days, which was a great encouragement to us. He preached the word of God in both our churches here to great blessing and with youthful freshness and power, and we all greatly appreciated his visit among us. Pastor A. Knudsen is, after all, the nestor of Norwegian and probably also Danish Methodism among the preachers, and we would hope that he will be able to remain among us for a long time, for blessing and joy follow wherever he goes.

Courtesy of Holly Scheyer

Four generations

Asle (standing) with his daughter Adella (Knudsen) Swenson (right), his granddaughter Synette (Swenson) Scheyer (left), and his great-grandson David Scheyer. Photo taken in 1928 at 3812 Portland Avenue, Minneapolis.

Evangelisk Tidende
December 19, 1929

Portland, Oregon

Arrived in Portland, Oregon, the 13th of November. Pastors Haver and Jacobsen were at the station. Then, it was time to get into Haver's fine car and drive to Jacobsen's home, where his wife had readied a festive meal. In the evening, there was a prayer meeting in Pastor Haver's church, where we were able to participate; a large crowd was gathered, and the Lord's blessing was strongly felt. During my stay in Portland, I had the pleasure of being a guest in the parsonage with Pastor H. S. Haver, and his wife was a good hostess, so I lived in royal fashion.

There was also a great church holiday in Portland in those days, as 18 of our bishops gathered and met for four days and decided to collect 10 million for the Foreign Mission for the coming year. We heard a lot about the Mission.

At the invitation of Pastor H. O. Jacobsen, we went to Astoria, where he is employed to serve our congregation there. Was there on Sunday, the 24th of November. Large congregations gathered in the church morning and evening. Finding so many we got to know over 40 years ago was so encouraging. Some we could mention are Rev. Olson, Mrs. Amundsen, Mrs. Stenvaag, Mrs. Spande, and more.

Monday, the 25th of November, we traveled back to Portland and then got to join the preacher's meeting in the evening at Jacobsen's home. There was a large crowd, and the meeting was very informative and instructive. So, thanks to all the kind friends in Portland and Astoria. We are now on our way to California—to the great city of San Francisco. More later.

Evangelisk Tidende
January 9, 1930

Arrived in the metropolis of San Francisco, California, on the 28th of November and was met at the station by Pastor M. L. Olson, who took me in his automobile to his home, where his wife had dinner ready. After eating and resting for a while, we got to see the well-equipped church building, which is in a good location and is an adornment to the congregation and the city. That same evening, the congregation organized a Thanksgiving party with a good program, music, singing, speeches, and entertainment, and everything was excellent. It was very encouraging for me to meet many acquaintances, and I feel so grateful to my friends for all the love shown to me in so many ways. It was a true joy to be a constant guest in the lovely home of Brother and Sister A. Ipson. One day, we had a lovely excursion to Golden Gate Park and Cliff House. Our host, Brother Tobson, took us all (10 in number) to chicken dinner, and I was honored to be given the key to Golden Gate Park, so now I can go there any time and open up the park to all the great sights. Thank you, Mrs. Tobson, for the gift.

One day, Brother Ipson took his car and drove out 100 miles to the Tokay Colony (my sister, Rina Knudsen, lives there), where I stopped for a week. She is doing so well in her small country house and now lives with Brother and Sister Lund. It was also dear to me to meet Brother Smeland in Stockton. He has recently lost his wife by death but has a capable daughter at home who looks after the house.[43] So, the journey continues to Los Angeles.

---

[43] Hans G. Smeland was married to Asle's daughter-in-law, Emma Olson, widow of Asle's son, Charles T. Knudsen. Emma died on 5 November 1928 in a Stockton area hospital.

Evangelisk Tidende
February 20, 1930

California

Dear Editor Andersen!

Arriving in Los Angeles, Brother Rohr and Brother Dahl were waiting to receive me. So, I got into their car and, in company with Pastor Martinus Nelsen, drove to our church together. There, we met Reverend Bringdale, and a large crowd gathered to hold a party in honor of Miss Gerkin, who had been manager of the girls' home but was now to end her service there and enter married life. It was indeed a grand evening of celebration with song and music, speeches by Pastor M. Nelsen, the undersigned, and others, and excellent hospitality.

After the party, I got to go to Dahl's and Rohr's homes as their guest. On Sunday, it fell to my lot to preach in the morning, and it was a real joy to see the church room and the side room filled with attentive listeners, and in the evening, the congregation was just as large when Pastor Bringdale preached.

On Christmas Eve, December 24th, we traveled to Hemet, a town 100 miles southeast of Los Angeles. Every home had a decorated Christmas tree, and many of my relatives and friends gathered in Mr. K. Utigaard's home.[44] The Christmas presents were then distributed and received, and a good part fell on me, for which I am grateful. During my stay in Hemet, we got to see many great sights that would take too much column space to mention.

---

[44] This was Knut B. Utigaard. He was a nephew of Knud K. Utigaard, who was married to Asle's sister Astrid.

On Sunday, January 19, my grandson, Arthur Knudsen,[45] came with his family from Los Angeles. We then enjoyed a magnificent feast in Mr. and Mrs. E. N. Neste's home. I lived in Neste's home for 25 days (Mrs. Tille Neste is my sister's daughter).[46] Then we accompanied Arthur K. to Rivera[47] on the outskirts of Los Angeles, which is now my place of residence, and I have occasion to go into our church every Sunday and during the week. Last Tuesday, we were in First M. E. Church in Los Angeles.[48] There was a big meeting. Bishop Burns spoke in the evening when 36 nurses from the Methodist Hospital graduated and received their diplomas. First Church is large and beautiful and has seating for five thousand people. There are some great churches in Los Angeles.

Yesterday, I had a ride in the air over the sprawling city of Los Angeles, was 3,000 feet up; yes, it was enjoyable!

Kind regards to all the paper's readers. Our paper has, to be sure, many subscribers out here in this part of the world, and it is well talked about.

Your brother in the Lord,
Asle Knudsen

---

[45] Arthur Knudsen was the son of Charles T. Knudsen, Asle's oldest son.
[46] Daughter of his sister Astrid.
[47] An unincorporated town in Downey Township that is today part of the city of Pico Rivera.
[48] This was the American First Methodist Church, not the Norwegian-Danish First Methodist Church.

Evangelisk Tidende
February 27, 1930

Los Angeles, California

This city is growing at a restless pace. It now has almost a million inhabitants. On Sunday, the 2nd of February, I was in San Pedro, California. There, we have a sailors' mission, which is looked after by Pastor Theodor Pederson, who is the right man for the job. He understands the life of a sailor so well. There had been 260 ships from Norway in the harbor last year. San Pedro seaport is very excellent—good and spacious. It was my pleasure to speak, morning and evening, to large gatherings in our church in San Pedro.[49] This mission is maintained mainly by our Norwegian-Danish Methodist congregation in Los Angeles. There are plans to build a new church suitable for the work, which will probably go well.

Last Sunday, the 9th of February, was my last Sunday in Los Angeles, and it fell to my lot to speak both morning and evening, and both rooms were filled to capacity. Pastor Bringdale finally spoke, and when he speaks, everyone's ears in the congregation are open. So, this time, he ended his speech by expressing a brotherly thanks to the undersigned for the visit and arranging for a table to be set at the altar and offerings to be made for this visitor. The offering was large; it wasn't crumbs, but just what I needed. Yes, the Lord bless you, congregation, and friends.

---

[49] Asle spoke at the morning service, and in the evening, his topic was "His Life In the Ministry, 57 Years." See "Scandinavian Sailors' Mission," *San Pedro (California) News-Pilot,* 1 February 1930, page 5, col 1.

Asle's Relatives in California

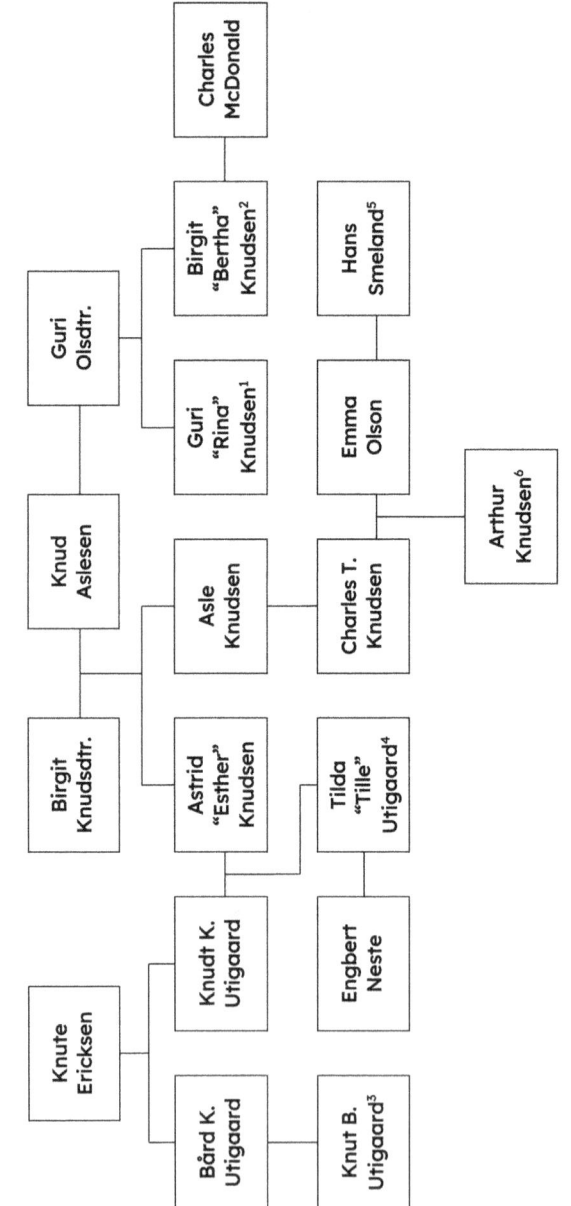

1. Rina, Asle's half-sister, lived in the Tokay Colony near Lodi.
2. Bertha, another half-sister, lived in Santa Cruz.
3. Knut B. Utigaard and 4. Mrs. Tille Neste, Asle's niece, lived in Hemet.
5. Hans Smeland and his wife Emma Olson, Asle's daughter-in-law, lived in Stockton.
6. Asle's grandson, Arthur Knudsen, lived in Rivera.

Evangelisk Tidende
April 10, 1930

On the Way Home

On the 6th of March, a great congregational feast was prepared in Tacoma, Washington, and Pastor Storaker, the minister of the congregation, was so kind as to invite us to participate in this solemn function. Over 300 people had cream porridge, and it was delicious, so one wanted more.

After stopping a few days in Puyallup, I came to Seattle and stopped there over Sunday, and on Monday morning, together with our pastors, I was able to take part in the city's big clergy meeting. And after dinner, we were guests in Reverend F. A. Scarvie's good home. Mrs. Scarvie was then on her feet after being ill for some time.

On Tuesday evening, a celebration was organized in Pastor R. P. Petersen's church with a program and entertainment; yes, we spent a festive evening there. During my stay in Seattle, my place of residence was with Rev. L. C. Knudsen and his wife.

On Wednesday morning, Rev. R. P. Petersen took me to Everett, where there was a meeting in our church in the evening, and a good gathering was present.

On Thursday evening in Spokane, we attended a large women's association celebration and met many acquaintances who had moved there from Minneapolis. Pastor Elvigen and his wife are doing excellent work in gathering and building up our little congregation in Spokane. God grant them great success.

Friday evening, I arrived in the town of Kalispell, Montana, where I met Pastor H. W. Hansen, who took me home. That same evening, there was a meeting in the church, and we had a blessed sermon by Pastor Hansen; many people had turned up. I have never been to this city before. It is a beautiful city, spread out over a wide, spacious valley with fine mountains all around and pretty lakes not far from the city, so you can fish and get a lot of good fish. We were allowed to eat all we wanted at the home of my old friends, Mr. Knud H. Robbin and his wife. I had the honor of being a guest in Dr. John Breset's home. It was 20 years since they had their wedding, and I married them in Minneapolis. Dr. Breset is the city's best doctor and is in high demand.

On Sunday, there was a service in our church morning and evening, and almost every seat was occupied. Brother Pastor Hansen has secured a good foothold among the people, and he and his wife are doing good work: the pastor with his sermon and the wife with her music and singing. Mrs. Pastor Hansen is the daughter of Pastor C. A. Andersen, who is the editor of our church paper, *Evangelisk Tidende* (she is the number-one singer). Then, we went out in the country to visit Mr. Kunstad and Mr. Grova. They live in their fine country estates in happiness and prosperity.

On Monday, March 17th, the voyage went home to Minneapolis, arriving there Wednesday morning, March 19th, after being gone for four months and 20 days. In all respects, it has been an encouraging and pleasant journey, and I thank my son, Albert, who paid my expenses.

So, a friendly greeting to everyone in California, Oregon, Washington, Idaho, and Montana for all the kindness shown to me by laymen and scholars, relatives and friends.

The Lord bless you all.
Asle Knudsen

Evangelisk Tidende
November 27, 1930

A Visit to the West Coast

On Wednesday evening, October 29th, 1930, we left Minneapolis on the train and arrived at Everett, Washington, on Saturday morning, November 1st.

Sunday, the 2nd of November, we went to the Norwegian-Danish Methodist church both morning and evening, and there were large gatherings at both meetings. Pastor M. T. Larson is the pastor and has made a good beginning with the people, and a good future is secured with the help of God and man.

Many thanks to Brother and Sister C. M. Petersen because we stopped at your place in Lowell, Washington. On Sunday, the 9th of November, we had the opportunity to be in both of our churches in Seattle, which have fine congregations. Pastor H. E. Andersen is minister of First Church, and Pastor R. P. Petersen is at the second, which is called Emanuel Church. The ministers and their congregations are faithfully working together, and their progress is on track.

On Monday, the 10th of November, we got to join Pastor A. Vereide for dinner and see the great Goodwill institution. They are now in the process of constructing another building, which will cost $50,000. The money is collected. Brother Vereide is busy with all his strength in this good work.

So, on Monday afternoon and evening, we had the pleasure of a meeting at Pastor and Mrs. Scarvie's home, where a group of 10 ministers, their families, and several other acquaintances had gathered. The company was assembled to honor the old undersigned.

> In the same issue of *Evangelisk Tidende*, there is the following letter from Pastor L. C. Knudsen:
>
> *... we had the great joy of having pastor Asle Knudsen from Minneapolis with us these days and as a guest in our home, which was a great comfort and encouragement to us personally, because he is such a friendly brother in the Lord....*
>
> *Brother Knudsen has now also preached this time in both our Norwegian churches here, to great encouragement and blessing.*
>
> *It is truly remarkable that a man of his advanced age, 87 years, can be so spirited, clear and powerful in his preaching of God's word.*

* * *

Evangelisk Tidende
January 15, 1931

Lodi California

Dear Editor, Pastor J. M. Beckstrøm![1]

Some reflections from the trip—during my stay in Puyallup, I went to Seattle, which is only 30 miles away, and spent the 27th of November, which was Thanksgiving day, with Pastor Andersen at First Church. There was a party that

---

[1] John M. Beckstrøm was editor of *Evangelisk Tidende* from 1930-1933 (Andersen, *Salt of the Earth*, page 264).

evening in the church, a large gathering, good singing, and music, so we spent a very pleasant evening there. On Wednesday, the 3rd of December, there was a clergy meeting at Pastor Storaker's in Tacoma, and he was kind enough to pick me up with his car, and I got to attend the meeting, which was very instructive and awesome. And I got to meet Pastor R. B. Langness, District Superintendent; F. A. Scarvie, chairman of the meeting; C. Aug. Petersen, ex-chairman; R. P. Peterson of Emanuel Church, Seattle; H. E. Andersen of First Church, Seattle; O. T. Field of Bellingham; Martin T. Larsen of Everett; Grebert Andersen of Aberdeen; and several brothers and sisters. Many thanks for the blessed time together!

On the 13th of December, we arrived in Portland, Oregon, and were met at the station and escorted to Reverend H. O. Jacobsen's home. Then, on Sunday, the 14th, I got to be in Pastor H. S. Haver's church on Vancouver Avenue. In the morning Bible class, a large class, the leader was Pastor Gjerding, and he was, in my opinion, a master Bible teacher. Then the sermon, and the church was packed. The choir was excellent. The evening meeting was very well attended.

Then, on Tuesday, Pastor Haver took me around to visit Brothers Ant. Strand and Enevoldsen, near Vancouver, Washington,[2] and our friend and brother, H. M. Jensen and family. The following day, Pastor H. Haver took me out into the countryside in his car to greet Brother Pastor Hansen sitting in his chair, and he has been sitting in this chair for 30 years. He has not been able to take a step in these many years, but he is still happy and thanks God. Pastor Haver brought a good sum of money that he had collected from his

---

[2] The Columbia River forms the border between Washington and Oregon and separates Vancouver, Washington, from Portland, Oregon.

congregation and a Christmas present, and they should have seen how happy he and his wife were with the gift.

Then, we were a few miles further out in the country to see and greet Pastor Hans Nordvig, whom we knew in our youth but had not seen for many years. And there was a stream of joyful tears when we met in his good home. Brother Nordvig has been the means of salvation for many souls. He is still warm and fresh in spirit, although his body is weakened.

Then there was the journey to San Francisco, California. Arriving there, Pastor M. L. Olsen met me at the station and took me to his home. I stayed with him over Sunday and met many familiar friends in the Lord. The church was well attended.

A friendly greeting to all friends. *Tidende* is well spoken of, and we send our New Year's greetings to Editor Beckstrøm.

* * *

Evangelisk Tidende
February 5, 1931

Lodi, California

Dear brother, Pastor Beckstrøm!

You will be kind enough to make room for my little article in our dear paper, *Evangelisk Tidende*. Also, to your delight and encouragement, we can say that our paper is very well-liked—and as proof of that, I am sending a bank instruction from some friends to pay for the paper.

I would like to send my New Year's greetings to my many friends and acquaintances spread all over the country and say thank you for the many Christmas and New Year's cards, letters, and presents. It has been a great encouragement to me in my old age. I spent most of this winter here with my sister, Rina Knudsen. Mr. Hans Lund and his wife live in the same house, and we have such a festive time together. We go to church every Sunday, and there we meet a nice group of God's children and get to witness about our precious Savior and what he has done for us—and we have a good time.

Yesterday was a holiday for us when we were visited by several of our friends from San Francisco, namely, Pastor M. L. Olsen and wife, Pastor R. B. Langness, Pastor D. Hassel, Pastor M. Nelson, Mr. C. Tobson and wife, Mr. O. S. Arntson, and Mr. Andrew Ipson and wife.[3] Just about everyone gave us encouraging speeches and songs. Thank you for the gifts you brought on the occasion of the day. And then we will immediately send thanks for the letters and cards with birthday wishes from our many friends. God is good and has so many good-hearted, genial people who encourage us old pilgrims. May the Lord continue to bless his people everywhere!

Your humble servant,
Asle Knudsen

---

[3] On Wednesday, the 21st of January a party was held in honor of Asle, his sister Rina, and Mrs. M. L. Olsen, all of whom had January birthdays. ("Three Honored on Their Anniversaries," *Stockton (California) Record*, 24 January 1931, page 15; *Newspapers.com*.)

Evangelisk Tidende
April 30, 1931

Memories from the Trip

Now that we have come home to Minneapolis, Minnesota, we will have editor Rev. J. M. Beckstrøm record a short article in our paper, *Evangelisk Tidende*. By doing so, we bring a fraternal greeting from people in the West who subscribe to *Evangelisk Tidende*. As a general thing, there is great satisfaction with the paper, even if in the West, you have to wait a whole week to get it in your hands after it is printed in Chicago; one then waits with patient longing and is happy when it comes!

Arriving in Lodi (Tokay Colony) two days before Christmas, where my sister Miss Rina Knudsen lives, I stayed there until the end of March and could probably have stayed even longer on a friendly invitation. There were four of us: Mr. and Mrs. Hans Lund, my sister, and I. And I have to say, I was waited on like a great gentleman, with big, fine rooms and all kinds of good food to eat.

There is a Norwegian Methodist church in the neighborhood, and the venerable Pastor Martinus Nelsen is the assigned minister, but as he lives far away and it is a difficult railway connection, it fell to my lot to be Brother Pastor Nelsen's chaplain, so the small, nice congregation was content to sit and listen to me preach every Sunday for two and a half months. And now let me send you my brotherly thanks for all the kindness that you all showed me, and as I sit and think about the many friendly companions that were there to encourage me, yes, thank you again for all the good food and drink, cream, porridge, buttermilk, roast chicken, etc. And thank you for the nice surprise with the gift of money. Dear friends, remember me in prayer.

So now the journey home begins, stopped for a few days in San Francisco. They have built on and improved their church building at a cost of $2,000 and have brought many good members into the congregation this year. The Annual Conference will be held there in June. During my stay in San Francisco, I visited many of our genial friends, and A. Ipson's was my headquarters. Brother Tobson took his big car one day, and that day, we visited 12 towns (small places) and drove out to President Hoover's home. So, thank you, my friends in San Francisco, for all your kindness to me, not forgetting Pastor Olsen and his wife.

Arriving in Portland, Oregon, met Pastor Haver with his fine car, stopped at his home over Sunday, and met many friends. The church is well-attended, and people have a good time there.[4]

Next stop is Puyallup, Washington, where I stayed with my granddaughter, Mrs. Dr. Scheyer, and on Sunday, I must speak at the American First M. E. Church.

In Seattle, I stopped at Pastor L. C. Knudsen's, and in the morning, there were five of our ministers, namely Revs. R. P. Petersen, E. A. Andersen, F. A. Scarvie, L. C. Knudsen, and H. O. Jacobsen, at the station to say goodbye to me. Stopped one day in the beautiful city of Spokane and greeted our dear Pastor Elvigen and his wife. Then, the journey was complete, and arrived in Minneapolis on Saturday evening, March 28th.

---

[4] While he was visiting Portland, Asle preached twice in the Vancouver Avenue Church, in Norwegian at the morning service and in English at the evening service ("Former Pastor Touring Along Pacific Coast," *Lake Mills Graphic*, 7 January 1931, p, 1, column 4).

Evangelisk Tidende
February 4, 1932

Minneapolis, Minnesota

There is an old saying that it is better late than never, and this time, I will make use of it and herewith send my New Year's greetings to editor J. M. Beckstrøm and his family.

And, as time flies by quickly, just think, it is only a few days since we attained the age of 89, and I would like to say thank you and thank you very much to everyone, far and near, who, in so many ways, sent congratulations in the form of cards, letters, and gifts. My health is better than can be expected at my advanced age. Thank God for everything good to me, and thank you to everyone who has been so undeservedly kind to me.

The peace of our Lord Jesus Christ be with you all.
Asle Knudsen

Evangelisk Tidende congratulates this stout giant of the Lord and wishes him many more happy working days. — Ed.

Evangelisk Tidende
April 7, 1932

Lake Mills, Iowa

As I understand it, our editor, Rev. Beckstrøm, is happy to receive reports from pastors and congregations, so we will let you hear from us in Lake Mills.

This fine town is conveniently located 25 miles south of Albert Lea, Minnesota. Here, it is just 8 miles to the Minnesota state line. We have two rail lines: the Minneapolis & St. Louis Railroad and the Chicago & Northwestern Railroad. Both have stations in the city and many trains a day. The town recently had a large, magnificent schoolhouse built, which cost a large sum of money. Here, there are cement streets, etc. Of churches, the town has three Lutheran, two Methodist, and one Catholic.

We have just finished a series of meetings in the Norwegian Methodist church. Our district superintendent, Reverend Edward Evensen, was with us for a week and was kind enough to preach every evening and twice on Sunday. The people were very good at attending, so there were always good gatherings, and God's word was preached with clarity and the power of conviction, so we felt that God is truly powerful with his word. Jesus was held up in His fullness—mighty to save us lost sinners. The closing meeting on Sunday evening was magnificent; seeing the entire altar surrounded by praying souls was solemn. May our dear Savior Jesus continue to bless us all.

There are many here who support our church newspaper, *Evangelisk Tidende*. I have sent four renewals and two new subscribers this year and will get a few more. We feel the hard times here, as hard as we can bear. So, we sit down and ask from the bottom of our hearts: "What will

Vesterheim Norwegian-American Museum

Lake Mills Norwegian Methodist Church

become of us here in this great, rich country?" God help us poor, unworthy ones.

Before I lay down my pen, let me thank all the kind friends in Lake Mills and vicinity for all the help and kindness shown during our meetings.

Asle Knudsen, Pastor

Evangelisk Tidende
February 23, 1933

From California

The journey from Minneapolis to Portland, Oregon, took just 52 hours on the Great Northern Railroad's Empire Builder, about 2,000 miles. At the station in Seattle, we were greeted by Pastors L. C. Knudsen, F. A. Scarvie, H. O. Jacobsen, and Brother Mr. Elias Hove. They all welcomed me to the warm country in the West. Arrived in Portland on Saturday, the 28th of January, where a smiling Reverend M. L. Olson welcomed us and we entered Brother Valdemar Petersen's nice car. After a few minutes, we sat down together at a set table in the parsonage, Mrs. Olson and her daughter as attendants.

Sunday, the 29th of January, I participated in three church services. They were good gatherings—a lovely singing choir. Pastor Olson is a good worker in the Lord's vineyard, and good co-workers in the vineyard could be mentioned: Erikson, Gjerding, Andersen,[5] and more. On Monday evening, we had a very festive time at Reverend O. T. Field's home. He is pastor at First Norwegian-Danish Church, Portland. On Tuesday, the 31st of January, Brother Madsen came with his nice car and picked up Pastor M. L. Olson, J. Eriksen, and me. Together, we went to Washington to visit Brother Albert Strand with his family and Brother Hansen, who has been sitting for 32 years and could not walk. It was emotional to see, but there was no complaint. That same evening, we were guests of Reverend Gjerding and had the opportunity to congratulate him and his wife.

---

[5] Probably Rev. H. E. Andersen.

On Wednesday morning, the 1st of February, the journey was made to Lodi, California. So, on Thursday morning, I arrived there. My sister, Mr. Lund, and Smeland showed up to accompany me home. Thanks to everyone who made me feel at home with them.

Sincerely.
My address is now:
Rev. Asle Knudsen
Route 1, Box 229
Lodi, California

***

Evangelisk Tidende
March 16, 1933

From California

It was very encouraging for me to meet my sister and friends in Lodi, California. Some of the genial friends have moved higher up and are singing their song of victory there. Brother Pastor Lundegaard is so weak that he is completely helpless and almost aimless, but he lies smiling and waiting for Jesus to take him home in heaven.[6] We also had the pleasure of meeting the district superintendent, Pastor Langness. He is constantly at work in his extensive district. Pastor Storaker and Brother C. Tobson from San Francisco were also here in Lodi at the same time, so it was a real holiday party in our church that evening.

---

[6] Pastor Lundegaard passed away later that year.

On Thursday, the 16th of January, Brother Tobson came from San Francisco to bring me to that big, lovely city, and that same evening, there was a most divine atmosphere in the church, and it was such a great encouragement to me to meet Brother Pastor Storaker and many familiar friends.

On Friday evening, January 17th, there was a large, well-attended mission meeting in our church. There was a very good program. Then, on Saturday morning, February 18th, Brother Tobson came in his big roomy car, and five of us left for the city of Napa, California, to visit Mrs. Støring, who came there about a year ago. She lives with her daughter, Mrs. Burens. We had a good time together in prayer, singing, and reading God's Word. Sister Støring sends her greetings to friends in Minneapolis.

During my stay in San Francisco, I made my home with Brother and Sister Andrew Ipson, and I was the guest of many kind friends. Sunday the 19th was spent in our beautiful church in San Francisco. And it was an inspiration to listen to the excellent singing choir led by Sister Johnson and to listen to Pastor Storaker's clear exposition of the Word of God. Thank you to all of you in the great city of San Francisco.

Brother Tobson will come on Wednesday morning, February 2nd, and take me to Lodi, so now I'm here, and tomorrow I leave for Los Angeles, Calif.

Your Brother,
Asle Knudsen

Evangelisk Tidende
November 9, 1933

Minneapolis, Minnesota

Dear Brother Pastor Fosdal,[7]

At our Annual Conference in Chicago last fall, I finished my service as pastor of the Norwegian Methodist Church in Lake Mills, Iowa. It was then 21 years that I had gone in and out of that lovely little town and preached the gospel about the saving power of Jesus.

The end was a solemn summer day on August 27. The weather was clear with customary heat. The bell in our church tower struck its resounding strokes to invite us to the morning service, and people came from town and country, so there was not enough room for everyone to sit down. Mrs. Hall, our organist, gave us beautiful organ music, and we had some extra songs both before and after the sermon. Then N. L. Thoe stood up and said: "Now we take up a farewell offering which will be given to Pastor A. Knudsen." And for this welcome and great sacrifice, I say many thanks! I would also like to express my humble thanks to everyone who has shown kindness to me in so many ways over these many years.

So, we wish Pastor J. A. Amundsen a warm welcome to Lake Mills to serve this small, friendly congregation.

Yours in Christ Jesus,
Asle Knudsen

---

[7] Sigbjørn Fosdal was editor of *Evangelisk Tidende* from 1933 to 1934.

Evangelisk Tidende
January 11, 1934

You have to resist old age

Most people, when they get a little older and feel that they are starting to get stiff in their limbs, sit down and say, "Yes, now my working days are about over." But therein lie many mistakes. We tend to think of ourselves as prematurely old.

Many years ago, I read a book written by Cicero, and in this book it says, among other things, that one must resist old age. To help with this, he states three rules: one is moderation in food and drink, the second is daily physical exercise, and the third is continuing one's studies. I have tried to comply with all three rules and, I believe, with good results. Anyone who observes the rules given by Cicero and never neglects daily exercises will reap great fruits.

The relevant passage from Cicero is as follows:

And so we must, dear friends,
Fight still against old age, and all its faults
Endeavour to make good by taking pains:
Fight it, as we would fight disease; attend
To health; use moderate exercise; of food
And drink as much as will sustain our strength,
Not burden it. Nor is the body all:
That must be cared for, but far more than it
The soul, the intellect; unless you feed
Them like a lamp with oil, they soon go out
When age comes on.

Cicero, *On Old Age*, Robert Allison, translator (London: Arthur L. Humphreys, 1916), page 22.

Other Writings

Vinter!

Asle Knudsen

Se ud det er vinter,
Der er sne over mark, over eng.
Se ud, al naturen
Ligger i sin snehvide seng.

Se ind i det hjerte;
Du tvivler vel slet ikke paa
At liv faar det døde,
Naar foraaret første falder paa.

Se op til Livsherren,
Som skaber hvert vaarliv paa jord,
Og kan du da tvivle
Paa liv, som bag gravene bor.

Look out—it's winter,
The snow lies on the ground.
Look out—at nature
Wrapped in its snow-white shroud.

Look in—to your heart,
You don't doubt at all
That life follows death
After the first spring thaw.

Look up—to the Lord of Life,
Who creates life every spring.
Can you doubt the rebirth
That every death shall bring?

This poem was printed in the March 3, 1932 issue of *Evangelisk Tidende*. Translation by the author.

A Brief Visit to Hol, Hallingdal, in 1902[1]

It had been 38 years since I had seen the place of my birth in Hallingdal. I thought I would see great changes. The mountains and the valley were the same. On some farms, a little change could be seen with new houses, etc., but the people were not the ones I had known. The old ones had died, and the young ones had grown up so that I did not recognize them.

My oldest sister was Mrs. Ole Simonsen Pukerud on Lien, Hallingdal.[2] She did not know that I, her eldest brother, had come to Norway, and she did not recognize me when I came to her home. She thought I was the sheriff who had come to give orders for road work. It was that time of year when everyone had to do their share in keeping the King's highway in good shape.

"So, the sheriff is out and about today," she said. "You will probably want to talk to Ole, my husband, but he is not home today. He will be home tomorrow."

---

[1] A. Knudsen, "Fra en kort besøg til Hol, Hallingdal, i 1902," *Hallingen*, March 1929, pages 11–12. Translation by the author with help from Leif Biberg Kristensen, based on an earlier translation by Edna Rude.

[2] This was his sister, Eli.

But then she began to look more closely at me and said: "No, you are not the sheriff; you have a long beard, and he does not. There's something about your face," she continued, "that almost makes me believe that you could be my brother." And with that, the tears flowed freely. It became an unforgettable moment of overwhelming joy for us both.

Soon, there was coffee, and the table was set with many good things to eat: goat *prim*, bacon, cheese, rum bread, *goro*, butter, and old-style flatbread.[3] Then Ola came home, and the three of us were together and could thank God that his great grace had preserved each of us during our long separation.

My cousin, Asle L. Trøo, had a farm nearby.[4] I was soon over there. I met him outside his beautiful house and greeted him:

"Good day, Asle Trøo."

"And good day to you," he answered. "Who are you?"

"Oh, I am from America."

"Would you, by any chance, know a man by the name of Asle Knudsen?"

"Yes, I know him really well."

"No! Is that so! But tell me, is he a Pastor? I have heard that, but I don't know if it is true."

"Yes, it's true."

"Do you know him? Have you heard him preach?"

"Many times."

"I would really like to hear him."

"He is talking to you right now."

---

[3] Prim is a soft, spreadable cheese made from whey; goro is a kind of wafer baked on a patterned, rectangular iron (Haugen, *Norwegian English Dictionary*, page 159, "goro," and page 314, "prim").

[4] Asle Larsen Trøo was the eldest son of Asle Knudsen's paternal aunt, Kristi.

He was very quiet for a long time. Then he said, in a loud voice, "I suppose you have come to take a bunch of Norwegians to America?"

"No. People have much that is good here in Norway—things we do not have in America. So, if they want to stay here, I think they should stay. And if they want to go, let them go."

"You talk like you have good sense," he said, adding, "Come into the house so we can talk more."[5]

---

[5] Thirty years later, on his deathbed, Asle Trøo told his neighbors that this conversation with Asle resulted in his conversion (Albert C. Knudson, "Father" in "Asle and Susan Knudsen: A Tribute," memorial booklet [1940], page 7).

Appendix

Courtesy of Sue Daigle

Knudsen family, circa 1904

Back row: Stella, Albert, Nettie
Front row: Adella, Susan, Asle, Tina

Lineage of Asle Knudsen

1. Asle Knudsen was born on 19 January 1844 on the Flåten farm in Hol, Hallingdal, Norway, and was baptized on 25 February 1844 in the Hol *gamle kirke* (old church).[1] He died on 29 September 1939 at his home in Minneapolis, Minnesota,[2] and was buried on 2 October 1939 in Forest Lawn Memorial Park, Maplewood, Minnesota.[3]

Asle married **Synnøve "Susan" Torkelsdatter Fosse** on 27 November 1866 in the Winneshiek County Courthouse, Decorah, Iowa.[4] Susan was born on 12 September 1842 on the Tveit farm in Feios, Sogn, Norway, the daughter of Torkel Torkelson Fosse and Christi Anfindsdatter Tveit. Susan was baptized on 8 October 1842 in the Rinde stavkirke.[5] She died on 11 February 1916 in Minneapolis[6] and was buried on 14 February in Forest Lawn Memorial Park.[7]

Asle and Susan were parents of the following children:

    i. CHARLES THEODORE was born on 10 December 1867 in Pleasant Township, Winneshiek County, Iowa.[8] He died on 8 June 1894, at age 26, in Saint Paul, Minnesota,[9] and was buried in Forest Lawn Memorial Park.[10] He married Emma Olson on 20 October 1892 in Saint Paul.[11] She was born in March 1869 in Saint Paul.[12] Emma died on 2 November 1928 in San Juaquin General Hospital near Stockton, California,[13] and was buried in Park View Cemetery in Manteca, California.[14]

During his short career, Charles worked as a bookkeeper.[15] After Charles' death, Emma married Hans G. Smeland,[16] a Methodist minister who served pastorates in Illinois, Wisconsin, New York, North Dakota, and Los Angeles.[17] Hans resigned from the ministry in 1909[18], and he and Emma moved to Stockton, California, where he worked in the real estate business.

ii. TINA ALVINA was born on 22 June 1869 in Pleasant Township.[19] She died on 7 September 1913 in Saint Paul[20] and was buried on 10 September 1913 in Roselawn Cemetery, Roseville, Minnesota.[21]

Tina married Halvor O. Helgeson on 14 September 1888 in Saint Paul.[22] Halvor was born on 11 March 1863 in Newburg Township, Fillmore County, Minnesota.[23] He died on 7 November 1940 in Minneapolis[24] and was buried on 9 November 1940 in Roselawn Cemetery.[25]

Halvor's first job was as a station agent at the train depot in Canton, a small town in Fillmore County.[26] Next, he was the cashier at the Bank of Canton and the editor of the *Canton Leader* newspaper.[27] In 1895, he moved to Lanesboro, Minnesota, and was the bank cashier for Citizens State Bank. Two years later, the bank failed. Halvor and Tina then moved to Saint Paul, where they lived with her parents, Asle and Susan, while getting established.[28] Halvor worked as a telegraph operator for the Northern Pacific Railroad and later as a clerk in the Merriam Park Post Office. He eventually became the superintendent of the Grant Post Office, a position he held until he retired.[29]

iii. HENRY BETHUEL was born on 7 March 1871 in Pleasant Township, Winneshiek County, Iowa.[30] He died on 25 October 1888, at age 17, in Saint Paul, Minnesota,[31] and was buried in Forest Lawn Memorial Park.[32]

iv. ALBERT CORNELIUS was born on 23 January 1873 in Grand Meadow Township, Mower County, Minnesota.[33] He died on 28 August 1953 in Cambridge, Massachusetts,[34] and was buried on 31 August 1953 in Mount Auburn Cemetery in Cambridge.[35]

Albert married Mathilde Johnson on 7 July 1899 in Chicago, Illinois.[36] They were married by Mathilde's father, Rev. John H. Johnson, who had baptized Albert 26 years earlier. Mathilde was born on 20 July 1872 in Racine, Wisconsin.[37] She died on 13 December 1948 in Cambridge[38] and was buried on 16 December 1948 in Mount Auburn Cemetery.[39]

Albert finished high school in Saint Paul at age 16 and enrolled in the University of Minnesota. He graduated second in his class in 1893, earning a Bachelor of Arts degree. It was then that Albert decided to become a preacher and study theology. He accordingly enrolled in Boston University. During his junior and senior years, in addition to his studies, he preached at a church in South Boston. In 1896, he graduated with a Bachelor of Sacred Theology degree. The following year, he began his post-graduate work, and in 1900, he received his Doctor of Philosophy degree. At Boston University, he was Professor of Systematic Theology, Dean of the School of Theology from 1926 until his retirement in 1938, and the author of nine books.[40]

v. ROSE ADELLA was born on 27 October 1875 in Freeport, Iowa, and was baptized on 19 February 1876 in the Washington Prairie Methodist Church.[41] She died on 8 September 1963 in Seattle, Washington,[42] and was buried on 11 September 1963 in Acacia Memorial Park, Lake Forest Park, Washington.[43]

Adella married John Henry Swenson on 22 June 1898 in Saint Paul, Minnesota.[44] John was born on 28 August 1871 in Watsessing, New Jersey.[45] He died on 18 April 1963 in Seattle[46] and was buried on 20 April 1963 in Acacia Memorial Park.[47]

John H. Swenson was the owner and operator of Standard Press, a printing shop in Minneapolis, for many years. After Asle's wife, Susan, died, Adella and John moved in with Asle at his home on 3812 Portland Avenue. Shortly before 1942, John retired, and he and Adella moved to Puyallup, Washington, where their daughter lived. In 1948, they moved to Seattle, where they lived out their lives.[48]

vi. OSCAR TYROL was born on 1 June 1877 in Freeport and was baptized on 29 June in the Washington Prairie Methodist Church.[49] He died on 31 January 1887 in Saint Paul[50] and was buried in Forest Lawn Memorial Park.[51]

vii. STELLA CHARLOTTE was born on 29 December 1878 in Newburg Township, Fillmore County, Minnesota. She was baptized on 23 February 1879 in the Newburg Methodist Church.[52] She died on 4 January 1975 in St. Louis Park, Minnesota,[53] and was buried in Oakdale Memorial Gardens, Davenport, Iowa.[54]

Stella married Hans Petersen on 27 November 1900 in Minneapolis.[55] Hans was born on 4 March 1872 in Fakse, Præstø, Denmark.[56] He died on 25 December 1924 in Davenport, Iowa,[57] and was buried on 27 December 1924 in Oakdale Memorial Gardens.[58]

Hans emigrated to Minnesota with his parents when he was ten years old. At the age of 12, he left school and went to work for a local Norwegian-language newspaper as a compositor. Hans worked as an itinerant printer for several years. Eventually, he took a job at one of the first papers that used a Linotype type-setting machine. He learned to operate the Linotype but felt it could be improved. He is credited with inventing the Linograph machine, which was superior to the Linotype in many ways. With the help of investors, Hans and his brothers established the Linograph Company in Davenport, Iowa, in 1912. By 1920, the company had produced more than 700 machines, which were sold in 22 countries.[59]

After Hans died, Stella and her children joined her sister Adella and her brother-in-law John at Asle's home in Minneapolis.[60]

viii. SOPHIA ANZONETTIE was born on 21 August 1881 in Newburg Township.[61] She died on 7 March 1966 in New York City[62] and was buried on 9 March 1966 in Kensico Cemetery, Westchester, New York.[63]

Nettie married, first, Ivar Sivertsen on 12 September 1907 in Minneapolis.[64] They had no children. The marriage ended in divorce.

Nettie married, second, Lawrence Arthur Heimark

on 3 June 1912 in Minneapolis.⁶⁵ Lawrence was born on 13 January 1887 in Clarkfield, Minnesota.⁶⁶ He died on 10 March 1960 in St. Joseph's Hospital, Park Rapids, Minnesota, and was buried on 14 March 1960 in Greenwood Cemetery in Park Rapids.⁶⁷

As a young man, Lawrence emigrated to Canada and filed a claim on a homestead in Waldeck, Saskatchewan.⁶⁸ After their wedding, Nettie and Lawrence lived in Waldeck. They returned to the United States in 1913⁶⁹ and lived in Ridgeway, Iowa, where Lawrence was engaged in the jewelry business.⁷⁰

In 1915, he and Nettie moved to Decorah, Iowa, where he worked in a jewelry store.⁷¹ On the first of June, 1916, northeastern Iowa was battered by a storm that dropped 3 inches of rain in two hours, which caused heavy flooding in Decorah. The Heimark home on Main Street was filled with several feet of water. Nettie, Lawrence, and their two children survived by climbing onto the tables and chairs.⁷²

Lawrence owned jewelry stores in small towns in Iowa and Minnesota, and from about 1923 to 1928, he had a store in Portland, Oregon.⁷³ He then moved back to Minneapolis, where, in 1930, he was a traveling jewelry salesman.⁷⁴ Lawrence and Nettie divorced on 28 December 1932.⁷⁵ Nettie kept custody of the children and went to live with her father at his home on 3812 Portland Avenue.⁷⁶

At the time of their marriage in 1912, Lawrence was a naturalized Canadian citizen. Under the law in effect at the time, married women always took the nationality of their spouse, so by marrying Lawrence, Nettie became a Canadian citizen. The law changed in 1922 when Congress passed the Married Women's Act, allowing a married woman to have a separate nationality from her spouse. Unfortunately for Nettie, this meant that when Lawrence regained his US citizenship in 1925, Nettie remained a Canadian citizen. Nettie may not have realized this since it was not until 1934 that she filed a petition for citizenship, which was granted on 9 May that year.[77] Ironically, two years later, Congress simplified the rules so that a woman in Nettie's situation would only have to take the oath to regain citizenship.[78]

ix. CYRUS ALVIN was born on 17 March 1883 in Millville, Minnesota.[79] He died on 22 April 1883 in Millville and was buried on 24 April 1883 in Oakwood Cemetery, Wabasha County, Minnesota.[80]

2nd Generation

Asle Knudsen was the son of Knud Aslesen and his first wife, Birgit Knudsdatter.

2. Knud Aslesen was born on 28 February 1813 on the Nygard farm in Hol, Hallingdal, Norway, and was christened on 11 April 1813 in the Hol Gamle Kirke.[81] He died on 18 November 1885 on the Vestreim farm in Hol.[82]

Knud married, first, **Birgit Knudsdatter on** 3 July 1841 in the Hol Gamle Kirke.[83] Birgit was born on 24 October 1818 on the Flåten farm in Hol and was baptized on 15 November 1818 in the Hol Gamle Kirke.[84] She died on 18 February 1850 on the Kaupang farm in Hol and was buried in the Hol Gamle Kirke cemetery.[85]

After their marriage, Knud and Birgit lived on the Flåten farm. In 1844, they moved to the Annfinnset farm, and in 1846, they moved to the Kaupang farm.[86]

They had the following children:

    i. ELI was born on 20 February 1842 on the Flåten farm and baptized on 24 March 1842 in Hol Gamle Kirke.[87] She died on 3 October 1913[88] and was buried in Geilo Cemetery in Hol.[89]

    Eli was eight years old when her mother died, and she went to live with her grandmother, Eli Haagensdatter, on Nygard.[90] Eli married Ole Simonsen on 21 June 1872 in the Hol Gamle Kirke.[91] Ole was born on 23 January 1847 on the Pukerud farm in Hol.[92] He died on 27 December 1939 and was buried on 5 January 1940 in Geilo Cemetery.[93]

+ 1 ii. ASLE, born on 18 January 1844 on the Flåten farm, died on 29 September 1939 in Minneapolis, Minnesota.

    iii. ASTRID "ESTHER" was born on 12 December 1846 on the Kaupang farm and baptized on 1 January 1847 in the Hol Gamle Kirke.[94] She died on 17 March 1888 in Oakwood Township, Wabasha County, Minnesota,[95] and was buried in the Oakwood Methodist Cemetery.[96]

    Astrid emigrated to America in 1868 and was living with her brother, Asle, at the time of the 1870 census.[97] Sometime after that, she began using the name Esther.

Esther married Knud K. Utigaard on 26 May 1874 in Oakwood Township.[98] Knud was born on 27 October 1837 in Nesset, Romsdalen, Norway.[99] He died on 30 March 1919 in Millville, Minnesota,[100] and was buried on 5 April 1919 in the Oakwood Cemetery.[101]

After Birgit's death, Knud married **Guri Olsdatter** on 15 November 1852 in the Hol Gamle Kirke.[102] Guri was born on 1 November 1817 on the Tufto farm in Kvisla in Hol and baptized on 30 November 1817 in the Hol Gamle Kirke.[103] Guri died in childbirth on 21 December 1871 and was buried at the Hol Gamle Kirke on 7 January 1872.[104]

In 1853, Knud sold Kaupang and bought, apparently the same year, the Vestreim farm.[105] He and Guri lived there the rest of their lives.

They had the following children, all born on Vestreim:

    iv. BIRGIT was born on 17 March 1853 and baptized on 22 May 1853 in Hol Gamle Kirke.[106] She died young on 22 December 1870, at age 17.[107]

    v. GURI "RINA" was born on 20 January 1855 and baptized on 29 March 1855 in Hol Gamle Kirke.[108] She died on 12 December 1955 and was buried in the Geilo Cemetery in Hol.[109]

Guri was called Rina to distinguish her from her mother. Guri is generally the shortened version of Gurina. So, the mother went by Guri, and the daughter went by Rina.

Rina emigrated to America in 1899[110] and possibly

lived in San Pedro, California, before purchasing a six-acre lot in the Tokay Colony near Lodi, California, in 1911.[111] She lived there until 1933 when she returned to Norway.[112] At the time of her death, Rina was living with relatives on the Pukerud farm.[113] She was 100 years, 10 months, and 22 days old when she died.[114]

vi. MARI was born on 4 August 1857 and baptized on 27 September 1857 in Hol Gamle Kirke.[115] She died on 24 February 1841 on the Jakobsplass farm in Hol.[116]

Mari married Iver Larsen on 20 June 1901 in Hol Gamle Kirke, his second marriage.[117] He was born on 29 January 1853 on the Jakobsplass farm and baptized on 30 March in the Hol Gamle Kirke.[118] He died on 3 May 1934 on Jakobsplass.[119]

vii. BIRGIT "BERTHA" was born on 19 April 1862 and baptized on 9 June 1862 in Hol Gamle Kirke.[120] In 1891, she was living with her uncle Hermund on the Thorrud farm in Skoger.[121] Sometime after that, she migrated to North America, where she went by the name Bertha Knudsen.

On 23 September 1913, she married Charles McDonald in Vancouver, British Columbia.[122] Charles was born on 18 September 1871 in St. Mary's Road, Kings County, Prince Edward Island.[123]

He and Bertha moved to the United States in 1914[124] and lived first in San Jose, California,[125] where he was naturalized; they later lived in Santa Cruz, California,[126] from about 1922 to 1933.[127]

3rd Generation

Knud Aslesen was the son of Asle Hermundsen and his second wife, Eli Haagensdatter.

3. Asle Hermundsen was born about 1773 on the Uthus farm in Hol, Hallingdal,[128] and died on 12 February 1831.[129]

Asle married, first, in January 1800[130], **Kristi Eriksdatter,** born, probably in 1766, on the Rue farm in Hol and baptized on 1 January 1767 in the Hol Gamle Kirke.[131] She died, most likely during the winter of 1806–1807, on Fjellberg and was buried on 28 March 1807.[132]

When Asle and his first wife, Kristi, married, they lived on Raunsgard, where Asle's mother was born. Asle's uncle Svein Olsen built Raunsgardstugu, a one-room log cabin with a sod roof that was initially a guest cottage on Raunsgard. The walls and ceiling were painted by folk artist Kristen Aanstad about 1790 in a traditional Norwegian decorative style known as *rosemaling*. Due to the cultural significance of the rosemaling, this building is now in the Hol Bygdemuseum.[133]

After their marriage, they moved to Fjellberg, where they were listed on the 1801 census. Their status is given as *husmann med jord* (cottar with land).[134] Kristi died in 1807, and the following year, Asle bought Nygard.

Asle and Kristi did not have any children.

Asle married, second, **Eli Haagensdatter** on 7 May 1809 in Ål Parish.[135] Eli was born in 1774 on the Finnesgard farm in Gol, Hallingdal,[136] and died on 7 April 1862 on Nygard.[137]

In 1824, Asle bought Fjellberg and owned both farms thereafter. One day in February 1831, he was returning home with a load of grain in icy conditions when he apparently had an accident. The next day, he was found dead under the overturned load. After Asle's death, Eli and her children continued to live on the farm. She sold it to her son-in-law and daughter, Kristi, ten years later.[138]

Asle and Eli had the following children, all born on the Nygard farm;

    i. HERMUND was born on 2 March 1810 and baptized on 25 March in the Hol Gamle Kirke.[139] He died on 22 January 1891 on the Thorrud farm in Skoger, Vestfold, Norway,[140] and was buried on 31 January in the Skoger Church Cemetery.[141]

Hermund married, first, on 6 February 1844, Ingeborg Knudsdatter.[142] She was born on 5 October 1811 on the Fossgard farm in Hol[143] and died in childbirth on 18 February 1847.[144]

Ingeborg was a widow who had inherited the Nordre Breie farm in Ål from her first husband. By marrying her, Hermund became the new owner of Breie.

Hermund married, second, on 2 March 1853, Kari Olsdatter in the Gol stavkirke.[145] She was born on 10 June 1831 on the Storla farm in Gol, Hallingdal.[146] She died in childbirth on 19 September 1856 and was buried at the Ål stavkirke.[147]

Hermund married, third, on 24 June 1857, Ingeborg Vilhelmsdatter.[148] She was born on 18 April 1832 on the Eidsgard farm in Gol.[149] She died on 27 February 1875 on the Thorrud farm in Skoger and was buried on 11 March.[150]

In 1860, Hermund moved his family to Lier kommune,[151] adjacent to the city of Drammen, a major port city located 27 miles southwest of Oslo. Hermund bought the Thorrud farm in Skoger kommune in 1863[152] and lived there until his death. Skoger was incorporated into the city of Drammen in 1964.

+ 2   ii.   KNUD, born on 28 February 1813, died on 18 November 1855.

iii.   KRISTI was born on 14 October 1814 and baptized on 1 January 1815, presumably in the Hol Gamle Kirke.[153] She died on 22 October 1876 on the Thorrud farm in Skoger and was buried on 29 October.[154]

Kristi married Lars Larsen on 7 June 1834.[155] Lars was born in 1799 on the Pukerud farm in Hol and baptized in the Hol Gamle Kirke.[156] He drowned in Nygardsvatnet[157] on 31 July 1854 and was buried at the Hol Gamle Kirke.[158]

In 1841, Kristi and Lars bought the Nygard and Fjellberg farms from her mother, Eli. After Lars' death, Kristi went to live with her brother Hermund. She is listed in her brother's household in Skoger in both the 1865 and 1875 censuses.[159]

iv.   ELLING was born on 12 January 1817 and baptized on 23 March 1817 in the Hol Gamle Kirke.[160] He died on 9 October 1912 at his home in Highland Township, Winneshiek County, Iowa,[161] and was buried on 14 October[162] in Big Canoe Lutheran Church Cemetery.[163]

Elling married Ragnhild Kittelsdatter on 24 March 1842 in the Hol Gamle Kirke.[164] Ragnhild was born on 14 November 1815 on the Foss farm in Hol and was baptized on 25 November in the Hol Gamle Kirke.[165] She died at home on 9 August 1910 and was buried on 12 August[166] in the Big Canoe Lutheran Church Cemetery.[167]

Elling purchased the Fosshaugen farm in Hol from his father-in-law in 1845 and lived there until 1850 when he sold it to a brother-in-law and migrated with his family to America.[168] They went first to the Rock Prairie settlement in Rock County, Wisconsin,[169] and later relocated to Winneshiek County, Iowa, where Elling bought a farm in Highland Township.[170] He went by the name Elling Foss in America.

v. OLE was born on 27 September 1822 and baptized on 20 October in the Hol Gamle Kirke.[171] He died on 22 May 1885 on the Jeglum farm in Hol and was buried on 7 June.[172]

Ole married Gro Olsdatter on 28 April 1858 in Hol Gamle Kirke.[173] She was born on 9 February 1828 on the Tufto farm in Kvisla in Hol and baptized in the Hol Gamle Kirke on 16 March 1828.[174] Gro died on 26 May 1880 on Jeglum and was buried on 6 June 1880, presumably in the Hol Gamle Kirke cemetery.[175]

Ole's wife, Gro Olsdatter, and his brother Knud's wife, Guri Olsdatter, were sisters.

Notes for the Lineage of Asle Knudsen

These notes use the following initialisms:

FHL Family History Library
NARA National Archives and Records Administration
UMC United Methodist Church

---

1. Asle's birthplace is in dispute since there is conflicting evidence from several sources. Asle himself, in a letter to *Hallingen*, states that he was born on Kaupang ("Brev fra Pastor A. Knudsen" [Letter from Pastor A. Knudsen], *Hallingen*, January 1917, page 30).

   The Hol *bygdebok* (farm history book) authors dismiss this by pointing out that the family didn't move from Annfinnset to Kaupang until 1846, two years after Asle was born. The authors argue that Asle probably doesn't remember Annfinnset because he was so young when they moved. He spent the rest of his childhood on Kaupang, so he remembers Kaupang as his birthplace. They conclude that Asle was born on Annfinnset. See Lars Reinton and Sigurd S. Reinton, *Folk og Fortid i Hol* [People and Past in Hol], volume 6, *Ætt og Eige: Kvisla og Lio* (Oslo: Hol Sparebank, 1977), page 76.

   However, the bygdebok authors themselves, in a different volume, report that Asle's father purchased Annfinnset on 28 June 1844, five months after Asle was born. See Reinton and Reinton, *Folk og Fortid I Hol*, volume 5, *Ætt og Eige: Sør-Hovet Framhald, Nord-Hovet, Sudndalen og Strønde* (Oslo: Hol Sparbank, 1975), page 177.

   The Ål church records contain the baptismal records for Asle and his older sister, Eli. In both instances, their father's name is Knud Aslesen Flåten, indicating that they were living on Flåten at the time. See Ål Parish (Buskerud County, Norway), Ministerialbok nr. 5, folio 114, Piger [Girls], line 19, "Ælie" and folio 127, entry 12, "Asle"; National Archives of Norway, *Digitalarkivet* (media.digitalarkivet.no), parish registers.

Based on the church records and the timing of the purchase of the Annfinnset and Kaupang farms, we must conclude that Asle was born on the Flåten farm.

2. Minnesota Department of Health, death certificate, number 22195 (1939), Asle Knudsen, informant was Albert C. Knudsen, son of deceased; certified copy (1984).
3. Forest Lawn Memorial Park, Maplewood, Minnesota (formerly Forest Cemetery), Knudson monument, section 3, "Father Asle 1844-1939"; transcribed and photographed 28 July 2014.
4. Winneshiek County, Iowa, Marriage Register, Book A, page 118, Asle Knudsen–"Susan Torklesen"; Recorder's Office, Winneshiek County Courthouse, Decorah.
5. Leikanger Parish (Sogn og Fjordane County, Norway), Leikanger Ministerialbok nr. 7 (1838-1851), page 49, entry 105, "Synneve"; FHL microfilm 126,468.
6. Minnesota Department of Health, death certificate, number 17689 (1916), "Susana Knudsen," informant was A. Knudsen, husband of deceased; certified copy (1984).
7. Forest Lawn Memorial Park, Knudson monument, "Mother Susan 1842-1916."
8. Asle Knudsen Diary, MS (1844-1937), page 3. Typescript translation (1977) of an unpublished autobiography and journal written in Norwegian by Asle Knudsen; photocopies provided by Sue Daigle and Stan Petersen.
9. Saint Paul, Minnesota, Certificate of Death, "Charles T Knudson," 6 June 1894; "Minnesota, Birth and Death Records, 1866-1916," digital images, *FamilySearch* (familysearch.org); citing Vital Records, Ramsey County Public Health Center, Saint Paul; FHL microfilm 1,309,246.
10. Forest Lawn Memorial Park, Knudson monument, "Charles Theodore, Born Dec 10 1867, Died June 6 1894."
11. Ramsey County, Minnesota, Marriage Record, volume 12 (1892-1893), page 332, Charles T. Knudsen–Emma Olson; "Marriage indexes, 1850-1917; marriage records, 1850-1916," *FamilySearch* (familysearch.org); FHL 7,579,666, item 1.

12. 1900 US Census, Ramsey County, Minnesota, population schedule, Saint Paul, ward 9, page 51 (stamped), enumeration district (ED) 141, sheet 4-A, dwelling 57, family 66, Edward Olson household.
13. California Department of Public Health, death certificate, local number 824 (1928), Emma Smeland, informant was F. J. Bradley, unknown relationship; "California, County Birth and Death Records, 1800-1994," digital images, *FamilySearch* (familysearch.org : accessed 1 February 2022).
14. *BillionGraves*, digital images (billiongraves.com), grave record for Emma Smeland (1869-1928), BillionGraves Record 29546893, Cl. 20 #7A-25; citing Parkview Cemetery, Stockton, California.
15. *St. Paul City Directory* (St Paul : R. L. Polk & Co., 1888), page 770; (1890), page 794; (1891), page 792; (1893), page 811.
16. Ramsey County, Minnesota, Marriage Record, volume 26, page 147, Hans Smeland-Emma Knudson, 2 October 1900; "Minnesota, County Marriages, 1860-1949," digital images, *FamilySearch* (familysearch.org).
17. *Minutes of the Annual Conferences of the Methodist Episcopal Church* (New York: [various publishers], 1895-1904). H. G. Smeland served the Norwegian and Danish Conference (1895-1900, 1904-1905), the New York East Conference (1901-1903), and the Western Norwegian-Danish Conference (1906-1908).
18. Vestre Norsk-Danske Konferense af den Biskoppelige Metodist-Kirke, *Forhandlings-Protokol for det Femtende Aarsmøde* [Proceedings of the Fifteenth Annual Meeting] (Ballard, WA: By the Conference, 1909), page 15; digital images, California-Pacific Conference UMC, *Archives & History* (calpacumc.org/ archiveshistory), Digital Archives, Journals and Minutes, "Western Norwegian Danish Conference, M.E.C. (1888-1939)."
19. Asle Knudsen Diary, page 3.
20. Minnesota Department of Health, death certificate, number 22464 (1913), "Tena A. Helgeson," informant was H. O. Helgeson, husband of the deceased; certified copy (1984).

21. Roselawn Cemetery (Roseville, Ramsey, Minnesota), "Tena A. Helgeson" grave marker, division 1, lot 225 W½, space 3; transcribed and photographed by the author, 1999.
22. Ramsey County, Minnesota, Marriage License and Certificate, Halvor O. Helgeson-Tina Alvina Knudsen; "Minnesota, County Marriages, 1860-1949," digital images, *FamilySearch* (familysearch.org : accessed 7 May 2017).
23. "Social Security Applications and Claims Index, 1936-2007," database, *Ancestry* (ancestry.com), Halvor O. Helgeson.
24. Minnesota Department of Health, death certificate, number 22698 (1940), Halvor O. Helgeson, informant was Mrs. Frank S. Hazen, daughter of the deceased; certified copy (1984).
25. Roselawn Cemetery, Halvor O Helgeson grave marker, division 1, lot 225 W½, space 2.
26. "Halvor Helgeson Passed Away," *Mabel (Minnesota) Record*, 15 November 1940, page 1, column 4; microfilm, Minnesota Historical Society.
27. Canton Minnesota 1879-1979: The Life and Legend of a Small Town (Canton Centennial Committee, 1979), page 63.
28. Traditional Helgeson Family History (no date), Larson Family Archives. This is an untitled typewritten document inherited by the author from Doris Helgeson Larson.
29. *St. Paul City Directory* (R. L. Polk & Co.: St. Paul, 1898-1933), entries for Helgeson, Halvor O; "U.S. City Directories, 1822-1995," digital images, *Ancestry* (ancestry.com).
30. Asle Knudsen Diary, page 3.
31. Saint Paul, Minnesota, Certificate of Death, "Henry Knudsen," 25 October 1888; "Minnesota, Birth and Death Records, 1866-1916," digital images, *FamilySearch* (familysearch.org); citing Vital Records, Ramsey County Public Health Center, Saint Paul; FHL microfilm 1,309,220.
32. Forest Lawn Memorial Park, Knudson monument, "Henry Bethuel, Born Mar 7, 1871, Died Oct 25, 1888."

33. "United States Passport Applications, 1795-1925," digital image, *FamilySearch* (familysearch.org), certificate #12302, Albert C Knudson, 1910; citing *Passport Applications, January 2, 1906-March 31, 1925*, NARA microfilm publications M1490 and M1372; FHL microfilm 1,498,048.

34. "Dean Knudson of B. U. Dies, Author, 80," *The Boston Herald*, 29 Aug 1953, page 5; digital images, *GenealogyBank* (genealogybank.com : accessed 6 Sep 2016).

35. *Mount Auburn Cemetery*, database (mountauburn.org/locate-a-grave : accessed 20 July 2016), search result for Albert C. Knudson, citing Glen Avenue, lot 7995, space 2, includes image.

36. "Illinois, Cook County Marriages, 1871-1920," *FamilySearch* (familysearch.org): Albert C. Knudson-Mathilda Johnson, 07 Jul 1899; citing Chicago, Cook, Illinois, 294578, Cook County Courthouse, Chicago; FHL microfilm 1,030,299.

37. "New York, New York Passenger and Crew Lists, 1909, 1925-1957," *FamilySearch* (familysearch.org : accessed 17 January 2016), SS *Rex,* 15 March 1938, page 1, line 24, Mathilde J. Knudson; citing NARA microfilm publication T715.

38. "In Loving Memory of Mathilde Johnson Knudson: Service at Harvard-Epworth Methodist Church, Cambridge, Massachusetts," booklet, 16 Dec 1948.

39. *Mount Auburn Cemetery*, burial search for Mathilde Knudson, citing Glen Avenue, lot 7995, space 1, includes image.

40. Elmer A. Leslie, "Albert Cornelius Knudson, the Man," in Edgar Sheffield Brightman, editor, *Personalism in Theology: A Symposium in Honor of Albert Cornelius Knudson* (Boston: Boston University Press, 1943), pages 4-17.

41. Washington Prairie Norwegian Methodist Church (Springfield Township, Winneshiek County, Iowa), "Record of the Norwegian Methodist Episcopal Church, Washington Prairie, Iowa" (1851-1902), unpaginated, "Record of Baptisms," 8th page, "Rose Adala"; "Norwegian Methodist Episcopal Church – Springfield Twp," WC 0226, folder #3; Winneshiek County Historical Society, Decorah, Iowa.

42. Washington State Department of Health, death certificate, state number 18835 (1963), "Rosa Adella Swenson," informant was Mrs. Synette Scheyer, daughter of deceased; digital image, *Washington State Archives - Digital Archives* (digitalarchives.wa.gov : accessed 3 February 2022).

43. *Find A Grave,* digital image (findagrave.com), memorial 84547378, "Della Knudson Swenson" (1875–1963); citing Acacia Memorial Park and Funeral Home (Seattle, Washington), mausoleum MC103 (Rose), L-F, crypt 25; maintained by Stephen Kronberg (contributor 46985297).

44. Ramsey County, Minnesota, Marriage Record, volume 21 (1897–1898), page 644, John H. Swenson–R. Adella Knudsen; "Minnesota, County Marriages, 1860–1949," digital images, *FamilySearch* (familysearch.org : accessed 16 June 2022); FHL 007,728,508, item 5.

45. "United States Passport Applications, 1795–1925," digital images, *FamilySearch* (familysearch.org), certificate #400690, Lisle Burroughs Swenson, 1924; citing Passport Applications, January 2, 1906–March 31, 1925, NARA microfilm M1490, roll 2486; FHL microfilm 1,750,292. This document states that Lisle's father was John Henry Swenson and gives John's place of birth as Watsessing, New Jersey.

46. Washington State Department of Health, death certificate, state number 7734 (1963), John H. Swenson informant was Mrs. Synette Scheyer, daughter of deceased; digital image, *Washington State Archives - Digital Archives* (digitalarchives.wa.gov : accessed 3 February 2022). Note that the place of birth on this document is Sterling, New Jersey.

47. *Find A Grave*, memorial 84547192, John H Swenson (1872–1963); citing Acacia Memorial Park and Funeral Home (Seattle, Washington), mausoleum MC103 (Rose), L-F, crypt 19; maintained by Stephen Kronberg (contributor 46985297).

48. "John H. Swenson," obituary, *Seattle Times*, 19 April 1963, page 48, column 3; digital images, *GenealogyBank* (genealogybank.com).

49. Washington Prairie Norwegian Methodist Church, Record Book, unpaginated, "Record of Baptisms," 8th page, "Tyrel Oscaer."

50. Saint Paul, Minnesota, Certificate of Death, "Oscar Cyrel Knudson," 31 January 1887; "Minnesota, Birth and Death Records, 1866–1916," digital images, *FamilySearch* (familysearch.org); citing Vital Records, Ramsey County Public Health Center, Saint Paul; FHL microfilm 1,309,218.

51. Forest Lawn Memorial Park, Knudson monument, "Oscar Tyrol, Born June 1 1877, Died Jan 30 1887."

52. Newburg Methodist Church (Newburg, Minnesota), "Record of the Newburg Scandinavian Mission Methodist Episcopal Church, Fillmore County, Minnesota," unpaginated, Baptisms, 1879, "Stella Sharlotte."

53. Minnesota Department of Health, Certificate of Death, number 122-75-003448 (1975), Stella Petersen, informant was Mrs. Stella Nylander, daughter of the deceased; Minnesota Historical Society, Saint Paul.

54. Oakdale Memorial Gardens (Davenport, Scott, Iowa), Stella Petersen grave marker, section 28; photographed by Janice Petersen.

55. Hennepin County, Minnesota, Marriage License and Certificate, Hans Petersen–"Stella Sharlotte Knudsen," 27 November 1900; certified copy (2021), Vital Records, Hennepin County Government Center, Minneapolis.

56. Fakse Parish (Præstø, Denmark), Hovedministerialbog (1814–1891), 1844 F–1883 F [Births], page 110, entry 12; Danish National Archives, "Kirkebøger fra hele landet" [Church books from the whole country], digital images, *Rigsarkivet* [The National Archives] (rigsarkivet.dk : 10 July 2016).

57. Iowa Department of Vital Statistics, Certificate of Death, number 082-2421 (stamped), Hans Petersen, the informant was P. O. Petersen, brother of deceased; digital image, "Iowa, U. S., Death Records, 1880–1972," *Ancestry* (ancestry.com); citing State Historical Society of Iowa, Des Moines.

58. Oakdale Memorial Gardens, Hans Petersen grave marker, section 28; photographed by Janice Petersen.
59. "The Linograph," *Metal Type* (metaltype.co.uk/wpress/early-machines/the-linograph).
60. 1930 US Census, Hennepin County, Minnesota, population schedule, Minneapolis, ward 13, p. 135 (stamped), enumeration district (ED) 27-248, sheet 1-A, dwelling 4, family 7. This census record lists Asle Knudsen, John and Adella Swenson, and Stella Petersen and her children all living at 3812 Portland Avenue.
61. Asle Knudsen Diary, page 11.
62. New York City, Manhattan death certificate, no 66-104973, "Nettie Knudson Heimark," informant was Lester Laurence, son of deceased; digital image received from Sue Daigle, 21 July 2016.
63. *Find A Grave*, memorial 11368640, Nettie Knudson Heimark (1881–1966); citing Kensico Cemetery (Valhalla, Westchester County, New York); maintained by Ginny M (contributor 253). Includes a biography by Bess Armstrong.
64. Hennepin County, Minnesota, Marriage License and Certificate; "Minnesota, County Marriages, 1860-1949," digital images, *FamilySearch* (familysearch.org), Ivar Sivertsen-Anzonettie Knudsen, 1907.
65. Hennepin County, Minnesota, Marriage License and Certificate, "Lawrence A. Himack"-Sophia A. Knudsen, 3 June 1912; certified copy (2021), Vital Records, Hennepin County Government Center, Minneapolis.
66. "United States World War I Draft Registration Cards, 1917–1918," digital images, *FamilySearch* (familysearch.org), Lawrence A. Heimark; citing Steele County, Minnesota, United States, NARA microfilm publication M1509; FHL microfilm 1,682,644.
67. Minnesota Department of Health, Certificate of Death, number 007022 (1960), Lawrence Arthur Heimark; Minnesota Historical Society, Saint Paul.

68. Homestead Register, volume 83, unpaginated, entry number 348480, application date 17 September 1909, grant date 13 May 1913; "Manitoba, Saskatchewan and Alberta, Canada, Homestead Grant Registers, 1872–1930," *Ancestry* (ancestry.com); citing Homestead Grant Registers, R190-75-1-E, Library and Archives Canada, Ottawa.
69. U.S. District Court For the District of Oregon, Naturalization Records, volume 21, page 86, Lawrence Arthur Heimark, Declaration of Intention, number 9504, 5 March 1925; "Oregon, U.S., Naturalization Records 1865–1991," *Ancestry* (ancestry.com); NARA microfilm M1540, roll 6.
70. 1915 Iowa state census, Winneshiek County, Ridgeway town, card number 94 (Lawrence A. Heimark), and card number 95 (S. Nettie Heimark).
71. "L. A. Heimark to Organize Mystic Workers," *Decorah (Iowa) Journal,* 17 November 1915, page 1, column 5; Winneshiek County Historical Society and Preus Library Luther College, *Winneshiek County Newspaper Archives*, digital images (winneshiekcounty.advantage-preservation.com).
72. "Great Flood Strikes County," *Decorah (Iowa) Journal,* 7 June 1916, pages 1 and 7.
73. *Polk's Portland City Directory* (Portland: R. L. Polk & Co., 1923, 1925–1927), page 800 (1923), page 768 (1925), page 694 (1926), page 741 (1927); "U.S., City Directories, 1822–1995," digital images, *Ancestry* (ancestry.com).
74. 1930 US Census, Hennepin County, Minnesota, population schedule, Minneapolis, ward 8, enumeration district (ED) 27-134, sheet 3-B, dwelling 56, family 65, "Al A. Heimark" household.
75. Hennepin County, Minnesota, District Court, book 459, pages 191–192, affidavit re: divorce of Nettie Heimark vs. Lawrence Heimark, 4 August 1945; digital image, *Record EASE Web Access* (https://txpr-reinq-d.co.hennepin.mn.us/search.aspx).

76. 1940 US Census, Hennepin County, Minnesota, population schedule, Minneapolis, Ward 7, enumeration district (ED) 89-184, sheet 1A. This census lists Nettie Heimark, Adella and John Swenson, and Stella Petersen all living at 3812 Portland Avenue.
77. Hennepin County, Minnesota, District Court, Naturalization Records, Sophia Anzonettie Heimark, Petition for Citizenship (20 April 1934) and Oath of Allegiance (9 May 1934); "Minnesota Naturalization Records and Indexes, 1872–1962," *FamilySearch* (familysearch.org).
78. For an excellent article on this subject, see Marian L. Smith, "Women and Naturalization, ca. 1802–1940," *Prologue*, volume 30, number 2 (Summer 1998); *National Archives* (archives.gov/publications/prologue/1998/summer), Genealogy Notes.
79. Wabasha County, Minnesota, Birth Register, book A, page 249, "Knutson"; Recorder's Office, Wabasha County Courthouse, Wabasha. The date is recorded as 26 March 1883, no first name, parents are "Alex," a minister, and Susan.
80. Asle Knudsen Diary, page 12.
81. Ål Ministerialbok nr. 3 (1807–1814), page 55, ninth entry, "Knud."
82. Hol Parish (Buskerud County, Norway), Hol Ministerialbok nr. I 2 (1870–1886), folio 355, entry 15, "Knud Aslesen Vestreim"; digital images, National Archives of Norway, *Digitalarkivet* (media.digitalarkivet.no), parish registers.
83. Ål Ministerialbok nr. 5 (1825–1848), folio 301, entry 26, "Knud Aslesen og Birgit Knudsdatter."
84. Ål Klokkerbok nr. 1 (1815–1829), page 99, entry 57, "Birgit."
85. Ål Ministerialbok nr. 6 (1849–1864), folio 164, entry 6, "Birgit Knudsdatter."
86. Reinton and Reinton, *Folk og Fortid I Hol*, volume 5, page 177.
87. Ål Ministerialbok nr. 5 (1825–1848), folio 114, line 19, Piger (Girls), "Ælie."

88. Buskerud County, Norway, Dødsfallsprotokoll [Death Register] nr. 4 (1911–1916), folio 19, Eli Knudsdatter Pukerud; digital images, National Archives of Norway, probate records, *Digitalarkivet* (media.digitalarkivet.no).

89. "Finn en Grav," *Slekt og data*, database (slektogdata.no/gravminner/finn-en-grav), "Eli Pukerud," Viken fylke, Hol kommune, Geilo gravplass, includes image.

90. Dorothy Petersen Swaney, "Nygaard-Knudsen and Related Families from Norway," typescript, final draft (1985), page 1.

91. Hol Ministerialbok nr. I 2 (1870–1886), folio 244, 1872, entry 11, "Ole Simonsen Pugerud"–"Eli Knudsdtr. Flaaten."

92. Ål Ministerialbok nr. 5 (1825–1848), folio 147, entry 31, "Ohla."

93. "Finn en Grav," *Slekt og data*, "Ole S. Pukerud," Viken fylke, Hol kommune, Geilo gravplass, includes image.

94. Ål Ministerialbok nr. 5 (1825–1848), folio 145, line 1, "Astri."

95. Wabasha County, Minnesota, Death Register, Book A, page 260, line 5, "Austria Knutson"; Recorder's Office, Wabasha County Courthouse, Wabasha.

96. Oakwood Methodist Cemetery (Wabasha County, Minnesota, behind Hilltop Fellowship Church), Knut K. and Esther Utigard grave marker, 5th row, 9th marker.

97. 1870 US Census, Winneshiek County, Iowa, population schedule, Pleasant Township, Locust Lane Post Office, p. 2, dwelling 9, family 9.

98. Wabasha County, Minnesota, Marriage Register, unknown volume, page 237, "Knud Knudson"–Esther Knudson, 26 May 1874; "Minnesota, County Marriages, 1860–1949," digital images, *FamilySearch* (familysearch.org : 13 June 2016).

99. Nesset Parish (Møre og Romsdal County, Norway), Nesset Ministerialbok nr. 551A04 (1831–1845), pages 55–56, entry 9, "Knud Knudsen Utigaard"; digital images, National Archives of Norway, *Digitalarkivet* (media.digitalarkivet.no), parish registers.

100. Wabasha County, Death Register, book E, page 180, line 6, "Knute M. Utigard"; Recorder's Office, Wabasha County Courthouse, Wabasha. Also:

    "Knut K. Utigard," obituary, *Wabasha County Herald (Wabasha, Minnesota)*, 17 April 1919, page 1, column 4; digital images, Minnesota Historical Society, *Minnesota Digital Newspaper Hub* (mnhs.org/newspapers : accessed 3 Jan 2017).

101. Oakwood Methodist Cemetery, Knut K. and Esther Utigard grave marker.

102. Hol Ministerialbok nr. I 1 (1850–1870), folio 138, 1852, line 9, "Knud Aslesen"–"Guri Olsdtr," 15 November 1852.

103. Ål Ministerialbok nr. 4 (1815–1825), page 57, entry 64, "Guri."

104. Hol Ministerialbok nr. I 2 (1870–1886), folio 328, 1871, entry 25, "Guri Olsdtr.," Vestreim.

105. Reinton and Reinton, *Folk og Fortid i Hol*, volume 6, page 75.

106. Ål Ministerialbok nr. 6 (1849–1864), folio 37, 4th entry, "Birgit."

107. Hol Ministerialbok nr. I 2 (1870–1886), folio 327, 1870, entry 35, "Birgit Knudsdtr.," Vestreim.

108. Ål Ministerialbok nr. 6 (1849–1864), folio 58, 5th entry, "Guri."

109. "Finn en Grav," *Slekt og data*, "Guri Knudsen," Viken fylke, Hol kommune, Geilo gravplass, includes image.

110. 1930 US Census, San Joaquin County, California, population schedule, O'Neal Township, enumeration district (ED) 39-72, sheet 8-B, Tokay Road, Rt. 1, Box 198, dwelling 190, family 192, Hans Lund household.

111. San Joaquin County, California, Deed of Sale, non-certified copy, H. G. Smeland and Emma Smeland to Rina Knutsen, 22 November 1911, West 6 acres of East 10.06 acres, lot 3, Jory Tract 1, $10; citing Book A, volume 206 of Deeds, page 391; San Joaquin County Recorder, Stockton.

112. "101-Åring i Hol" [101-Year-Old in Hol], *Buskeruds (Norway) Blad*, 8 November 1955, page 8, column 4; digital images, National Library of Norway, *Nasjonalbiblioteket,* Newspaper collection (nb.no/search?mediatype=aviser).
113. Reinton and Reinton, *Folk og Fortid i Hol*, volume 6, page 76.
114. Swaney, "Nygaard-Knudsen Families," page 8.
115. Ål Ministerialbok nr. 6 (1849–1864), folio 75, 4th entry, "Mari."
116. "Buskerud Bygder Døde, 1941" [Buskerud Death Register, 1941], unpaginated, Hol sokn, Hol herred, 1st Quarter, 1941, Kvinner, entry 5, Mari Knudsdtr. Jakobsplass; "Norway, Death Registers, 1928–1941," digital images, *Ancestry* (ancestry.com); citing National Archives of Norway, *Death Registers 1928–1960*.
117. Hol Ministerialbok nr. I 3 (1887–1918), folio 263, 1901, entry 5, "Ivar Larsen Jakobsplads"–"Mari Knudsdtr. Pukerud."
118. Ål Ministerialbok nr. 6 (1849–1864), folio 37, "Døbte af Mandkjøn" [Male Baptisms], entry 24, "Iver."
119. Buskerud County, Norway, Dødsfallsprotokoll [Death Register] nr. 7 (1933–1941), "Protokoll over anmeldte dødsfall i Hol lensmannsdistrikt," unpaginated, 1934, entry 5, Ivar Jakobsplass.
120. Ål Ministerialbok nr. 6 (1849–1864), folio 227, entry 28, "Birgit."
121. 1891 Census of Norway, Vestfold County, Skoger kommune, Tællingskreds 4, huslist 12, personseddel 11, "Birgit Knutsdatter," born 1862 in Hol, Hallingdal; digital images, National Archives of Norway, *Digitalarkivet* (media.digitalarkivet.no).
122. British Columbia, Division of Vital Statistics, Marriage Registrations, volume 72 registrations 029081 to 029990 (1913), number 29937 (stamped), "Chas McDonald"–"Bertha Knudsen"; "Canada Marriages, 1661–1949," digital images, *FamilySearch* (familysearch.org : accessed 3 October 2021).

123. Santa Clara County, California, Record of Declarations of Intention, volume 6 (numbers 1901–2400), page 144, number 2044, "Charles MacDonald"; "California County Naturalizations, 1831–1985," digital images, *FamilySearch* (familysearch.org : accessed 10 October 2021).

124. United States Department of Labor, "List or Manifest of Alien Passengers Applying for Admission to the United States from Foreign Contiguous Territory," sheet 24, Port of Vancouver, B.C., Month of July 1914, line 15, Charles MacDonald; "U.S., Border Crossings from Canada to U.S., 1895–1960," digital images, *Ancestry* (ancestry.com : accessed 4 October 2021); citing The National Archives at Washington, D.C., "Manifests of Passengers Arriving at St. Albans, VT, District through Canadian Pacific and Atlantic Ports, 1895–1954."

125. 1920 US Census, Santa Clara County, California, population schedule, San Jose, precinct 22, enumeration district (ED) 168, sheet 8-A.

126. 1930 US Census, Santa Cruz County, California, population schedule, Santa Cruz, page 138 (stamped), enumeration district (ED) 44-3, sheet 5-A.

127. "U.S., City Directories, 1822–1995," digital images, *Ancestry* (ancestry.com); citing Santa Cruz city directory for the years 1922, 1924–1930, 1932–1933.

128. Reinton and Reinton, *Folk og Fortid i Hol*, volume 7, *Ætt og Eige: Ustedalen og Skurdalen* (Oslo: Hol Sparebank, 1979), page 407. Swaney, "Nygaard-Knudsen Families," page 1. Ål Ministerialbok nr. 2 (1771–1806), page 209, confirmation record for "Asle Hermundsen Rognsgaard." Ål Ministerialbok nr. 5 (1825–1848), folio 308, line 21, burial record.

The Reinton brothers place Asle Hermundsen's birth in 1770, while Swaney places his birth in 1773. The Ål Parish baptism records list several children named Asle between 1770 and 1773. Unfortunately, the handwriting is barely legible. Reading the fathers' names was impossible, so one could not identify which Asle was which.

There *is* a legible confirmation record for Asle Hermundsen in 1792. Given that Asle was confirmed in 1792, it is more likely that he was born in 1773 rather than 1770. Also, his burial record states that he was 58 years old when he died in 1831, making his year of birth 1773.

129. Ål Ministerialbok nr. 5 (1825–1848), folio 308, line 21.
130. Ål Ministerialbok nr. 2 (1771–1806), page 341, 1800, entry 6, "Asle Hermondsen R??"–"Christi E??dtr ??."
131. Ål Ministerialbok nr. 1 (1744–1769), page 260, 2nd entry, "Kristi," daughter of Erik Jacobsen.
132. Ål Ministerialbok nr. 3 (1807–1814), page 432, 7th entry, "Christi Ericksdatter Fjeldberg," 40 years old.
133. "Raunsgardstugu fra Raunsgard i Ustedalen, kårstugu," *Hallingdal Museum* (digitaltmuseum.no/021055992029/raunsgardstugu-fra-raunsgard-i-ustedalen-karstugu).
134. 1801 Census of Norway, Buskerud County, Ål Parish, Hol sokn, folio 233, "Fieldberg" farm, family 9, Asle Hermundsen household; digital images, National Archives of Norway, *Digitalarkivet* (media.digitalarkivet.no).
135. Ål Ministerialbok nr. 3 (1807–1814), page 529, 1809, entry 12. The record does not indicate in which church the wedding took place.
136. Reinton and Reinton, *Folk og Fortig i Hol*, volume 7, page 407.
137. Ål Ministerialbok nr. 6 (1849–1864), page 178, line 17, "Eli Haagensdatter."
138. Reinton and Reinton, *Folk og Fortid i Hol, volume* 7, pages 407–408.
139. Ål Ministerialbok nr. 3 (1807–1814), page 32, "Hermun."
140. Skoger Parish (Vestfold County, Norway), Skoger Ministerialbok nr. I 6 (1885–1910), folio 353, entry 2, "Hermünd Aslesen Breien"; digital images, National Archives of Norway, *Digitalarkivet* (media.digitalarkivet.no), parish registers.
141. "Finn en Grav," *Slekt og data*, "Hermund A. Breien," Viken fylke, Drammen kommune, Skoger gravplass, includes image.

142. Ål Ministerialbok nr. 5 (1825–1848), folio 173, entry 5, "Hermünd Aslesen"–"Ingeborg Knudsdatter."

143. Ål Ministerialbok nr. 3 (1807–1814), page 43, 4th entry, "Ingebor."

144. Ål Ministerialbok nr. 5 (1825–1848), folio 345, females, entry 4, "Ingeborg Knudsdatter."

145. Gol Parish (Buskerud County, Norway), Ministerialbok nr. I 2 (1837–1863), pages 394–395, entry 8, "Hermünd Aslesen Breen af Aal"–"Kari Olsdatter Storla"; digital images, National Archives of Norway, *Digitalarkivet* (media.digitalarkivet.no), parish registers.

146. Gol Ministerialbok nr. I 1 (1821–1837), page 102, entry 77, "Kari."

147. Ål Ministerialbok nr. 6 (1849–1864), folio 172, "Døde af Qvindkjøn" [Female Deaths], entry 33, "Kari Olsdatter."

148. Ål Ministerialbok nr. 6 (1849–1864), folio 149, entry 26, "Hermünd Aslesen"–"Ingeborg Vilhelmsdat."

149. Gol Ministerialbok nr. I 1 (1821–1837), page 110, entry 47, "Ingeborg."

150. Skoger Ministerialbok nr. I 5 (1873–1884), page 523, entry 14, "Ingeborg Vilhelmsdatter."

151. Ål Ministerialbok nr. 6 (1849–1864), folio 277, Utflyttede [Transfers Out], 1860, entry 46.

152. Skoger Ministerialbok nr. I 4 (1862–1872), page 628, Inflyttede [Transfers In], entry 20, "Hermünd Aslesen Breein."

153. Ål Ministerialbok nr. 4 (1815–1825), page 1, entry 2, "Kristi."

154. Skoger Ministerialbok nr. I 5 (1873–1884), page 533, entry 38, "Enke Kristi Aslesdatter Nygaard fra Aal."

155. Ål Ministerialbok nr. 5 (1825–1848), folio 283, entry 34, "Lars Larsen Pugerud" – "Christi Aslesdatter Nÿegaard."

156. Ål Ministerialbok nr. 2 (1771–1806), page 711, left column, entry 10, "Lars."

157. Swaney, "Nygaard-Knudsen Families," page 1.

158. Ål Ministerialbok nr. 6 (1849-1864), folio 171, entry 22, "Lars Larsen."
159. 1865 Census of Norway, Vestfold County, Skoger parish, Ekhaugen school district, Thorrud farm (number 65), and 1875 Census of Norway, Vestfold County, Skoger parish, Tellingskrets 4, Ekhaugen school district, list 35, Thorrud farm (number 65); digital images, National Archives of Norway, *Digitalarkivet* (media.digitalarkivet.no).
160. Ål Ministerialbok nr. 4 (1815-1825), page 46, entry 19, "Elling."
161. "Elling Asleson," death notice, *Decorah (Iowa) Journal*, 15 October 1912, unpaginated.
162. Big Canoe Lutheran Church (Pleasant Township, Winneshiek County, Iowa), Record Book 2 (1893-1931), unpaginated, Jordfæstede [Burials], 1912, entry 11, "Elling Asleson Foss"; "Evangelical Lutheran Church in America Church Records, 1781-1969," digital images, *Ancestry* (ancestry.com). Note that the church records report a death date of 10 October.
163. Big Canoe Lutheran Church Cemetery (Pleasant Township, Winneshiek County, Iowa), Ellingson/Foss monument, Elling A. Foss, died 9 October 1912; transcribed by the author.
164. Ål Ministerialbok nr. 5 (1825-1848), folio 356, entry 6, "Elling Aslesen"-"Ragnhild Kittelsdatter."
165. Ål Ministerialbok nr. 4 (1815-1825), page 21, entry 68, "Ragnild."
166. Big Canoe Lutheran Church, Record Book 2, unpaginated, Jordfæstede [Burials], 1910, entry 11, "Mrs. Elling A. Foss."
167. Big Canoe Lutheran Church Cemetery, Ellingson/Foss monument, Ragnhild K. Foss, 9 August 1910; transcribed by the author.
168. Reinton and Reinton, *Folk og Fortid i Hol*, volume 6, page 457-458.

169. Elling had a son named Asle who was born in the Rock Prairie settlement in 1851. See Luther Valley Church (Rock County, Wisconsin), Ministerial Records, Book 1 (1846-1856), page 133, entry 252, "Asle"; "Evangelical Lutheran Church in America Church Records, 1781-1969," digital images, *Ancestry* (ancestry.com : accessed 1 June 2021).
170. Winneshiek County, Iowa, Deed Record Book C, page 247, Samuel Brown to Elling Asleson, 2 July 1855; County Recorder's Office, Decorah.
171. Ål Ministerialbok nr. 4 (1815-1825), page 156, entry 73, "Ole."
172. Hol Ministerialbok nr. I 2 (1870-1886), folio 354, entry 6, "Ole Aslesen," Jeglum.
173. Ål Ministerialbok nr. 6 (1849-1864), folio 151, entry 17, "Ole Aslesen"-"Gro Olsdatter."
174. Ål Ministerialbok nr. 5 (1825-1848), folio 19, entry 43, "Gro Olsdatter."
175. Hol Ministerialbok nr. I 2 (1870-1886), folio 338, 1880, Kvinde Kjön, entry 10, "Gro Olsdr Jeglum."

Illustration Credits

Page
4. **Nygard farm, circa 1920.** Photo by Lars K. Ødegaard. Hol Bygdearkiv (HBA.96001-0246). The image is dedicated to the public domain under CC0. / cropped.
8. **The steamship Belgian, formerly Hammonia.** Digital image courtesy of Norway-Heritage (norwayheritage.com). / cropped and converted to black and white.
22. **Washington Prairie Norwegian Methodist Church.** Photo by the author, 2012. Creative Commons CC BY-SA 3.0 / converted to black and white.
33. **First Norwegian-Danish Methodist Church.** Digital image courtesy of Minnesota United Methodist Church Archives, Minneapolis. The quote is from the Norwegian and Danish Annual Conference Minutes, 1887, p. 22.
38. **Bethlehem Methodist Church, North Minneapolis.** "Bethlehem United Methodist Church, 1901–1969," typescript, page 3 (5); Minneapolis, Bethlehem, Box 7, Folder 3 ("History Scrapbook"); Minnesota Conference UMC Archives, Minneapolis. / cropped and retouched.
46. **Asle Knudsen on his 94th birthday.** Hennepin County Library, Minneapolis Newspaper Photograph Collection (P14070). Photo taken by a

Minneapolis Tribune staff photographer and originally published 20 January 1938, page 15.

49. **1925 Norse-American Centennial program.** Norse-American Centennial Executive Committee, *Norse-American Centennial 1825–1925*, souvenir booklet (Saint Paul: Augsburg Publishing House, 1925); digital images, courtesy of Norwegian-American Historical Association. Image created by cropping and merging parts of pages 73 and 75. / converted to white background and increased contrast.

63. **Railroad map of Southeast Minnesota, circa 1885.** Detail from *Map of the Grand Trunk and Great Western of Canada and their Connections* (Boston: Rand Avery Supply Co., 1885); digital image, *David Rumsey Historical Map Collection* (davidrumsey.com/luna/servlet/detail/RUMSEY~8~1~24509~900031).

80. **Asle Knudsen, circa 1875.** Photograph by A. W. Adams, Decorah, Iowa. Studio portrait printed on card stock, 2¼" x 4" from the author's personal collection. This photo was a gift from Nancy N., a descendant of one of the early members of the Washington Prairie Methodist Church. / cropped and retouched.

84. **Oakwood Methodist Church, 1881.** Digital image courtesy of the Rochester, Minnesota, *Post Bulletin.* Used by permission / lightly retouched.

96. **A page from Asle's handwritten history of Bethlehem Church.** Asle Knudsen, "Menighedens Begyndelse" [The Congregation's Beginning], manuscript (1906), page 4; Congregations Papers (P0537), box 11, folder 21; Norwegian-American Historical Association, Northfield, Minnesota.

Illustration Credits

130. **1819 Engraving of a Methodist camp meeting.** M. Dubourg, engraver, "Camp meeting of the Methodists in N. America"; Library of Congress, Prints and Photographs Division (LC-USZ62-2497). / converted to black and white.
134. **Trinity Methodist Church, Deer Park, circa 1910.** This photo is part of an "Our Heritage" display in the nave of the church. Digital copy used by permission. / cropped and retouched.
142. **Veterans C. F. Eltzholtz and A. Knudsen.** Photo and quote from *Evangelisk Tidende*, 22 March 1923, page 8.
174. **Four generations.** Digital image, courtesy of Holly Scheyer. / cropped.
192. **Lake Mills Norwegian Methodist Church.** Digital image, courtesy of Vesterheim Norwegian-American Museum, Decorah, Iowa. / cropped and retouched to remove a telephone pole.
208. **Knudsen Family, circa 1904.** Digital image, courtesy of Sue Daigle, from the estate of Lester L. A. Heimark, son of Nettie (Knudsen) Heimark. / cropped and retouched.
217. **Rina Knudsen.** Photocopy, Dorothy Petersen Swaney Papers, courtesy of Bob Swaney.
220. **Hermund Aslesen Breien.** Photocopy, Dorothy Petersen Swaney Papers, courtesy of Bob Swaney.
221. **Elling Aslesen Foss.** Photocopy, Dorothy Petersen Swaney Papers, courtesy of Bob Swaney.

Resources

Published Works

Alexander, W. E. *History of Winneshiek and Allamakee Counties, Iowa.* Sioux City, Iowa: Western Publishing Co., 1882.

Anderson, Arlow W. "Norwegian-Danish Methodism on the Pacific Coast." *Norwegian-American Studies and Records*, volume 19 (1956): pages 89–115.

———. *The Salt of the Earth: A History of Norwegian-Danish Methodism in America.* Nashville: Parthenon Press, 1962.

Barnes County History: Barnes County, North Dakota. Barnes County Historical Society, 1976.

Bergh, H. P. *Femtiaarsskrift Udgivet ianledningaf [sic] Den norske-danske Methodismes Femtiaarsjublæum, 1901* [Year Book Published on the Occasion of Norwegian-Danish Methodism's Fiftieth Anniversary]. Chicago: Den norsk-danske Boghandel, 1901.

Blegen, Theodore C. *Norwegian Migration to America, 1825–1860.* 1931. Reprint, New York: Arno Press and the New York Times, 1969.

———. *Norwegian Migration to America: The American Transition.* Northfield, Minnesota: Norwegian-American Historical Association, 1940.

Boeder, Thelma Ballinger, compiler. "Planting United Methodist Roots in Minnesota, 1837–2018." PDF. *Minnesota Annual Conference of the United Methodist Church.* www.minnesotaumc.org/files/websites/www/Planting+UM+roots+in+MN.pdf.

California. San Pedro. *San Pedro News-Pilot,* 1 February 1930.

———. Stockton. *Stockton Record*, 24 January 1931.
Canton, Minnesota, 1879-1979: The Life and Legend of a Small Town. Canton Centennial Committee, 1979.
Cicero. *On Old Age.* Robert Allison, translator. London: Arthur L. Humphreys, 1916.
Curtiss-Wedge, Franklyn, editor. *History of Goodhue County, Minnesota.* Chicago: H. C. Cooper, Jr. & Co., 1909.
———. *History of Mower County, Minnesota.* Chicago: H. C. Cooper, Jr. & Co., 1911.
Davison's Minneapolis City Directory. Minneapolis Directory Co., 1899, 1901.
The Doctrines and Discipline of the Methodist Episcopal Church. New York: Nelson & Phillips, 1876. Image copy. University of Michigan Library Digital Collections. *Making of America Books.* name.umdl.umich.edu/agv9068.0001.001.
Fladby, Rolf. *Liers historie,* volume 2, *Gårdshistorie.* Lier Bygdeboknemnd, 1963.
Gesme, Ann Urness. *Between Rocks and Hard Places.* Hastings, Minnesota: Caragana Press, 1993.
Haagensen, A. *Den Norsk-Danske Methodismes Historie, Paa begge Sider havet* [The History of Norwegian-Danish Methodism on Both Sides of the Ocean]. 1894. Reprint, Scholar Select, no date.
Hansen, Carl G. O. *My Minneapolis.* Minneapolis: Standard Press, 1956.
Hanson, Lars G. and Ole Jorgensen. *A Brief History of the Bear Creek Community, Mower County, Minnesota.* Privately published, [1915]. Image copy. Adams Area Historical Society and History Center. adamsmnhistory.com/bear-creek-community.html.
Hassing, Arne. "Methodism from America to Norway." *Norwegian-American Studies,* volume 28 (1979): pages 192-216.

Haugen, Einar. *The Norwegians in America.* Localized History Series. New York: Teachers College Press, Columbia University, 1967.

Haugen, Einar, editor. *Norwegian English Dictionary.* Madison, Wisconsin: University of Wisconsin Press, 1967.

History of Ottawa County, Michigan. Chicago: H. R. Page & Co., 1882.

History of Vernon County, Wisconsin. Springfield, Illinois: Union Publishing Co., 1884.

History of Wabasha County [Minnesota]. Chicago: H. H. Hill & Co., 1884.

Hobart, Chauncey. *History of Methodism in Minnesota.* Red Wing, Minnesota: Red Wing Printing Co., 1887.

Holand, Hjalmar Rued. *De Norske Settlementers Historie* [History of the Norwegian Settlements]. Ephraim, Wisconsin: Forfatterens Forlag, 1909.

Illinois. Chicago. *Den Kristelige Talsmand,* 1877–1921.

———. Chicago. *Evangelisk Tidende: the Norwegian-Danish Christian Advocate,* 1922–1939.

———. Chicago. *Skandinaven,* 12 June 1925.

An Illustrated Historical Atlas of the State of Minnesota. Chicago: A. T. Andreas, 1874. Digital images. Minnesota Historical Society. *Minnesota Reflections.* reflections.mndigital.org/catalog/mhs:1192.

Iowa. Decorah. *Decorah Journal,* 1912–1984.

———. Forest City. *Forest City Summit,* 15 October 1936.

———. Lake Mills. *Lake Mills Graphic,* 1928–1936.

Knudson, Albert C., and John H. Swenson. "Asle and Susan Knudsen: A Tribute." Memorial booklet, [1940]. *Our Immigrant Ancestors.* ourimmigrantancestors.com. Profile for Rev. Asle Knudsen. Histories section

Larson, Martin T., editor. *Memorial Journal of Western Norwegian-Danish Methodism.* By the Conference, 1944.

Leslie, Elmer A. "Albert Cornelius Knudson, the Man." Edgar Sheffield Brightman, editor, *Personalism in Theology: A Symposium in Honor of Albert Cornelius Knudson.* Boston: Boston University Press, 1943.

"The Linograph." *Metal Type.* metaltype.co.uk/wpress/early-machines/the-linograph.

Massachusetts. Boston. *Boston Herald,* 29 August 1953.

Minnesota. Mabel. *Mabel Record,* 15 November 1940.

———. Minneapolis. *Minneapolis Daily Tribune,* 20 July 1885.

———. Minneapolis. *Minneapolis Journal,* 18 October 1933.

———. Minneapolis. *Minneapolis Tidende,* 1900–1931.

———. Minneapolis. *Minneapolis Tribune,* 1934–1938.

———. Minneapolis. *Minneapolis Star,* 1938–1939.

———. Red Wing. *Red Wing Argus,* 1883–1886.

———. Saint Paul. *Skaffaren,* 12 August 1885.

———. Wabasha. *Wabasha County Herald,* 17 April 1919.

Minutes of the Annual Conferences of the Methodist Episcopal Church. New York: [various publishers], 1866–1939.

Minutes of the Norwegian and Danish Annual Conference [various titles]. Chicago: By the Conference, 1880–1943. Digital images. Minnesota Conference UMC Archives, Minneapolis. From 1880 to 1884, the Norwegian and Danish Conference was known as the Northwest Norwegian Conference.

Neill, Edward D. *History of Fillmore County.* Minneapolis: Minnesota Historical Co., 1882.

New York. New York. *Nordisk Tidende,* 5 March 1936.

"New York Passenger Lists, 1820–1891," database with images, *FamilySearch* (familysearch.org); citing National Archives and Records Administration microfilm publication M237, roll 091.

Nilsen, C. F. "Our Church History." *Souvenir Program of the Eightieth Anniversary of the Newburg Methodist Church.*

Pamphlet (1940); Congregations Papers. Norwegian-American Historical Association, Northfield, Minnesota.

Norlie, Olaf Morgan. *History of the Norwegian People in America.* Minneapolis: Augsburg Publishing House, 1925.

Norse-American Centennial Executive Committee. *Norse-American Centennial 1825-1925.* Souvenir booklet. Saint Paul: Augsburg Publishing House, 1925.

Norway. Drammen. *Buskeruds Blad,* 8 November 1955.

———. Oslo. *Kristelig Tidende,* 1909-1939.

North Dakota. Grand Forks. *Hallingen*, a monthly publication of the Hallinglag of America, 1917-1929.

Palmer, Michael P. "Palmer List of Merchant Vessels." *GeoCities.* 2001. Archived at *OoCities.* oocities.org/mppraetorius. Search for *Hammonia* (1855).

"Passenger Lists: Quebec 1865-1921." Digital images. *Library and Archives Canada.* collectionscanada.gc.ca.

Polk's Portland City Directory. Portland: R. L. Polk & Co., 1923, 1925-1927.

Preble, Geo. Henry. *A Chronological History of the Origin and Development of Steam Navigation.* Philadelphia: L. R. Hamersly & Co., 1883.

"Raunsgardstugu fra Raunsgard i Ustedalen, kårstugu." *Hallingdal Museum.* digitaltmuseum.no/021055992029/raunsgardstugu-fra-raunsgard-i-ustedalen-karstugu.

Reinton, Lars and Sigurd S. Reinton. *Folk og Fortid i Hol* [People and Past in Hol]. 8 volumes. Oslo: [various publishers], 1938-1982.

Reinton, Sigurd S. "Hol Herad." Lars Berg et al., editors. *Norske Gardsbruk* [Norwegian Farmsteads], volume 7, *Buskerud Fylke 1.* Oslo: Norske Gardsbruk, 1948.

Solem, Børge. *Emigrant Ship Databases.* Norway-Heritage. norwayheritage.com.

Sowinski, Carolyn Mankell. *The Great Storm: Minnesota's Victims in the Blizzard of January 7, 1873*. Amazon.com: Kindle Direct Publishing, 2022.
Smith, Marian L. "Women and Naturalization, ca. 1802–1940." *Prologue*, volume 30, number 2 (Summer 1998). *National Archives*. archives.gov/publications/prologue/1998/summer. Genealogy notes.
South Dakota. Sioux Falls. *Argus-Leader.* 14 May 1927.
St. Paul City Directory. St. Paul: R. L. Polk & Co., 1884–1933.
Strand, A. E., compiler and editor. *A History of the Norwegians of Illinois*. Chicago: John Anderson Publishing Co., 1905.
Swaney, Dorothy Petersen. "Nygaard-Knudsen and Related Families from Norway." Typescript, final draft (1985). Copy privately held by Bob Swaney.
Swenson, Adella Knudsen. Knudsen correspondence. Privately held by the author.
United States. National Park Service. *National Register of Historic Places*. Digital Asset Search. npgallery.nps.gov/NRHP/GetAsset/NRHP/80001463_text.
Veblen, Thorstein B. "The Price of Wheat Since 1867." *Journal of Political Economy*, volume 1, issue 1 (December 1892): pages 68–103. *The University of Chicago Press: Journals.* doi.org/10.1086/250116.
Warberg, Thor. *Aal bygdesoga*. 10 volumes. Ål, Norway: Ål Kommune/Sparebank, 2008.
———. *Nye Ål bygdebok*. aal-bygdebok.no.
Washington. Seattle. *Seattle Times,* 19 April 1963.
Western Norwegian and Danish Conference. Journals and Minutes [Various titles]. By the Conference, 1906–1931. Digital images. calpacumc.org/archiveshistory.
Who's Who in America, volume 13, *1924–1925*. Chicago: A. N. Marquis & Co., 1924.
Wisconsin. Eau Claire. *Reform,* 1899–1939.

Archives

California-Pacific Conference, United Methodist Church. *Archives & History.* calpacumc.org/archiveshistory. Western Norwegian Danish Conference annual reports.

Decorah Genealogy Association, Decorah, Iowa. Photo collection.

Evangelical Lutheran Church of America Archives, Chicago. Microfilmed church record books.

Library and Archives Canada. collectionscanada.gc.ca. Ships' passenger lists.

Minnesota Conference United Methodist Church Archives, Minneapolis. Congregation papers and Norwegian-Danish Conference annual reports.

National Archives of Norway. *Digitalarkivet.* Database with images. media.digitalarkivet.no. Census records, parish registers, and probate records.

Norwegian-American Genealogical Center and Naeseth Library, Madison, Wisconsin. Bygdebok collection.

Norwegian-American Historical Association, Northfield, Minnesota. Congregation papers.

Pierce County Historical Association. History Sites. piercecountyhistorical.org/history-sites.

Vesterheim Norwegian-American Museum, Decorah, Iowa. Photo collection.

Waseca County History Center, Waseca, Minnesota. wasecacountyhistorycenter.org. Photo collection.

Winneshiek County Historical Society, Decorah, Iowa. Congregation papers.

Local Sources

Iowa

Big Canoe Lutheran Church Cemetery (Pleasant Township, Winneshiek County, Iowa). Grave markers.

Winneshiek County. County Recorder's Office, Decorah. Deed books, marriage registers, and naturalization books.

Minnesota

Forest Lawn Memorial Park (Maplewood, Ramsey County, Minnesota). Grave markers. Office records.

Newburg Methodist Church (Newburg, Minnesota). Record Book 1 (1867–).

Oakwood Cemetery (Wabasha County, Minnesota; two miles south of Millville, behind the Hilltop Fellowship Church). Grave markers.

Wabasha County. County Recorder's Office, Wabasha. Marriage register.

Index

This index lists all the persons and places mentioned in the text, as well as more general topics such as Annual Conferences, Churches, and Norwegian Farms. Similarly spelled names have been conflated together for the reader's convenience.

Married women are listed under their maiden name and all married names. Individuals born in Norway are also listed under each farm name where they are known to have lived.

Bold page numbers indicate an entry in the Lineage.
Italic page numbers indicate a photograph.

Aanstad
    Kristen 219
Aase
    Anders 60
Ames
    Edward R., Bishop 73
Amundsen
    J. A. 196
    Mrs. —?— 175
Andersen/Anderson
    Andrus G. 133
    Carl A. 104, 112, 161, 170, 182
    E. A. 189
    Elmer 126, 149, 152, 167
    Emelia (Hedemark) 133
    Grebert 185
    H. E. 172, 183, 184–85, 193
    Ivar 85
    Jens P. 145, 153
Andrews
    Edward G., Bishop 79, 86

Anfindsdatter
    Christina 9, 56, 61, 70, 209
    Sigrid 10, 56, 63
Annfinnset
    Birgit Knudsdatter (1818–
        1850) 4, 57, 70, 180, **215**
    Eli Knudsdatter 5, 57, 203–4, **216**
    Knud Aslesen ... 3, 5, 56, 57, 70, 180, **215–17**
Annual Conferences
    1872 – Winona 19
    1873 – Anoka 18, 68
    1874 – St. Paul 20, 73, 75
    1875 – Red Wing 18, 76
    1876 – Minneapolis 77
    1877 – Faribault 23, 79
    1878 – Rochester 81
    1879 – Winona 82
    1880 – Racine 83
    1881 – Chicago 25, 73, 85

Annual Conferences (continued)
  1882 – St. Paul 85
  1883 – Racine 26, 86
  1884 – Forest City 87
  1885 – Cambridge 87
  1886 – Minneapolis 88
  1887 – Chicago 88
  1888 – St. Paul 88
  1889 – Racine 27, 89
  1890 – La Crosse 29, 91, 108
  1891 – Chicago 91
  1892 – Duluth 91
  1893 – Chicago 92
  1894 – Minneapolis 92
  1895 – Milwaukee 92
  1896 – Hillsboro 93
  1897 – Forest City 93
  1898 – Racine 36, 93
  1899 – Minneapolis 93
  1900 – Milwaukee 94
  1901 – St. Paul 94
  1902 – Chicago 94
  1903 – Racine 94
  1904 – Duluth 94
  1905 – Minneapolis 95
  1906 – Chicago 39, 95
  1907 – Forest City 95
  1908 – St. Paul 95
  1909 – Duluth 97
  1910 – Chicago 40, 97
  1918 – Chicago 114
  1933 – Chicago 196
Arntson
  O. S. 187
Arvesen
  Engebret 77
Aslesdatter
  Kristi 3, 204, **221**
Aslesen
  Elling. 3, 7, 9, 10, 56, 59, 60, 61, **221–22**, *221*
  Hermund 3, 5–6, 14, 56, 57–58, 218, **220–21**, *220*
  Knud 3, 5, 56, 57, 70, 180, **215–17**
  Ole **222**
Ausland
  Daniel 143

Bakke
  H. O. 118
Bakken
  M. O. 126, 149
Bast
  Anton, Bishop 134
Beckstrøm
  John M. ... 104, 106–7, 184, 186, 188, 190, 191
Belgian
  Steamship 7–9, *59*
Bergh
  Hans P. 146
Berry
  Joseph F., Bishop 95
Bethany Home for the Aged .. 139
Bowman
  Thomas, Bishop 77, 87
Breien/Breen
  Hermund Aslesen 3, 5–6, 14, 56, 57–58, 218, **220–21**, *220*
  Ingeborg Knudsdatter 220
  Ingeborg Vilhelmsdatter ... 58, 220
  Kari Olsdatter 220
Breset
  John 182
Bringdale
  J. G. 177, 179
British Columbia
  Vancouver 218
Burens
  Mrs. —?— 195
Burns
  Charles W., Bishop 178
California
  Burbank 141
  Colton 141
  Cupertino 42
  Hemet 141, 177
  Lodi 42, 194–95, 218
  Long Beach 141
  Los Angeles 141–44, 176, 177–79, 195, 210
  Manteca 209
  Napa 195
  Oakland 139–40
  Pasadena 141

California (continued)
  Pico Rivera.................................. 178
  Rivera............... *See* Pico Rivera
  Riverside..................................... 141
  San Bernardino....................... 141
  San Diego.........................141, 143
  San Francisco....... 139-40, 176, 186, 187, 189, 195
  San Jose..................................... 218
  San Pedro.............. 141, 179, 218
  Santa Ana................................. 141
  Santa Cruz.....................141, 218
  Stockton............... 139, 176, 209
  Tokay Colony......... 42, 139, 176, 188, 218
Camp Meetings
  Belvidere....................................72
  Chesborg.................................... 82
  Corn (Coon) Prairie............... 78
  Devils Lake 113
  Forest City................................. 68
  Grantsburg.................................75
  Lake Elizabeth...........................77
  New Centerville........................76
  Newburg......................68, 77, 82
  Swan Lake..................................77
  Washington Prairie.......... 73, 78
Canada
  Quebec City............................ 7, 9
  St. Mary's Road, PEI 218
  Vancouver, BC 218
  Waldeck, Sask......................... 214
Carlsen
  B. E. 110
  G. A. 139
Christe
  C. 66
Christensen
  Andrew...................................... 172
Christiansen
  Casper O. 147
  Herman....................................... 58
Christophersen
  Christopher......................77, 107
  Nils 68, 73, 77, 146
Churches
  Aberdeen.................................. 185
  Ål stavkirke............................ 6, 58

Churches (continued)
  Bear Creek.............. *See* Grand Meadow
  Bellingham............................... 185
  Belvidere 44, 72
  Bethlehem.......37-38, *38*, 94, 95
  Big Canoe........15-16, 20, 62, 64
  Blooming Grove 32, 40, 87, 97
  Columbia Heights.. 38, 115-16, 118
  Cove.. 160
  Diamond Bluff..........................39
  Eidsvold................................35, 93
  Emanuel (Seattle) 138, 156, 171-72, 183, 185
  Everett 172, 183, 185
  First (Chicago) 88, 91
  First (Los Angeles).. 143, 177-78
  First (Minneapolis).. 32, *33*, 36, 42, 43, 44, 87-88, 92-95, 134-35
  First (Portland) 137, 157-59, 193
  First (San Francisco) 140, 189, 195
  First (Seattle)....... 156, 172, 183, 184-85
  First (St. Paul)....26, 32, 73, 159
  First (Tacoma) 160, 172
  Forest 133
  Forest City 43, 162
  Grand Meadow.......... 19, 65, 69
  Hartland......73, 146-48, 168-69
  Hol gamle kirke.... 209, 215-22
  Lake Mills........121, 126-27, 132, 135, 145, 149-57, 161-65, 167, 169-70, 191-92, *192*, 196
  Long Creek.............. *See* Millville
  Maplewood......................... 92, 94
  Martell.................................146-47
  Matilda Ave. (St. Paul)... 26, 87
  Millville..........20, 69, 72, 74, *84*
  Moline..122
  New Centervillle.... *See* Martell
  Newburg............... 23-25, 68, 212

Churches (continued)
   North Minneapolis .... *See* Bethlehem
   Oakland 140
   Olalla 173
   Palmer ... *See* Blooming Grove
   Plainview .... *See* Millville
   Rinde stavkirke 9, 209
   Rock River .... *See* Martell
   Roxbury (Boston) 110
   Saint Paul Mission .... *See* Matilda Ave.
   Scandia Grove 32
   Scandinavian Sailors' Mission (San Pedro) 179
   Second (St. Paul) .... *See* Matilda Ave.
   Simpson (Minneapolis) 45
   South Fork 23–25
   Tokay 42, 139, 188, 194
   Trinity (Deer Park) 35–36, 133, *134*
   Vancouver Ave. (Portland) 137, 157–59, 185, 189
   Viking 146–47, 168–69
   Washington Prairie 20–23, *22*, 212

Cicero 197
Clausen
   Fredrik C. 61
Colby
   C. E. 126
Dahl
   E. 141, 177
Dakken
   Mrs. Ole E. 127, 135
   Ole E. 106, 117, 121, 126, 135, 149, 161
Danielsen
   Henry 108
Denmark
   Fakse 213
   Præstø 213
Doublough
   O. A. 144
Drafna
   Norwegian bark 60

Dummerud
   Ole 60
Eidsgard
   Ingeborg Vilhelmsdatter ... 58, 220
Elim Home for the Aged .. 47, 106, 128
Ellefsen
   P. M. 139
Ellingson
   Kittel 62
   Sever 61
Eltzholtz
   Carl F. *142*, 143–44
Elvigen
   Hagbarth 171, 181, 189
Endresen
   Endre 62, 64, 68, 72–76
Enevoldsen
   J. P. 159, 185
Engebretsen
   Frederick 140
England
   Hull 7, 58
   Liverpool 7–8, 58
Ericksen/Eriksen
   J. 193
   Knute 180
Eriksdatter
   Kristi **219**
Evanston Theological School 128, 156, 164
Evensen
   Edward 191
Field
   O. T. 137, 185, 193
Finnesgard
   Eli Haagensdatter **219–20**, 221
Fitzgerald
   James N., Bishop 89
Fjellberg
   Asle Hermundsen 56, **219–20**
   Eli Haagensdatter **219–20**, 221
   Kristi Aslesdatter ... 3, 204, **221**
   Kristi Eriksdatter **219**
   Lars Larsen 221

Fjellberg (continued)
  Ole Aslesen 222
Flåten
  Birgit Knudsdatter (1818–1850) 4, 57, 70, 180, **215**
  Eli Knudsdatter 5, 57, 203–4, **216**
  Knud Aslesen ... 3, 5, 56, 57, 70, 180, **215-17**
Folkestad
  Halvard 133–35
Fosdal
  Sigbjørn 104, 196
Foss
  Anne 56, 60
  Cyrus D., Bishop 85, 92, 93
  Elling Aslesen 3, 7, 9, 10, 56, 59, 60, 61, **221-22**, *221*
  Ragnhild Kittelsdatter 222
Fosse
  Betsy 70, 74
  Christina 9, 56, 61, 70, 209
  Lewis T. 9, 11, 56, 59
  Susan ... 9–10, 15–16, 37, 47, 56, 61, 67–68, 70, 71, 73, 79, 82–83, 85, 86, *208*, **209**, 210, 212
  Torkel .. 9–11, 47, 56, 61, 64, 65, 70, 209
Fossgard
  Ingeborg Knudsdatter 220
Fosshaugen
  Elling Aslesen 3, 7, 9, 10, 56, 59, 60, 61, **221-22**, *221*
Foster
  Randolf S., Bishop 81, 87
Fowler
  Charles H., Bishop 88, 91, 94
Gabrielsen
  G. 65
Garberg
  Lorensa (Kittleson) 137
Gerkin
  Bessie 177
Gifstad
  Herman Christiansen 58
  Sicilia "Sille" 14, 58
  Siri 14, 58

Gilberts
  Gilbert 162
Gjerding
  Elias 138, 159, 185, 193
Goodsell
  Daniel A., Bishop 91, 94, 95
Great Britain
  Steamship 8
Grova
  Mr. —?— 182
Grove
  Martin 66
Haagensdatter
  Eli **219-20**, 221
Haagensen
  Anders "Andrew " ... 25, 68, 123
  Julia (Thompson) 123
Hall
  John O. 156
  Mrs. —?— (organist) 196
Hallinglag of America 48
Halstensen
  Harold 60
Halverson
  Gunder 68
Hamilton
  Steamship .... See *Hammonia*
Hammonia
  Steamship 7–9, *59*
Hansen
  Albert M. 111
  B. 68, 72–73, 75
  Brother —?— 185, 193
  H. W. 181–82
  Helina 71, 73
  Herman 71, 72
  Mrs. Jens 116
  Oliver L. 73, 77, 108
Harris
  William L., Bishop 83
Hassel
  David C. 156, 187
Hauge
  Christian N. 140
  Hans Nielsen 14
Haugland
  P. O. 160

Haver
  Hans S. 139–40, 175, 185–86, 189
Hedemark
  Emelia 133
  Sofie 133
Heimark
  Lawrence Arthur 213–15
  Sophia Anzonettie (Knudsen) 83, *208*, **213–15**
Helgeson
  Halvor O. 210
  Hans A. 82
  Tina (Knudsen) 63, 65, *208*, **210**
Hermundsen
  Asle 56, **219–20**
Holland
  Halvor H. 68, 76
  Mr. —?— 126
Holm
  H. M. 51, 113
Hoover
  Herbert 189
Hovde
  Ole 60, 61
Hove
  Elias 193
Hughes
  Edwin H., Bishop 112
Hurst
  John F., Bishop 88
Illinois
  Chicago .. 39, 85, 88, 91, 92, 94, 95, 97, 114, 115, 119, 122–23, 188, 196, 211
  Evanston 122–23, 128, 156, 164
  Fox River 24
  Moline 122
  Rock Island 122
Ingerslew
  J. P. 111
Iowa
  Big Canoe 9, 16, 75, 79, 221
  Conover 76
  Davenport 119, 122, 212–13

Iowa (continued)
  Decorah 21, 61–63, 75–76, 209, 214
  Des Moines 32, 88, 105–6
  Forest City 43, 68, 87, 93, 95, 106, 145, 153, 162, 170
  Freeport 21, 75–77, 82, 212
  Highland Township 11, 222
  Lake Mills 40–42, 97, 105–6, 115, 117, 119, 121, 126–27, 132, 135–36, 145, 149–57, 161–66, 167, 169–70, 191–92, 196
  Lansing 9, 59, 61
  Missouri Valley 32, 88
  Pleasant Township 10, 209, 210, 211
  Ridgeway 214
  Washington Prairie .. 73, 75–79
Ipson
  Andrew M 139, 176, 187, 189, 195
Jacobs
  O. B. 77
Jacobsen
  Hans O. 138, 175, 185, 189, 193
  J. A. 108
  John 67, 72–73, 75, 77
  Ole 77
Jakobsplass
  Ivar Larsen 218
  Mari Knudsdatter **218**
Jansen
  Anders 7, 58
Jeglum
  Gro Olsdatter 222
  Ole Aslesen **222**
Jensen
  H. M. 185
  Peter 83
Johnsen/Johnson
  Andrew (first couple married) 71, 73
  Andrew (traveling companion) 7, 58
  Arne .. 15–16, 62–63, 65, 68, 122
  B. 73

Johnsen/Johnson (continued)
  Helina (Hansen) 71, 73
  John H 18, 19, 66-69, 72-77, 146, 211
  Mathilde 110, 119-20, 123, 125, 211
  Sister —?— 195
Joyce
  Isaac W., Bishop 93
Kaupang
  Astrid "Esther" Knudsdatter... 5, 57, 70, 73, 180, **216-17**
  Birgit Knudsdatter (1818-1850) 4, 57, 70, 180, **215**
  Eli Knudsdatter 5, 57, 203-4, **216**
  Knud Aslesen ... 3, 5, 56, 57, 70, 180, **215-17**
Kittelsdatter
  Ragnhild 222
Kittelson
  Lorensa 137
Kjelstad
  M. L. 108
Kjelstrup
  Frederik C. A. 58
Knudsdatter
  Astrid "Esther" 5, 57, 70, 73, 180, **216-17**
  Birgit (1818-1850) 4, 57, 70, 180, **215**
  Birgit (1853-1870) **217**
  Birgit "Bertha" (1862-?) 141, 180, **218**
  Eli 5, 57, 203-4, **216**
  Guri "Rina" ... 42, 139, 176, 180, 194, **217-18**, *217*
  Ingeborg 220
  Mari **218**
Knudsen/Knudson
  Adella .... *See* Rose Adella
  Albert Cornelius 23, 45, 47, 50, 67, 110, 118-19, 123, 125, *208*, **211**
  Arthur E. 178, 180
  Birgit "Bertha" (1862-?) 141, 180, **218**
  C. W. 172

Knudsen/Knudson (continued)
  Charles Theodore 47, 62-64, 65, 180, **209-10**
  Cyrus Alvin 86, **215**
  Emma (Olson) 139, 176, 180, 209-10
  Guri "Rina" 42, 139, 176, 180, 194, **217-18**, *217*
  Henry Bethuel ... 47, 64, 65, 88, 211
  Knud 66
  Lars C. 156, 171-73, 181, 184, 189, 193
  Mathilde (Johnson) .. 110, 119-20, 123, 125, 211
  Oscar Tyrol 47, 78, 88, **212**
  Rina .... *See* Guri
  Rose Adella 77, *174*, *208*, **212**
  Sophia Anzonettie 83, *208*, **213-15**
  Stella Charlotte ... 81, 122, *208*, **212-13**
  Susan (Fosse) .9-10, 15-16, 37, 47, 56, 61, 67-68, 70, 71, 73, 79, 82-83, 85, 86, *208*, **209**, 210, 212
  Tina Alvina 63, 65, *208*, **210**
Kolberg
  Nels H. 146, 148, 168-69
Krogstad
  Albert 168
Krosby
  Brother —?— 148
  Mother —?— 168
Kunstad
  Mr. —?— 182
Landswick
  Annie M. 138
Langness
  R. B. 171, 185, 187, 194
Larsen/Larson
  Amelia 72
  Asle 204-5
  Carl J. 137, 159
  Christian 168
  Ivar 218
  Lars 221
  Lewis A. 73, 77

Larsen/Larson (continued)
   Martin T. 172, 183, 185
   Melvin 113
Lee
   Mathias 113
Linam
   Peter Pedersen 7, 58
Lindquist
   Carl Frederick 18, 64
Loberg
   Thor H. 164
Lorentz
   John 113, 146–47
Lund
   Emma 176, 187–88
   Hans 176, 187–88
Lundegaard
   Eilert J. 194
Madsen
   Hans K. 104, 114–15
Mallalieu
   Willard F., Bishop 94
Married Women's Act 215
Massachusetts
   Boston 110, 112, 211
   Cambridge 211
   Concord 112
Mathison
   Jennie 164, 167, 169
McCabe
   D. A. 81
McDonald
   Birgit "Bertha" Knudsdatter
      .... 141, 180, **218**
   Charles 180, 218
McDowell
   William F., Bishop 94
McIntyre
   Robert, Bishop 97
Merrill
   Stephen M., Bishop .. 18, 68–69,
      85, 88, 91, 92, 94
Michigan
   Detroit 9, 110
   Grand Haven 9
Minnesota
   Albert Lea 40, 170, 191
   Amherst 25, 82

Minnesota (continued)
   Anoka 68
   Belvidere . 18, 20, 66, 71–72, 85
   Blooming Grove 87
   Brighton 88
   Canton 210
   Choice 23–25, 81–83
   Clarkfield 214
   Columbia Heights . 37, 38, 115–
      16, 118
   Crookston 51
   Duluth 31, 91, 94, 97
   Eidsvold 93
   Faribault 79
   Fergus Falls 91
   Glenville 40, 97
   Goodhue County 20
   Grand Meadow .. 18, 19, 65–68,
      85, 211
   Halstad 91
   Hendricks 43
   Henning 31
   Lake Elizabeth 77
   Lanesboro 210
   Leon Township 35
   Maplewood 209, 211–12
   Millville 19–20, 66–67, 71–74,
      85, 94, 215, 217
   Minneapolis 36, 44–45, 77,
      87–88, 92–95, 106, 115, 119,
      121, 122, 125, 128, 135, 136,
      144, 153, 171, 181, 182, 183,
      188, 189, 190, 209, 212,
      213–14, 216
   Newburg 16, 23, 65, 68, 77,
      81–83, 210, 212–13
   Oakwood Township 216
   Palmer 40
   Park Rapids 214
   Plainview 18, 19–20, 66–67,
      71–74, 75, 85
   Preble Township 25
   Red Wing 20, 39, 72, 76, 85,
      94
   Rochester 81
   Roseville 210

Minnesota (continued)
   Saint Paul 32, 44, 48, 73, 85, 86, 87, 88, 94, 95, 108, 121, 147, 159, 209, 210, 211, 212
   Scandia Grove 88
   Spring Grove 61
   St. Louis Park 212
   Stephen 32
   Stevens Point 92
   Stringtown .... *See* Amherst
   Swan Lake 77
   Tordenskjold 32, 91
   Virginia 146
   Warren 32, 92
   Weaver 20, 68
   Winona 82
Monsen
   Anfind 56
Montana
   Kalispell 181–82
Munson
   Hans C. 122–23
Nebraska
   Omaha 32, 88
Nelson/Nielsen/Nilsen
   Arne 75
   Christ 105
   H. P. 157–58, 159
   Halvor "Oliver" 66
   Martinus 177, 187, 188
   Mrs. Ole 111
   Naomi 159
   O. 171
Neste
   Engbert N. 178, 180
   Tilda (Utigaard) 178, 180
New Hampshire
   Berlin 111
New Jersey
   Perth Amboy 111
   Watsessing 212
New York
   Buffalo 110, 111
   Clayton 119, 123
   Crescent Island 124
   Murray Island.. *See* Thousand Islands
   New York City 8, 213

New York (continued)
   Thousand Islands 110, 119–20, 123–25
   Westchester 213
Ninde
   William X., Bishop 92
Nobel
   Reuben, Judge 63
Norby
   Hans P. 116, 118
Nordvig
   Hans 186
Norlemann
   Sophus A. 115, 119
Norse-American Centennial ... 48–50
North Dakota
   Crary 113
   Devils Lake 113
   Enderlin 31, 128
   Grand Forks 113, 171
   Hillsboro 51, 93, 113
   Romness 128
   Valley City 31
Norway
   Aal/Ål 3, 5, 14, 58
   Christiania (Oslo) 6, 58
   Drammen 6, 7, 58
   Feios 9, 61, 209
   Geilo 4, 216, 217
   Hol .. 3, 57–58, 94, 203, 209, 215
   Kunslen .... *See* Kvisla
   Kvisla 57, 217, 222
   Leikanger 9
   Lien 203
   Lier 6, 14, 58
   Nes 60
   Nesset 217
   Oslo .... *See* Christiania
   Skoger 6, 58
   Sogn 9, 61, 209
   Ustedalen 57
Norwegian Farms
   Annfinnset 5, 216
   Breie 5, 220
   Eidsgard 220
   Finnesgard 219
   Fjellberg 219, 221

Norwegian Farms (continued)
- Flåten 4, 209, 215–16
- Foss 222
- Fossgard 220
- Fosshaugen 222
- Gifstad 14, 58
- Jakobsplass 218
- Jeglum 222
- Kaupang 5, 216
- Nygard 3–4, *4*, 215–16, 219–20, 221
- Pukerud ... 203–4, 216, 218, 221
- Raunsgard 219
- Rue 219
- Storla 220
- Thorrud 6, 58, 218, 220–21
- Trø 204–5
- Tufte 57
- Tufto 57, 217, 222
- Tveit 9, 209
- Utenga 58
- Uthus 219
- Vestreim 215–17

Nygard
- Asle Hermundsen ... 56, **219–20**
- Asle Larsen 204–5
- Eli Haagensdatter **219–20**, 221
- Eli Knudsdatter ... 5, 57, 203–4, **216**
- Elling Aslesen 3, 7, 9, 10, 56, 59, 60, 61, **221–22**, *221*
- Hermund Aslesen 3, 5–6, 14, 56, 57–58, 218, **220–21**, *220*
- Knud Aslesen ... 3, 5, 56, 57, 70, 180, **215–17**
- Kristi Aslesdatter ... 3, 204, **221**
- Lars Larsen 221
- Ole Aslesen **222**

O—?—
- Olin 66

Ofstie
- Hans A. 145, 147, 152–55
- Mrs. Joseph 168–69

Olin
- Bengt E. 77, 87, 94

Olsdatter
- Gro 222

Olsdatter (continued)
- Guri 57, 180, **217**
- Kari 220

Olsen/Olson
- Amund 43, 68, 72–74, 77–78, 81
- Carrie Amelia 71
- Charlie 71
- Emma 139, 176, 180, 209–10
- Fred 132
- Lydia M. 143
- Mathias 31
- Melvin L. 141–44, 156, 176, 186, 187, 189, 193
- Miss —?— 168
- Mrs. Julius 147
- R. E. 71
- Svein 219
- T. 73

Olufsen
- A. 68

Omlie
- Mrs. —?— 79

Opdahl
- Knud 76

Oregon
- Astoria 175
- Portland 136–38, 139, 156, 157–60, 175, 185, 189, 193, 214

Ossen
- Betsy (Fosse) 70, 74
- George 70, 74

Peck
- Jesse T., Bishop 82

Pedersen/Pederson
- Peder 7, 58
- Theodor 179

Petersen/Peterson
- C. August 160, 172, 185
- C. M. 183
- Edward 117, 153, 170
- Hans 122, 213
- Mable 117
- Peter M. 104, 128, 130, 131, 150
- Robert P. 108, 140, 171, 172, 183, 185, 189

INDEX

Petersen/Peterson (continued)
  Stella (Knudsen).. 81, 122, *208*, **212-13**
  Valdemar 193
Preachers' Aid Fund 108-9, 127, 128
  Financial Sec'y 40, 47, 95, 114-15
Prince Edward Island
  St. Mary's Road 218
Pukerud
  Eli Knudsdatter 5, 57, 203-4, 216
  Lars Larsen 221
  Ole Simonsen 203-4, 216
Quebec
  Quebec City 59
Raunsgard
  Asle Hermundsen 56, **219-20**
  Kristi Eriksdatter **219**
  Svein Olsen 219
Robbin
  Knud H. 182
Rohr
  P. H. 141, 143, 177
Røhrstaff
  Ole 50, 170
Romsdalen
  Nesset 217
Rue
  Kristi Eriksdatter **219**
Sæther
  L. T. 160
Sanaker
  Christian O. 77
  James 23
Saskatchewan
  Waldeck 214
Scarvie
  Annie M. (Landswick) 138
  Frank A. 137, 172, 173, 181, 183, 185, 189, 193
Schevenius
  Carl W. 2, 19, 47
Scheyer
  David *174*
  Fred L. 172

Scheyer (continued)
  Synette (Swenson) 172, *174*, 189
Schollert
  E. T. 44, 108, 114-15
Simonsen/Simonson
  Ole 203-4, 216
  T. 76
Sivertsen
  Ivar 213
  Sophia Anzonettie (Knudsen)
    .... 83, *208*, **213-15**
Smedstad
  Asbjorn 45, 47, 167
Smeland
  Emma (Olson) 139, 176, 180, 209-10
  Hans G. 139, 176, 180, 194, 210
Sorbon
  Engebret 67
  Kari 68
  Ole 65
South Minneapolis Temperance Assn 48
Spande
  Mrs. —?— 175
Spellmeyer
  Henry, Bishop 95
Stend
  Samuel 78
Stenvaag
  Mrs. —?— 175
Stoen
  Harold Halstensen 60
Storaker
  Gustav A. 137-38, 157-58, 159, 172, 181, 185, 194-95
Storhøi
  A. G. 143
Støring
  Mrs. —?— 195
Storla
  Kari Olsdatter 220
Strand
  Albert 159, 193
  Ant. 185

Swenson
  John Henry 212
  Rose Adella (Knudsen) 77, *174*, *208*, **212**
  Synette Adella 172, *174*, 189
Theological School, Evanston
  .... 128, 156, 164
Thoe
  Inger 126
  Lars N. 126, 149, 166
  Nels L. 117, 121, 126, 132, 135, 149, 152, 153, 161, 163, 166, 167, 170, 196
Thompson
  John 107
  Julia 123
  Simon 11, 56, 63
Thorson
  Anne (Foss) 56, 60
  Ole 56, 60
Tobson
  Charles 140, 176, 187, 189, 194–95
Tollefsen
  J. C. 108
Torkelsdatter
  Synnøve "Susan". 9–10, 15–16, 37, 47, 56, 61, 67–68, 70, 71, 73, 79, 82–83, 85, 86, *208*, **209**, 210, 212
Torkelsen
  Torkel .. 9–11, 47, 56, 61, 64, 65, 70, 209
Troø
  Asle Larsen 204–5
Tufte
  Gutorm 57
Tufto
  Gro Olsdatter 222
  Guri Olsdatter 57, 180, **217**
Tveit (Twedt)
  Anfind Monsen 56
  Christina Anfindsdatter . 9, 56, 61, 70, 209
  Sigrid Anfindsdatter 10, 56, 63

Tveit/Twedt (continued)
  "Susan" Torkelsdatter 9–10, 15–16, 37, 47, 56, 61, 67–68, 70, 71, 73, 79, 82–83, 85, 86, *208*, **209**, 210, 212
Ulland
  Amund Olsen 43, 68, 72–74, 77–78, 81
Utah
  Salt Lake City 144
Uthus
  Asle Hermundsen 56, **219–20**
Utigaard
  Astrid "Esther" 5, 57, 70, 73, 180, **216–17**
  Bård K. 180
  Knud K. 67, 70, 73, 180, 217
  Knut B. 177, 180
  Tilda 178, 180
Valder
  Hans 24
Veblen
  Andrew A. 143
Vestreim
  Birgit "Bertha" Knudsdatter (1862–?) 141, 180, **218**
  Birgit Knudsdatter (1853–1870) 217
  Guri "Rina" Knudsdatter 42, 139, 176, 180, 194, **217–18**, *217*
  Guri Olsdatter 57, 180, **217**
  Knud Aslesen ... 3, 5, 56, 57, 70, 180, **215–17**
  Mari Knudsdatter **218**
Vilhelmsdatter
  Ingeborg 58, 220
Vincent
  John H., Bishop 93
Wang
  John J. 170
Warren
  Henry W., Bishop 93
Washington
  Aberdeen 185
  Ballard 171
  Bellingham 185
  Beulah Park 160

Washington (continued)
- Cheney 137
- Everett 172, 181, 183, 185
- Lake Forest Park 212
- Lowell 183
- Olalla 173
- Puyallup 172, 181, 184, 189, 212
- Salmon River 159
- Seattle 156–57, 171–73, 181, 184, 189, 212
- Spokane . 136–37, 171, 181, 189
- Tacoma 160, 172, 181
- Vancouver 159, 185

Wiley
- Issac W., Bishop 18, 76

Wilhelmsen
- Rasmus F. 104, 121, 122

Willett
- G. R., Judge 61

Wilson
- Luther B., Bishop 95
- Ole H. 108

Wisconsin
- Bay City 148, 168
- Cambridge 87
- Chesborg 82
- Colfax 115
- Deer Park 35, 75, 93, 107, 133–35
- Diamond Bluff 39, 94
- Forest 35, 133
- Grantsburg 75
- Hartland Township 73, 148, 168–69
- La Crosse 9, 59, 91
- Martell 146–47
- Milwaukee 9, 59, 92, 94
- New Centerville 76, 146
- Prairie du Chien 9, 59
- Racine 83, 86, 89, 93, 94, 211
- Rock Prairie 222
- Salem 168
- Stoughton 122
- Viking 146–47, 168–69

Next Steps

If you would like more information about Asle Knudsen, please visit the companion website at

https://knudsen.familyarchive.online

There you will find more photos and images of many original documents, including

- Birth, marriage, and death certificates
- Census records, land records, newspaper articles, etc.
- Brief histories of the churches Asle served
- The memorial booklet about Asle and Susan Knudsen, written by Albert C. Knudsen and John Swenson.

www.ingramcontent.com/pod-product-compliance
Lightning Source LLC
Chambersburg PA
CBHW060453030426
42337CB00015B/1578